WHITAKER'S
LITTLE BOOK OF
KNOWLEDGE

B L O O M S B U R Y

LONDON · NEW DELHI · NEW YORK · SYDNEY

Copyright © 2012 Bloomsbury Publishing Plc
50 Bedford Square, London WC1B 3DP

www.bloomsbury.com

Bloomsbury Publishing, London, New Delhi, New York and Sydney

ISBN 978-1-4081-7830-0

Editorial Staff

Editor and Principal Contributor: Nathan Joyce
Contributors: Oli Lurie, Ruth Northey and Joel Simons
Illustration Design: Oli Lurie
Executive Editor: Ruth Northey

Thanks to Omer Ali, Sam Joyce, Marika Lysandrou and Wendy Palmer

Typeset by RefineCatch Ltd, Bungay, Suffolk NR35 1EF
Printed and bound by CPI Group (UK) Ltd, Croydon CR0 4YY

CONTENTS

Biggest and Best

School Condensed

CONTENTS

A Sporting Guide

How to Sound Clever

Nostalgia

Treasure Trove

Ready Reference

BIGGEST &
BEST

Most Expensive Items Sold on Ebay

1. A 405ft yacht dubbed the 'Gigayacht', designed by naval architect Frank Mulder – $168m (£104m) in 2006
2. A Gulfstream II twin-engine private jet – $4.9m (£3m) in 2001
3. Lunch with American business magnate Warren Buffett – $2.63m (£1.6m) in 2010
4. Albert, Texas, a five-person Texan hamlet – $2.5m (£1.5m) in 2007
5. 1909 Honus Wagner baseball card, one of only 50 ever made – $1.2m (£742,000) in 2000
6. 2003 Enzo Ferrari sports car – £650,000 in 2004
7. Samuel Allsopp's Arctic Ale c.1852, an extremely rare bottle of beer – $503,300 (£311,000) in 2007
8. Zagami Martian Meteorite, a valuable space-rock found in Nigeria – $450,000 (£278,000) in 2006
9. The ball hit by baseball star Barry Bonds for his 715th home run – $220,100 (£136,000) in 2006
10. *Bandai Stadium events*, a rare Nintendo video-game – $41,300 (£25,500) in 2010

'Forbes Fictional Fifteen' in 2012
(The Richest Fictional Characters in the World: Top Ten)

1. Smaug, treasure-hoarding dragon from *The Hobbit* – $62.0bn (£39.6bn)
2. Flintheart Glomgold, Scottish-South African duck, corrupt business tycoon and enemy of Scrooge McDuck – $51.9bn (£33.2bn)
3. Carlisle Cullen, vampire patriarch from *Twilight* – $36.3bn (£23.2bn)
4. Jed Clampett, patriarch of the Beverly Hillbillies – $9.8bn (£6.3bn)
5. Tony Stark, engineer, industrialist and alter ego of superhero Iron Man – $9.3bn (£5.9bn)
6. Richie Rich, aged around ten-years-old, an only child and the richest kid in the world – $8.9bn (£5.7bn)
7. Charles Foster Kane, enigmatic and tragic newspaper tycoon in *Citizen Kane* – $8.3bn (£5.3bn)
8. Bruce Wayne, business magnate and alter ego of superhero Batman – $6.9bn (£4.4bn)
9. Forrest Gump, table-tennis player, shrimp boat captain and fortuitous investor – $5.7bn (£3.6bn)
10. Mr Monopoly, legendary property developer – $2.5bn (£1.6bn)

Highest-earning Actors (2012) [Source: Forbes]

1. Tom Cruise – $75m (£48m)
2. Leonardo Di Caprio – $37m (£24m)
2. = Adam Sandler – $37m (£24m)
4. Dwayne Johnson – $36m (£23m)
5. Ben Stiller – $33m (£21m)
6. = Sacha Baron Cohen – $30m (£19m)
6. = Johnny Depp – $30m (£19m)
6. = Will Smith – $30m (£19m)
9. Mark Wahlberg – $27m (£17m)
10. Taylor Lautner – $26.5m (£17m)

Fastest Cars by Top Speed

1. Bugatti Veyron Super Sport – 267mph (430kph)
2. = Hennessey Venom GT – 260mph (418kph)
2. = Koenigsegg Agera R – 260mph (418kph)
4. = SSC Ultimate Aero – 257mph (414kph)
4. = 9ff GT9-R– 257mph (414kph)
6. Saleen S7 Twin-Turbo – 248mph (399kph)
7. Koenigsegg CCX – 245mph (394kph)
8. McLaren F1 – 240mph (386kph)
9. Zenvo ST1 – 233mph (375kph)
10. Gumpert Apollo – 225mph (362kph)

Best-selling Toys of all Time

1. 'Nerf' (Non-expanding Recreational Foam) assorted balls
2. Star Wars action figures
3. Barbie
4. Gameboy
5. Cabbage Patch Kids
6. Mr Potato Head
7. Zhu Zhu Pets (also known as Go Go Hamsters)
8. Pet Rock
9. The Slinky
10. The Viewmaster (with scenic reel of Mecca)

All-time Olympic Medals by Country

1. United States – 2,296 summer; 253 winter; 2,549 total
2. Soviet Union – 1,010 summer; 194 winter; 1,204 total
3. Germany – 851 summer; 248 winter; 1,099 total
4. Great Britain – 715 summer; 22 winter; 737 total

⑤ France – 636 summer; 94 winter; 730 total
⑥ Italy – 521 summer; 106 winter; 627 total
⑦ Sweden – 475 summer; 175 winter; 604 total
⑧ East Germany – 409 summer; 110 winter; 519 total
⑨ Hungary – 459 summer; 6 winter; 465 total
⑩ Finland – 298 summer; 156 winter; 454 total

World's Most Expensive Hotel Rooms per Night
① The Royal Penthouse Suite, President Wilson Hotel, Geneva – $65,000 (£40,100)
② The Royal Villa at the Grand Resort Lagonissi, Athens – $50,000 (£30,900)
③ Hugh Hefner Sky Villa/Palms Casino Resort, Las Vegas – $40,000 (£24,700)
④ = Ty Warner Penthouse, Four Seasons Hotel, New York City – $35,000 (£21,600)
④ = Penthouse Prestige Apartment, Hotel Martinez, Cannes, France – $35,000 (£21,600)
⑥ The Presidential Suite, Hotel Cala di Volpe, Costa Smeralda, Sardinia – $34,000 (£21,000)
⑦ Villa La Cupola Suite, Westin Excelsior, Rome – $31,000 (£19,100)
⑧ = The Penthouse at The Setai, South Beach, Miami – $30,000 (£18,500)
⑧ = The Royal Plaza Suite, The Plaza Hotel, New York City – $30,000 (£18,500)
⑩ The Ritz-Carlton Suite, Ritz-Carlton, Tokyo – $25,000 (£15,400)

Sport Stadiums by Number of Seats
① Rungrado May Day Stadium (football), Pyongyang, North Korea – 150,000
② Salt Lake Stadium (football), Calcutta, India – 120,000
③ Michigan Stadium (American football), Michigan, USA – 109,901
④ Beaver Stadium (American football) Pennsylvania, USA – 106,572
⑤ Estadio Azteca (football), Mexico City, Mexico – 105,000
⑥ Neyland Stadium (American football), Tennessee, USA – 102,455
⑦ Ohio Stadium (American football), Ohio, USA – 102,329
⑧ Bryant-Denny Stadium (American football), Alabama, USA – 101,821
⑨ Darrell K. Royal-Texas Memorial Stadium (American football), Texas, USA – 100,119
⑩ Melbourne Cricket Ground (cricket), Melbourne, Australia – 100,018

Largest Empires at their Respective Peaks
① British Empire (c.1583–c.1945) – 22.63 per cent of world land area
② Mongol Empire (c.1206–c.1370) – 16.11 per cent of world land area
③ Russian Empire (c.1721–c.1917) – 15.31 per cent of world land area

④   Spanish Empire *(c.1740–c.1790)* – 13.43 per cent of world land area
⑤   Qing Dynasty *(c.1636–c.1912)* – 9.87 per cent of world land area
⑥   Yuan Dynasty *(c.1271–c.1368)* – 9.4 per cent of world land area
⑦   = Umayyad Caliphate *(c.661–c.750)* – 8.73 per cent of world land area
⑦   = Second French colonial Empire *(c.1534–c.1980)* 8.73 per cent of world land area
⑨   Abbasid Caliphate *(c.750–c.1258)* – 7.45 per cent of world land area
⑩   Portuguese Empire *(c.1415–c.1822)* – 6.98 per cent of world land area

Best-selling Cars of all Time

①   Toyota Corolla (1966–present) – 32,000,000+
②   Ford F-Series (1948–present) – 30,000,000+
③   Volkswagen Golf (1974–present) – 25,000,000+
④   Volkswagen Beetle (1938–present) – 22,300,000+
⑤   Ford Escort (1968–2000) – 20,000,000
⑥   Honda Civic (1972–present) – 17,730,000+
⑦   Ford Model-T (1908–1927) – 16,500,000
⑧   Honda Accord (1976–present) – 15,800,000+
⑨   Volkswagen Passat (1973–present) – 14,100,000+
⑩   Chevrolet Impala (1958–present) – 14,000,000+

Highest-paid Civil Servants (2011)

①   Tony Fountain – Chief Executive of the Nuclear Decommissioning Authority – £379,999 per annum
②   Dennis Hone – Chief Executive of the Olympic Delivery Authority – £314,999 per annum
③   Howard Shiplee – Director of Construction at the Olympic Delivery Authority – £289,999 per annum
④   = Sir David Nicholson – Chief Executive of the NHS – £279,999 per annum
④   = John Fingleton – Chief Executive of the Office of Fair Trading – £279,999 per annum
⑥   = John Armitt – Chairman of the Olympic Delivery Authority – £254,999 per annum
⑥   = Andrew Haines – Chief Executive of the Civil Aviation Authority – £254,999 per annum
⑧   David Flory – Deputy Chief Executive of the NHS – £249,999 per annum
⑨   Joe Harley – Department for Work and Pensions and Government Chief Information Officer – £244,999 per annum
⑩   Stephen Geraghty – Commissioner and Chief Executive of the Child Maintenance and Enforcement Commission – £239,999 per annum

Highest-earning Heads of State (January 2012)

❶ Lee Hsien Loong – Prime Minister of Singapore – $1,700,000 (£1.09m) per annum

❷ Donald Tsang – Chief Executive and President of the Executive Council of Hong Kong – $513,245 (£317,000) per annum

❸ Raila Odinga – Prime Minister of Kenya – $427,886 (£264,300) per annum

❹ Barack Obama – President of the United States – $400,000 (£247,100) per annum

❺ Nicolas Sarkozy – President of France – $345,423 (£213,300) per annum

❻ Stephen Harper – Prime Minister of Canada – £296,400 (£183,100) per annum

❼ Julia Gillard – Prime Minister of Australia – $286,752 (£177,100) per annum

❽ Angela Merkel – Chancellor of Germany – $283,608 (£175,200) per annum

❾ Jacob Zuma – President of South Africa – $272,280 (£168,200) per annum

❿ John Key – Prime Minister of New Zealand – $271,799 (£167,900) per annum

Best-selling Single-volume Books (Approximate Sales)

❶ = *A Tale of Two Cities* by Charles Dickens (1859) – 200,000,000

❶ = *The Little Prince* by Antoine de Saint-Exupéry (1943) – 200,000,000

❸ *The Lord of the Rings* by J.R.R. Tolkien (1954–5) – 150,000,000

❹ = *The Hobbit* by J.R.R. Tolkien (1937) – 100,000,000

❹ = *Hong Lou Meng (Dream of the Red Chamber)* by Cao Xueqin (1759–91) – 100,000,000

❹ = *And Then There Were None* by Agatha Christie (1939) – 100,000,000

❼ *The Lion, The Witch and The Wardrobe* by C.S. Lewis (1950) – 85,000,000

❽ *She* by H. Rider Haggard (1887) – 83,000,000

❾ *The Da Vinci Code* by Dan Brown (2003) – 80,000,000

❿ *Think and Grow Rich* by Napoleon Hill (1937) – 70,000,000

Longest-running TV Shows

❶ *Meet the Press* (News show, USA) – 1947–present

❷ *Guiding Light* (Soap opera, USA) – 1952–2009

❸ *Tagesschau* (News show, Germany) – 1952–present

❹ *Hockey night in Canada* (Sports show, Canada) – 1952–present

❺ *Zenigata Heiji* (Historical drama, Japan) – 1952–present

❻ *NHK Nodo Jiman* (Music show, Japan) – 1953–present

❼ *Panorama* (Current affairs show, UK) – 1953–present

❽ *The Tonight Show* (Chat show, USA) – 1954–present

❾ *Gunsmoke* (Western drama, USA) – 1955–1975

❿ *It is Written* (Religious show, USA) – 1956–present

All-time Eurovision Winners
1. Ireland (1970, 1980, 1987, 1992, 1993, 1994, 1996)
2. France (1958, 1960, 1962, 1969, 1977); Luxembourg (1961, 1965, 1972, 1973, 1983); United Kingdom (1967, 1969, 1976, 1981, 1997); Sweden (1974, 1984, 1991, 1999, 2012)
3. Netherlands (1957, 1959, 1969, 1975)
4. Israel (1978, 1979, 1998); Norway (1985, 1995, 2009)
5. Denmark (1963, 2000); Germany (1982, 2010); Italy (1964, 1990); Spain (1968, 1969); Switzerland (1956, 1988);
6. Austria (1966); Azerbaijan (2011); Belgium (1986); Estonia (2001); Finland (2006); Greece (2005); Latvia (2002); Monaco (1971); Russia (2008); Serbia (2007); Turkey (2003); Ukraine (2004); Yugoslavia (1989)

Most Visited Museums in the World by Visitors per Year (2010 Estimate)
1. Musée du Louvre, Paris – 8,500,000
2. British Museum, London – 5,842,138
3. Metropolitan Museum of Art, New York City – 5,216,988
4. Tate Modern, London – 5,061,172
5. National Gallery, London – 4,954,914
6. National Gallery of Art, Washington DC – 4,775,114
7. Museum of Modern Art, New York City – 3,131,238
8. Centre Georges Pompidou, Paris – 3,130,000
9. National Museum of Korea, Seoul – 3,067,909
10. Musée d'Orsay, Paris – 2,985,510

Largest Individual Philanthropic Bequests
1. $31bn (£19.15bn) from American business magnate Warren Buffett to the Bill and Melinda Gates Foundation
2. $9bn (£5.56bn) from Irish-American businessman Chuck Feeney to Atlantic Philanthropies
3. $2bn (£1.24bn) from Indian businessman Azim Premji to the Azim Premji Foundation
4. $1bn (£618,000) from American media mogul Ted Turner to the United Nations
5. = $500m (£309m) from American financier T.Boone Pickens to Oklahoma State University
5. = $500m (£309m) from American publisher Walter Annenberg to public school reform in the USA
7. $350m (£216m) ($7bn [£4.32bn] in modern terms) from Scottish-American industrialist Andrew Carnegie in 1901, who distributed most of his wealth to good causes

8 $424m (£262m) from managers of the Reader's Digest fortune to the Metropolitan Museum of Art

9 = $350m (£216m) from singer Michael Jackson to over 39 different charities

9 = $350m (£216m) from musician Yank Barry and his Global Village Champions in food and medical supplies to the needy around the world

Largest Employers in the World (2011 Estimate)

1 Walmart (Supermarket chain, USA) – 2,100,000 employees
2 China National Petroleum – 1,649,992 employees
3 State Grid (China) – 1,533,800 employees
4 Indian Railways – 1,361,519 employees
5 Sinopec (Petroleum company, China) – 633,383 employees
6 G4S (Security company, UK) – 630,000 employees
7 Hon Hai Precision Industry (Electronics company, Taiwan) – 611,000 employees
8 US Postal Service – 574,000 employees
9 ISS A/S (Facilities company, Switzerland) –522,700 employees
10 Carrefour (Hypermarket chain, France) – 475,976 employees

Largest City Squares in the World

1 Lapangan Merdeka (Freedom Square), Jakarta, Indonesia – 1,000,000m² (247 acres)
2 Praca dos Girassóis (Sunflowers Square), Palmas, Brazil – 570,000m² (141 acres)
3 Tiananmen Square, Beijing, China – 440,000m² (109 acres)
4 Macroplaza, Monterrey, Mexico – 400,000m² (99 acres)
5 India Gate Complex, New Delhi, India – 306,600m² (76 acres)
6 Parade Square, Warsaw, Poland – 240,000m² (59 acres)
7 Kuybyshev Square, Samara, Russia, 174,000m² (43 acres)
8 Esplanade, Perm, Russia – 174,000m² (43 acres)
9 = Universitetskaya Square, Moscow, Russia – 130,000m² (32 acres)
9 = Moskovskaya, St Petersburg, Russia – 130,000m² (32 acres)

Largest Passenger Ships in the World (Measured by Gross Tonnage)

1 = Allure of the Seas – 225,282 tonnes (496,661,793lb)
1 = Oasis of the Seas – 225,282 tonnes (496,661,793lb)
3 Norwegian Epic – 155,873 tonnes (343,641,142lb)
4 = Freedom of the Seas – 154,407 tonnes (340,409,165lb)
4 = Liberty of the Seas – 154,407 tonnes (340,409,165lb)
4 = Independence of the Seas – 154,407 tonnes (340,409,165lb)

⑦   Queen Mary 2 – 151,400 tonnes (333,779,865lb)
⑧   = Navigator of the Seas – 138,279 tonnes (304,853,012lb)
⑧   = Mariner of the Seas – 138,279 tonnes (304,853,012lb)
⑩   MSC Fantasia – 137,936 tonnes (304,098,826lb)

World's Busiest Airports by Total Passengers
(Source: Airport Council International, 2011)
①   Hartsfield-Jackson Atlanta International Airport (Atlanta, Georgia, USA) – 93,575,299
②   Beijing Capital International Airport (Chaoyang District, Beijing, China) – 78,425,739
③   London Heathrow Airport (Hillingdon, London, UK) – 70,099,268
④   O'Hare International Airport (Chicago, Illinois, USA) – 67,492,388
⑤   Tokyo International Airport(Ota, Tokyo, Japan) – 63,446,998
⑥   Los Angeles International Airport (Los Angeles, California, USA) – 62,747,777
⑦   Paris Charles de Gaulle Airport (Ile-de-France, France) – 61,532,701
⑧   Dallas Fort Worth International Airport (Dallas, Texas, USA) – 58,327,154
⑨   Frankfurt Airport (Frankfurt am Main, Frankfurt, Germany) – 56,851,400
⑩   Hong Kong International Airport (Chek Lap Kok, Hong Kong, China) – 54,473,772

Most Expensive Paintings Ever Sold
①   *The Card Players* by Paul Cézanne (1892–3) – $250m (£154m) in 2011
②   *No 5, 1948* by Jackson Pollock (1948) – $140m (£86m) in 2006
③   *Woman III* by Willem de Koonig (1953) – $137.5m (£85m) in 2006
④   *Portrait of Adele Bloch-Bauer I* by Gustav Klimt (1907) – $135m (£83m) in 2006
⑤   *The Scream* by Edvard Munch (1893) – $119.9m (£74m) in 2012
⑥   *Nude, Green Leaves and Bust* by Pablo Picasso (1932) – $106.5m (£70m) in 2010
⑦   *Garcon á la pipe* by Pablo Picasso (1905) – $104.2m (£64m) in 2004
⑧   *Dora Maar au Chat* by Pablo Picasso (1941) – $95.2m (£52m) in 2006
⑨   *Portrait of Dr. Gachet* by Vincent Van Gogh (1890) – $82.5m (£51m) in 1990
⑩   *Bal du Moulin de la Galette* by Pierre-Auguste Renoir (1876) – $78.1m (£48m) in 1990

Biggest Underground Networks by Total Stations
①   New York City Subway – 421
②   Seoul Subway – 314
③   Paris Métro – 301

④ Metro de Madrid – 300
⑤ Shanghai Metro – 285
⑥ London Underground – 270
⑦ Beijing Subway – 218
⑧ Moscow Metro – 185
⑨ Mexico City Metro – 175
⑩ Berlin U-Bahn – 173

World's Largest Airlines by Fleet Size (2011)
① Delta Air Lines (USA) – 744 planes
② Sky West (USA) – 727 planes
③ United Airlines (USA) – 712 planes
④ Lufthansa (Germany) – 710 planes
⑤ Southwest Airlines (USA) – 700 planes
⑥ American Airlines (USA) – 624 planes
⑦ Air France-KLM (France and Netherlands) – 616 planes
⑧ International Airlines Group [British Airways and Iberia] (UK and Spain) –
420 planes
⑨ = Air Canada (Canada) – 362 planes
⑨ = China Southern Airlines – 362 planes

Tallest Buildings in the World
① Burj Khalifa (2010) – Dubai, United Arab Emirates – 830 metres (2,721ft)
② Taipei 101 (2004) – Taipei, China – 508 metres (1,667ft)
③ Shanghai World Financial Centre – Shanghai, China – 492 metres (1,614ft)
④ International Commerce Centre – Hong Kong – 484 metres (1,588ft)
⑤ Petronas Towers 1 & 2 – Kuala Lumpur, Malaysia – 452 metres (1,483ft)
⑥ Zifeng Tower – Nanjing, China – 450 metres (1,476ft)
⑦ = Willis Tower – Chicago, USA – 442 metres (1,450ft)
⑦ = Kingkey Tower – Shenzhen, China – 442 metres (1,450ft)
⑨ Guangzhou International Finance Centre – Guangzhou, China – 439 metres
(1,440ft)
⑩ Trump International Hotel & Tower – Chicago, USA – 423 metres (1,388ft)

Most Aces in a Tennis Match
① John Isner (USA) – 113, Wimbledon 2010
② Nicolas Mahut (France) – 103, Wimbledon 2010
③ Ivo Karlovic (Croatia) – 78, Davis Cup 2009
④ Ivo Karlovic (Croatia) – 55, French Open 2009
⑤ Gary Muller (South Africa) – 54, Wimbledon 1993 (qualifying)
⑥ = Joachim Johansson (Sweden) – 51, Australian Open 2005

⑥ = Ivo Karlovic (Croatia) – 51, Wimbledon 2005
⑦ = Chris Guccione (Australia) – 50, Wimbledon 2005 (qualifying)
⑦ = Grégory Carraz (France) – 50, Andrézieux 2004
⑦ = Roger Federer (Switzerland) – 50, Wimbledon 2009
⑩ Richard Krajicek (Netherlands) – 49, US Open 1999

Biggest Film Flops by Inflation-adjusted Net Loss
① *Cutthroat Island* (1995) – $147,157,681 (£90.9m)
② *The Alamo* (2004) – $146,644,313 (£90.6)
③ *The Adventures of Pluto Nash* (2002) – $145,877,124 (£90.1m)
④ *Sahara* (2005) – $144,857,030 (£89.5m)
⑤ *Mars Needs Moms* (2011) – $140,513,991 (£86.8m)
⑥ *The 13th Warrior* (1999) – $137,142,407 (£84.7m)
⑦ *Town & Country* (2001) – $124,202,203 (£76.7m)
⑧ *Speed Racer* (2008) – $114,479,584 (£70.7m)
⑨ *Heaven's Gate* (1980) – $114,281,677 (£70.6m)
⑩ *Stealth* (2005) – $111,700,123 (£69m)

Highest-paid Musicians by Net Earnings (Between May 2010 and May 2011) [Source: Forbes]
① U2 – $195m (£120m)
② Bon Jovi – $125m (£77m)
③ Elton John – $100m (£62m)
④ Lady Gaga – $90m (£56m)
⑤ Michael Bublé – $70m (£43m)
⑥ Paul McCartney – $67m (£41m)
⑦ Black Eyed Peas – $61m (£38m)
⑧ The Eagles – $60m (£37m)
⑨ Justin Bieber – $53m (£33m)
⑩ Dave Matthews Band – $51m (£31m)

SCHOOL
CONDENSED

PLOT SUMMARIES OF SHAKESPEARE'S PLAYS

All's Well that Ends Well (1603–4)

Helena, the orphaned daughter of a famous doctor, is the **ward** of the **Countess of Rousillon** and has fallen in love with the Countess's son **Bertram**, who has gone to the court of the **King of France**. Helena hears that the **king is ill**, and using her father's knowledge, she **cures him**. As a reward, he gives her a ring and **allows her to marry any man she wants**, and so she chooses Bertram. This makes Bertram deeply unhappy and **he soon flees France**. Helena returns home and receives a letter from Bertram, declaring that she could **only be his true wife if she falls pregnant with his child** and **if she is given the family ring**, two things that he says will never happen. Helena is inconsolable and goes on a pilgrimage. Meanwhile, Bertram becomes the **general** of the **Duke of Florence's army**. Coincidentally, Helena is travelling to **Florence**, where she learns that Bertram is wooing the virgin **Diana**. Helena learns that Diana has no desire to lose her virginity, **so she helps to fool Bertram**, who gives Diana **his ring** as a symbol of his love. He makes his way to Diana's bedchamber and **makes love to someone he thinks is Diana**, but is actually **Helena**. Bertram **receives news that Helena is dead** and returns to France, **secretly followed by Helena**. They arrive back at Rousillon, where the town is in mourning. The king is present and **allows Bertram to marry the daughter of a lord**, but notices that his **ring is the one the king had given to Helena** (Helena had given Diana the ring and she had given it to Bertram). Bertram cannot fathom how he got this ring, but Diana and her mother arrive, and explain what happened. **To Bertram's amazement, Helena appears** and informs him that **both his stipulations have been honoured, thus she is his true wife**. Bertram **repents** and **pledges to be an honourable husband**.

Antony and Cleopatra (1606)

Mark Antony, one of the three triumvirs of Rome is in Egypt, where he has an affair with **Queen Cleopatra**. A message arrives from Rome revealing that **Antony's wife, Fulvia, is dead and that, Sextus Pompey**, a rebel general, is **raising an army**. Antony returns to Rome, where he and fellow triumvir Octavius agree an **alliance to fight the rebels**, cementing it with a plan for **Antony to marry Octavius's sister Octavia**. Cleopatra receives news of the marriage and resolves to win Antony back. The triumvirs **make peace with Pompey and war is averted**. Antony and Octavia leave Rome; meanwhile **Octavius breaks his truce, and attacks and defeats Pompey's army**. He then falsely accuses third triumvir Lepidus of treason and has him imprisoned. Antony hears of this and is **incensed**, but his new **wife implores him to maintain the peace**. He sends her to Rome on a rapprochement mission, while he returns to Cleopatra. **Antony amasses an army**; when Octavius finds out that Antony has abandoned his sister, **he also raises an army and sails to Egypt**.

The **two armies clash** and **Octavius wins the day**. Cleopatra sends word to the victorious Octavius, pleading that Antony be allowed to live in Egypt and that her heirs can still rule Egypt. Caesar **refuses the former**, but **agrees to the latter, only if Cleopatra betrays Antony**. Antony's troops meet Caesar's forces and **win**, but the following day, the Egyptian army **deserts** Antony. He **curses Cleopatra, presuming she betrayed him and swears to kill her**. She hears of this and retreats to her **monument**, ensuring that Antony receives word that she has committed **suicide**. **Antony falls on his sword**, but does not die straight away. **He is carried to Cleopatra** where they **reunite**. Octavius plans to take Cleopatra as a **prize** but she hears of his plan and **kills herself**, by allowing **poisonous asps to bite her: 'I am fire and air; my other elements I give to baser life'**. She is buried next to Antony.

As You Like it (1599)

The wealthy Sir Rowland has died, and his fortune passes to his son **Oliver**, who betrays his father by failing to provide for his brother **Orlando**. Meanwhile, **Frederick** has seized the **dukedom** from his brother **Duke Senior**. Senior's daughter, **Rosalind**, is spared due to her friendship to Frederick's daughter, **Celia**. **Rosalind and Orlando fall in love** but she only reveals her feelings to Celia. Orlando learns of a **plot to kill him** and flees to the **Forest of Arden**. Frederick changes his mind and **exiles Rosalind**. Celia goes with her, **disguised as the pauper Aliena**, while **Rosalind disguises herself as Ganymede**, a young man. They are accompanied by the court jester, **Touchstone**. The three of them reach the forest, where Duke Senior is hiding. **Duke Frederick commands Oliver to find Celia, Rosalind and Orlando.** Orlando arrives in the forest and is welcomed by Senior. Ganymede (Rosalind) and Aliena (Celia) stumble across a shepherd called **Silvius** who moans about his love for **Phoebe**. They also run into Orlando, who **is taken in by Rosalind's disguise**. He reveals his feelings of lovesickness to Ganymede, so he (she) offers to help, instructing Orlando to come and **woo him** (her) **every day**. Later, **Phoebe falls in love with Ganymede**. **Oliver arrives** in the forest and **falls in love with Aliena**, and they **plan to marry**. Rosalind grows tired of the pretence and makes everyone promise to meet the next day, where they congregate before Senior. Rosalind, still disguised as Ganymede, **makes Phoebe promise that if she refuses to marry him, she will marry Silvius instead, and makes Senior promise that he would allow his daughter to marry Orlando if she were available**. Ganymede and Aliena leave and return as Rosalind and Celia. Honouring their promises, **Rosalind and Orlando, Celia and Oliver, Phoebe and Silvius**, and **Audrey** (a simple-minded shepherdess) and **Touchstone** are **all married**. **Duke Frederick repents** of his sins after visiting a holy man and **returns the dukedom to Senior**.

The Comedy of Errors (1594)

Elderly trader **Egeon**, who faces execution for breaking the law banning travel from **Syracuse** to **Ephesus**, recounts his tale to the **Duke of Ephesus** of how his **twin sons and the twins of a poor woman, whom he bought to be his sons' servants, were separated during a shipwreck**. He rescued one son and his slave, while his wife, one son and his slave were rescued by another boat; **Egeon has not seen them since**, hence his voyage to Ephesus to try and find them. Unbeknownst to his father, his son Antipholus of Syracuse also travelled to Ephesus, **but he has no idea that this city houses his long-lost twin**. He soon encounters his twin brother's wife, who takes him home for dinner. **His twin brother arrives at the house** but is refused entry. The situation becomes more confusing when a **goldsmith** arrives with a **gold chain that Antipholus of Syracuse supposedly ordered**, telling him that he will return for payment later. When the goldsmith runs into the Ephesian Antipholus, he demands payment, but this Antipholus claims he has received no chain and is **arrested**. The Ephesian Antipholus is later **tied up in the cellar** by his wife, who assumes that he has gone **insane**. Antipholus of Syracuse and his servant **leave Ephesus**, convinced that the city is plagued by some sort of **witchcraft**. However, they are pursued by Adriana and a number of guards, so they seek sanctuary in an **abbey**. Adriana implores the Duke to step in. Meanwhile, her real husband escapes the cellar and travels to see the Duke to bring charges forward against his wife. Finally, the **abbess brings out the Syracusians to face their twins** and everyone grasps the misunderstanding of the day as she reveals that she is Antipholus's mother and Egeon's wife. **Egeon is pardoned** by the Duke and the **family is reunited**.

Coriolanus (1608)

Deprived of grain, Roman citizens begin to riot, blaming General **Caius Martius** for the food shortage. Martius acts disparagingly towards the rioters and two Roman tribunes, **Brutus** and **Sicinius**, express their displeasure at his words. News reaches Martius of a marching **Volscian** army commanded by his old enemy **Tullus Aufidius**, and he leaves to join **Cominius**, leader of the Roman forces. They split their army; **Cominius will face the Volscii in the field**, while Martius will attack the Volscian city of **Corioles**. After a valiant assault, **Martius captures the city**. He rides to join forces with Cominius and **meets Aufidius on the battlefield**, but the latter is ushered away by his soldiers. After the battle, the heroic Martius is given the cognomen **Coriolanus**. His mother **Volumnia** persuades Coriolanus to **run for Consul**, and he wins the approval of both the Senate and the plebeians. However, **Brutus and Sicinius plot to scupper Coriolanus's rise to power** and engineer a riot, enraging Coriolanus to the point that he openly pours forth **wrath on the masses**. Coriolanus is **denounced as a traitor and banished**, but delivers a stinging speech: **'You common cry of curs! whose breath I hate/As reek o' the rotten fens,** whose loves I prize/As the dead carcases of unburied men/That do corrupt my air, – I banish you.' He travels to the Volscian capital of Antium, and suggests **Aufidius kills him to spite Rome**. Despite his fury at seeing his foe, **Aufidius embraces him** and they plan to assault Rome. The Romans hear of the **invading Volscian army** led by Coriolanus and are terrified. A plea from Cominius and **Menenius** falls on deaf ears. Volumnia, and Coriolanus's wife **Virgilia** and son **Martius** are finally allowed to approach him. Although initially resistant to their desperate words, he eventually breaks and **negotiates a treaty** between Rome and the Volscii. **Coriolanus returns to Antium**, but is **murdered by Aufidius** and co-conspirators for his treachery.

Cymbeline (1609)

Cymbeline, **King of Britain** at the time that **Augustus Caesar was Emperor of Rome**, has a daughter, **Imogen**, who has secretly married lowborn **Posthumus** and exchanged rings. The king has **banished** Posthumus because Imogen is his only child and therefore Posthumus would inherit the throne. Cymbeline had **two sons** years ago, but they were stolen as infants by **Belarius**. Meanwhile, the Queen is plotting to have **Cloten**, her son by an earlier marriage, married to Imogen. Posthumus flees to Italy where he meets **Iachimo**. On hearing of Imogen's beauty and chastity, he **bets Posthumus that he can seduce Imogen and bring proof of her infidelity**. He fails to seduce Imogen, but hides in her bedchamber and spies an unusual mole on her left breast. He steals her bracelet and returns to Italy, where he convinces Posthumus that he has won the bet, claiming the ring Imogen gave to him as his winnings. Posthumus sends a letter to his servant demanding he kill Imogen, but the servant helps her escape, disguising Imogen as a boy, **Fidele**. On her journey, **she takes refuge in a cave**, where she finds Belarius and two young men, **Polydore** and **Cadwal, who are actually her two long-lost brother**s. Cloten, dressed in Posthumus' clothes, has followed Imogen, and is determined to rape her and **kill Posthumus**. He enters into a fight with the brothers in which **he is killed** and his head cut off. **Imogen awakes to find the body of Cloten, but she thinks it is Posthumus**. Despairing, **she joins the Roman army which is invading Britain**. Posthumus and Imogen's two brothers help Cymbeline to defeat the Romans. As Fidele, Imogen is captured by Cymbeline, together with Iachimo. The king, not recognising her, but captivated by her beauty, grants her a favour. She demands to know why **Iachimo** is wearing **the ring she gave to Posthumus**. Plots are then uncovered, identities revealed, and as Imogen's brothers are restored to their inheritance, **she is free to marry Posthumus**.

Hamlet (1601)

King Hamlet is murdered by his brother **Claudius, who takes the throne and marries his late brother's wife Gertrude**. **Prince Hamlet** (King Hamlet and

Gertrude's son) is ordered by an apparition of his father to **avenge his murder**. Hamlet's behaviour gets increasingly erratic, alarming **Ophelia**, the woman he is courting, but her father **Polonius** assures her that it is symptomatic of his love for her. Polonius and his son **Laertes** convince Ophelia to talk to Hamlet, but he rants furiously at her and leaves her heartbroken, telling her **'Get thee to a nunnery'**. A troupe of **players** arrive at court and Hamlet's **hatches a plan** for the performers to **re-enact King Hamlet's murder**, while spying Claudius's reaction to the scene. Claudius leaves abruptly, proving his **guilt**. Gertrude demands an explanation from Hamlet, and the pair argue. Hamlet spots movement behind a **tapestry** and **stabs the intruder**, believing it to be Claudius, but it is in fact **Polonius**. **Hamlet is sent to England** supposedly on a diplomatic mission, but Claudius has actually planned for his **murder** there. Hamlet uncovers the plot and **escapes, returning to Denmark**. Meanwhile the news of her father's death **drives Ophelia to madness** and she is later discovered **drowned**. Claudius convinces Laertes that Hamlet is solely responsible for Polonius's death and they **plot to murder him with a poisoned sword** during a fencing match, and, failing that, **poisoned wine**. Gertrude unknowingly **drinks the poisoned wine and dies**. Hamlet and Laertes wound each other with the poisoned blade, sealing their fate. Laertes **reveals Claudius's plan**, reconciles with Hamlet, and **Hamlet finally kills Claudius**. Hamlet dies in the arms of his best friend Horatio, who says **'Now cracks a noble heart. Good-night, sweet prince; And flights of angels sing thee to thy rest.'**

Henry IV, Part I (1596–7)

The play opens with a worried **King Henry** speaking to his council about the civil unrest in the country. Henry feels he must postpone his intended Crusade to Jerusalem to sort out the troubles. Apart from **Welsh and Scots rebels**, he has fallen out with **Henry Percy** (known as Hotspur). Percy wants the king to ransom **Edmund Mortimer** from **Owen Glendower**, the leader of the Welsh rebels, who is holding him prisoner, but Henry refuses. After all, **Richard II**, who Henry deposed, had named Mortimer as his heir. Consequently, **the Percy family join the Welsh and Scots** in a rebellion to depose Henry. Henry's other worry is his degenerate son, **Prince Hal**, who is enjoying the low life of the taverns with his rotund and cowardly friend, **Sir John Falstaff**. However, once the king explains the seriousness of the rebellion, Hal promises to join him in battle: **'And I will die a hundred thousand deaths/Ere break the smallest parcel of this vow'**. Hal orders Falstaff to requisition a group of soldiers and meet him at the battle site in Shrewsbury. In the rebel camp, Hotspur learns that his father, **Northumberland**, is sick and won't be joining the battle. He also receives news that Glendower can't assemble his soldiers in time, but Hotspur decides to go ahead anyway, leading his troops into battle. Prince Hal is injured in the battle, but **tracks down Hotspur and kills him in single combat**. **Falstaff, who has been playing dead on the battlefield** to avoid injury, discovers

Hotspur's body, stabs it, and **pretends that he has done the deed himself**. But the war is not over: the king's army still have to deal with the **Archbishop of York**, who has joined forces with **Northumberland, Mortimer**, and **Glendower**. This sets the scene for Part II.

Henry IV, Part II (1597)

As in Part I, **Falstaff** is still drinking and enjoying the company of prostitutes and petty criminals in the **Boar's Head Tavern** in **Eastcheap**. Mistress Quickly attempts to get Falstaff arrested for debt, complaining **'He hath eaten me out of house and home'**. But then news comes of a second rebellion against the king, so **Falstaff joins the army again**, conscripting a motley band of rustics: Mouldy, Shadow, Wart, Feeble and Bullcalf for the purpose. The rebels are disappointed that the Earl of Northumberland has not sent soldiers to support them, but he has just received news that his son, **Hotspur, has been killed**. Henry's son **Prince John** leads his father's army to meet the rebels, claiming that he will meet all their demands, but as soon as they have dispersed their troops, he **arrests the leaders and has them executed**. Meanwhile, the King has become ill, and is increasingly worried (**'Uneasy lies the head that wears the crown'**) by the irresponsible behaviour of his son, Hal. Towards the end of the play, **Prince Hal takes the crown while his father is asleep, imagining his father has already died**. Henry is horrified when he wakes: **'Dost thou so hunger for mine empty chair?'** At this his son does his best to reassure him, and promises to be a good king so that Henry at last dies contented. On Henry's death, Prince Hal becomes **King Henry V**, and immediately **orders the taverns to be cleaned up and the criminals who haunt them to be imprisoned**. When Falstaff hears that his friend has succeeded to the throne, he hurries to London, expecting preferment, but the new king ignores his erstwhile friend: **'I know thee not, old man.'**

Henry V (1599)

Twenty-seven-year-old King Henry V has acceded to the throne in a **precarious situation** and is keen to **consolidate his power**. Citing an ancient law, **he lays claim to part of France**. The French **dauphin** learns of Henry's plans and sends a message in which he mocks Henry, who responds by **readying an invasion fleet**. Immediately before they are due to set sail from **Southampton**, Henry learns of a **plot to assassinate** him. He reacts decisively, **executing the three traitors**. The fleet makes for France and they win battle after battle, eventually overrunning the town of **Harfleur**, during which Henry rouses his soldiers with the exhortation: **'Once more unto the breach, dear friends, once more/Stiffen the sinews, summon up the blood/Follow your spirit, and upon this charge Cry "God for Harry, England, and Saint George!"'**. The English are met by a French army with nearly five times as many men. On the morning of the battle, he prays to God and delivers an awe-inspiring speech: 'This day is call'd the feast of Crispian/He that outlives this day, and comes safe home,/Will stand a tip-toe when this day is named,/ And rouse him at the name of Crispian/We few, we happy few, we band of brothers;/For he to-day that sheds his blood with me/Shall be my brother'. The English win the days against the odds and **the French are slaughtered and captured in their thousands**. The terms of the surrender negotiations include **a marriage between Henry and Catherine**, the daughter of the French King. **Henry's son will therefore be the King of France, and will unite the two kingdoms**.

Henry VI, Part 1 (1592)

The play opens with the **funeral of Henry V**. The nobles mourn his death: '**England ne'er lost a king of so much worth**', and fear that the French will now take advantage of them. Indeed, messengers arrive with news that the French, led by the **Dauphin, Charles**, are rebelling, and **Lord Talbot** has been taken prisoner. As the young **Henry VI** is considered inexperienced, the **Duke of Bedford** departs for France to take charge of the army, while his brother, **Gloucester** agrees to rule England. The **Bastard of Orleans** (the illegitimate son of the Duke or Orleans) tells Charles of a visionary young woman, **Joan la Pucelle**, who claims to know how to defeat the English. Charles challenges her to **single combat** to examine her resolve and, upon her victory, immediately **puts her in charge of the army**. Meanwhile, in England, an argument between **Richard Plantagenet** and the **Duke of Somerset** is disrupting the country. Richard has discovered from his uncle, **Edmund Mortimer**, that their family helped **Henry Bolingbroke** seize the throne from **Richard II**, but that **Henry V had Richard's father executed and his property stolen**. On Mortimer's death, Richard puts the case before the newly-crowned Henry VI **who agrees to reinstate his title and lands**. King Henry arrives in France and asks Richard and Somerset to **forget their quarrel** for the sake of the war against the French, but **they fail to support each other, and the English army is defeated**. However, Joan has been captured by Richard, and is **burned at the stake**. Henry then **sues for peace** with the French, which they reluctantly agree to. Meanwhile, a beautiful French princess, **Margaret of Anjou**, has been captured by the **Earl of Suffolk** as a bride for the king. However, the wily Suffolk is plotting to use her to influence the king. The play ends on this unsettled note.

Henry VI, Part 2 (1591)

The play opens with the marriage of **Henry** to **Margaret of Anjou**, a match organised by the **Duke of Suffolk**, not only to unite England and France, but so that he can **influence Henry** through Margaret, his lover. The **Duke of Gloucester**, who is trusted by the king, is an enemy of Suffolk, who has Gloucester **falsely accused of treason**. Before the trial takes place, however, Suffolk has him **killed**. Meanwhile,

Richard, Duke of York, presents his claim to the throne: that he is descended from **Edward III's third son,** whereas Henry is descended from his **fourth son.** The Earls of **Salisbury** and **Warwick** pledge their allegiance to Richard. When **Henry discovers Suffolk's part in Gloucester's murder, he banishes him,** to Margaret's distress. She plans Suffolk's return, but before she can carry this out, **he is killed by pirates,** and his **head is presented** to the unhappy Queen. Richard enlists an officer of his, **Jack Cade,** to **stage a rebellion** in order to find out if he, Richard, would have the support of the people if he were to seize power. Richard then **departs for Ireland** so that he will not be held accountable for the uprising. Cade proves popular with the common people, encouraging them to riot, but Lord Clifford persuades the people to abandon Cade's vain cause.

Richard then returns from Ireland with an army, **'To claim his right,/and pluck the crown from feeble Henry's head'.** He is supported by his sons, **Edward,** (the future Edward IV) and **Richard** (later Richard III). The English nobles take sides, either for the **House of York,** or for **Henry and the House of Lancaster.** A battle is fought at **St Albans** in which the Yorkists win and **Lord Clifford is killed by Richard, Duke of York.** Margaret persuades the **king to flee to London,** joined by **young Clifford** who is **determined to avenge his father's death.**

King Henry VI, Part 3 (1592)

The Yorkists, including **Richard, Duke of York,** his sons **Richard, George** and **Edward** (later Edward IV), and the **Earl of Warwick,** emerge victorious from the first **Battle of St Albans. King Henry has conceded** that the **throne** will pass to the **House of York** after his death. But Margaret, his Queen, is furious that this agreement disinherits their son, **Prince Edward.** Margaret and Edward leave the King, and with Clifford's support, **declare war on the Yorkists.** They attack the Duke of York's castle at **Wakefield** and **kill him** and his 12-year-old son, Rutland. The furious Yorkists retaliate at the **Battle of Towton** where **Clifford meets his death.** After Towton, **Warwick heads to France,** where he secures a **marriage for Edward** with **Louis XI's sister-in-law,** in order **to unite the two countries.** However, **Edward has met, and fallen in love with,** the recently widowed Lady Grey, **Elizabeth Woodville.** He is determined to **marry her** despite losing the support of both **George** and **Richard,** and **infuriating Warwick,** who **changes his allegiance to the Lancastrians** in disgust, **and leads a French invasion into England. Edward** is subsequently **taken prisoner** and **Henry is restored to the throne.** However, Edward is rescued by Richard, Hastings and Stanley, and they meet Warwick's army at the **Battle of Barnet,** which the **Yorkists win** at the expense of **Warwick and Montague.** A Lancastrian/French army arrives, led by Margaret and Prince Edward. Henry is **captured** by two gamekeepers loyal to Edward and **imprisoned** in the **Tower of London.** In the ensuing **Battle of Tewkesbury,** the **Yorkists rout the Lancastrians and capture Margaret and Prince Edward.** The **Queen is banished,** and **Prince Edward stabbed to death**. Richard goes to the Tower to kill Henry. With his dying breath, Henry predicts the later Richard III's treacherous career: '**Teeth hads't thou in thy head when thou wast born/To signify thou cam'st to bite the world**'. King Edward IV, as he now becomes, believes the wars to be over, unaware of Richard's plans.

Henry VIII (1613)

Thought to have been written by both Shakespeare and **John Fletcher**, the play is set entirely at **Henry VIII's court**. At the opening, the nobles, principally the **Duke of Buckingham**, are complaining about the influence that **Cardinal Wolsey** has over the king. Wolsey then enters, and makes it clear that Buckingham is not in his favour. Buckingham is swiftly arrested for **treason**. King Henry makes his entrance, followed by **Queen Katherine** (Henry's first wife). She is also unhappy with Wolsey's preferential treatment, and brings up the subject of Buckingham's arrest, but Henry **orders his trial to go ahead**. Buckingham is convicted of treason. Wolsey gives an elaborate banquet at which the king and his party enter in disguise. Henry dances with **Anne Bullen** (Boleyn) and is bewitched: '**The fairest hand I ever touch'd. O Beauty,/Till now I never knew thee.**' Henry **plans to divorce Katherine, and marry Anne**, but the Queen protests that she has always been a loyal and faithful wife. Anne hears the news, and is sorry for Katherine. Queen Katherine is put on trial, but she begins by accusing Wolsey of plotting against her: '**I am a simple woman, much too weak/T'oppose your cunning.**' She refuses to stay for the proceedings. The lords suspect Wolsey of double-dealing, and some of Wolsey's letters to the Pope have mysteriously been sent to the king instead, **proving Wolsey's duplicity**. Henry is justifiably angry, and Wolsey realises he has lost the king's favour. Katherine falls ill and talks of death, but continues to profess loyalty to the king and even good wishes for the new Queen. Anne's coronation takes place with much pomp and ceremony. In the last Act, **Queen Anne gives birth to a daughter, Princess Elizabeth**, and Archbishop Cranmer predicts that she will bring '**Upon this land a thousand thousand blessings.**'

Julius Caesar (1599)

Julius Caesar is welcomed back to Rome with a **triumphal parade** after defeating the sons of **Pompey**. A soothsayer calls to Caesar: '**beware the Ides of March**' (the next day), but he thinks nothing of it. Two friends and senators, **Cassius** and **Brutus**, discuss how Caesar is now lauded like a god, although he is just a man, and a man with **physical failings** to boot. **Cassius hatches a plan to kill Caesar**. Brutus travels home, where he finds **letters**, apparently penned by Roman citizens, but **actually forged by Cassius**, expressing concerns about Caesar's power. These words compound Brutus's fears about a dictator silencing the will of the people. Cassius arrives at Brutus's house and they **plot to kill Caesar the following day**. The next morning Caesar arrives at the Senate and is **stabbed to death**, giving up the fight when he sees his **best friend Brutus**; a heartbroken Caesar utters 'Et tu, Brute?' and dies. The conspirators do not flee, certain that they acted in the **best interests of Rome**. Brutus makes a funeral speech, claiming that **although he loved Caesar, he loved Rome more, and Caesar threatened the liberty of Rome**. Antony stands up and addresses the crowd: 'Friends, Romans, Countrymen, lend me your ears'. His speech is a masterpiece of rhetoric, in which he reminds the people that Caesar actually refused the crown. Antony **manipulates** the people so they **beg him to read out Caesar's will**, which reveals that Caesar promised **money to every citizen** and left his **gardens to become public property**. **The crowd turn** against the conspirators and **chase them out of Rome**. Cassius and Brutus **raise an army** and are met by an army headed by **Mark Antony** and Caesar's adopted son **Octavius**. The battle turns against the conspirators and **Cassius orders one of his men to kill him**. The following day, with defeat imminent, **Brutus falls on his sword**. Antony finds Brutus's body, proclaiming him **'the noblest Roman of them all'** for he was the **only conspirator who believed his actions were for the good of Rome**.

King Lear (1605–6)

King Lear wants to retire and decides to **split the country** among his three daughters, offering the largest share to the one who loves him the most. **Goneril** and **Regan** exuberantly proclaim their love, while **Cordelia** speaks candidly, which upsets Lear and **he disinherits her**. The **Earl of Kent** speaks out in protest and is **banished**. One of Cordelia's suitors abandons his pursuit of her, but the **King of France marries her**, impressed by her honesty. Meanwhile, **Edmund**, the illegitimate son of the **Earl of Gloucester** plots to kill his brother, **Edgar**, the legitimate heir to the earldom. Edmund pretends he's been attacked by Edgar, and the latter is **denounced** by his father as an **outlaw**. With no power, Lear is mistreated by Goneril and Regan. He ventures out into a storm to rant against his ungrateful daughters: 'How sharper than a serpent's tooth it is to have a thankless child!', where he meets Edgar, in the guise of a madman. Kent also follows them (disguised as a servant, Caius), vowing to protect Lear. Edmund betrays his father, whose **eyes are then gouged out** by Regan's husband, **Cornwall**, who is subsequently **killed by a servant**. Goneril and Regan meet Edmund, **become attracted to him**, and vie for his affection. Meanwhile, a **French army**, accompanied by Cordelia, **has landed in Britain**; Kent sees the army and leads Lear to them. Edgar finds a **letter** from Goneril to Edmund **suggesting that he murders her husband**, Albany, and then **marries her**. The British defeat the French in battle, and **Lear and Cordelia are captured**. Edmund sends them off with secret orders for execution. Regan declares she will marry Edmund, but Albany **exposes Goneril's plans to murder him**, proclaiming Edmund as a traitor. **Regan collapses**, having been **poisoned** by the jealous Goneril. No longer disguised, Edgar fights his brother Edmund and **kills** him in a duel. **Goneril stabs herself** and the dying **Edmund reveals his order to murder Cordelia and Lear**. But Cordelia is already **dead**. Lear collapses with grief and **dies**. Edgar is later crowned King.

The Life and Death of King John (1593–6)

King John is a play of unhappy disputes. **Richard I, the Lionheart, has died**, and his brother, **John**, has become king of England. But, according to **King Philip of France, the crown should rightfully belong to Arthur**, the son of John's deceased older brother, **Geoffrey**. King John oversees a land dispute in the Faulconbridge family, during which it emerges that Philip Faulconbridge, called **Philip the Bastard**, is an **illegitimate son of Richard the Lionheart**. The King knights Philip and invites him to join his army. King John then fights the French for possession of the town of **Angiers**, where a citizen, **Hubert** suggests that the solution might be to unite both sides with a marriage between **Louis**, the **Dauphin**, and **Lady Blanche, King John's niece**, a scheme that gives John a stronger right to the throne. Another dispute centres on the Church: **John is excommunicated** for not agreeing to the Pope's preferred candidate **for Archbishop of Canterbury. King Philip agrees to invade England**, after pressure from the Papal legate, **Cardinal Pandulph**, who tells him that his duty to the church is more important than his recent family connections. In a skirmish, **Arthur is captured** and John asks Hubert to execute him. While Hubert hesitates, **Arthur dies leaping off the castle walls** in an attempt to escape, but **the English nobles believe that John murdered him and defect to Louis**. John then changes his mind, and **swears allegiance to the Pope**, but only if **Pandulph can negotiate with the French army**. Pandulph fails to convince Louis and so the two armies meet in battle. A wounded French lord reveals that Louis plans to kill the English lords, so they rejoin John. Meanwhile, **John has been poisoned by a monk and dies**. Philip the Bastard **prepares to attack Louis**, but is presented with a **peace treaty** from Louis. **Philip the Bastard and the lords swear allegiance** to John's son, **Henry** (who becomes Henry III).

Love's Labour's Lost (1594–5)

The **King of Navarre** and his lords, **Berowne, Longaville** and **Dumaine** each swear to commit themselves to study and abstain from debauchery and women for three years. However, Berowne reminds the king that the Princess of France will be visiting Navarre with her three ladies-in-waiting, so in order to honour his oath, the king arranges to meet them outside the castle. Meanwhile, **Don Armado**, a Spanish guest of the king's, falls for the country girl, **Jaquenetta**. He asks the fool **Costard** to deliver a letter to her. When the king and the lords meet the ladies, the lords fall farcically in love. As Berowne puts it: '**For where is any author in the world,/ Teaches such beauty as a woman's eye?**' Berowne gives Costard a letter to deliver to **Rosaline**, the maiden he has fallen in love with. But Costard **accidentally gives**

Berowne's letter to Jacquenetta, mixing it up with Don Armado's. Berowne looks on, unseen, as **the king professes his love for the princess.** Longaville enters and both Berowne and the king hide, witnessing him professes his love for the **Lady Maria.** The same thing happens with Dumaine, who is secretly watched by Berowne, Longaville and the king as he reads out an ode about **Lady Katharine. The king then reveals himself** and rebukes Longaville and Dumaine for going back on their oath. However, **his bluff is called** when Berowne emerges accusing the king of the same. Jaquenetta then comes in to return Berowne's letter to him, which he immediately tears up, but he leaves a **fragment** and is **outed by Dumaine.** After the lords **agree to pursue their respective women,** the princess receives a message that **her father has died.** She returns to France with her maidens, stipulating that they will only receive the attentions of the men **after a year has passed** in order to **test the earnestness of their professed love.**

Macbeth (1606)

Victors in battle, **Macbeth** and **Banquo** come across **three witches,** who **prophesise that Macbeth will become Thane of Cawdor and then King of Scotland** and that Banquo will be the father of kings. Both men are shocked, but are even more shocked when Macbeth is subsequently named **Thane of Cawdor.** When **King Duncan** arrives as a guest at their household, Lady Macbeth, now aware of the prophecy, highlights the opportunity, and after Duncan is in bed, she convinces her husband to murder him. The next day, Duncan's son **Malcolm** learns of his father's death and flees, fearing for his own life. **Macbeth is named king,** but Banquo and the Thane of Fife, **Macduff,** suspect foul play. Macbeth, anxious about Banquo's knowledge of the prophecy and his future destiny, arranges the **murder of Banquo,** although **his son escapes.** At a banquet, Macbeth sees the **ghost of Banquo** and starts to lose his cool. Spooked, Macbeth seeks out the witches once more. They conjure apparitions who tell Macbeth that he will not be harmed by anyone born to a woman and that he will not be vanquished until '. . . **Great Birnam wood to high Dunsinane hill/Shall come against him.'** The latter he knows not to be possible as a forest cannot move, and the former makes him believe he is invulnerable, as all men and women are born to a woman. **Macbeth hears of Macduff's defection to England** and, in retaliation, **sends men to slaughter his wife and children.** Hearing this terrible news, Macduff plots with Malcolm to depose Macbeth. Lady Macbeth is haunted by the memory of blood on her hands, which she continually tries to wash clean. **She kills herself** and Macbeth sinks into a **deep depression.** He is terrified to learn that the English army are shielded with boughs cut from Birnham wood. **Macduff and Macbeth meet in battle.** Macduff reveals that he was not **'of woman born',** having been **'untimely ripp'd'** from his mother's womb. **Macduff kills Macbeth and Malcolm is crowned king.**

Measure for Measure (1604)

The **Duke of Vienna** pretends to leave the city on a diplomatic pretext and hands over power to the stern judge, **Angelo**. Secretly he will stay behind disguised as a friar and spy on Angelo to see how firmly the law stays in place. **Claudio**, a young gentleman, has recently wedded **Juliet** but, due to lack of funds, they have not observed all the legal formalities. Angelo decides **not to recognise their marriage** and has **Claudio arrested and sentenced to death** for having sex outside marriage. A lord says of Angelo's ruthless behaviour: **'Some rise by sin, and some by virtue fall'**. Claudio's sister, the nun **Isabella**, pleads to Angelo on her brother's behalf. The judge takes a shine to the young nun, and makes her an offer: **he will grant Claudio mercy if she sleeps with him**. Isabella – who cannot sacrifice her soul – **refuses**. The Duke now intervenes to help Isabella. They hatch a trick in which **Mariana** – Angelo's betrothed, whom he has not married because of her lost inheritance – **poses as Isabella** and sleeps with the judge. Even though Angelo thinks he has had his wicked way with Isabella, **he goes back on his promise to free Claudio**. The duke therefore arranges for the **head** of another man, who has recently died and happens to look like Claudio, to be sent in place of Claudio's head. Then the Duke **'returns'** to Vienna and **Isabella and Mariana petition him**, making accusations against Angelo. Angelo denies the accusations, blaming the friar. After re-disguising himself as the friar, the Duke **reveals his true appearance** and **exposes Angelo as a liar**. Angelo is forced to **marry Mariana** and is only **saved from execution** by her pleas for him. The **Duke then proposes to Isabella** but she does not reply (often interpreted in performances as silent acceptance).

The Merchant of Venice (1596–7)

In Venice, **Bassanio**, a young lad about town and something of a spendthrift, wants to travel to **Belmont** to win the hand of the beautiful and wealthy **Portia**. He asks his wealthy friend Antonio for a loan, but his money is tied up in his **ships**, which are at sea, so Antonio agrees to put his ships as **collateral** if Bassanio can find a lender. Bassanio asks the Jewish money-lender, **Shylock**, who detests Antonio for his anti-Semitism (**'You call me misbeliever, cut-throat dog,/And spit upon my Jewish gaberdine'**) and also for his business habit of undercutting him by charging customers no interest. However, Shylock agrees to the loan but adds the condition that if Antonio cannot pay him back by a specified date, he will be owed **a pound of Antonio's flesh**. Antonio, sure that his ships will return, agrees to the bond. Meanwhile, in Belmont, Portia is anxious about her dead father's **will** which states that her future husband **will have to choose the right casket** out of three – **lead**, **silver** and **gold** – for her hand in marriage. Portia takes a shine to Bassanio and luckily he chooses the right casket (**lead**) and **wins her hand**. Back in Venice, Shylock's daughter Jessica elopes with Lorenzo and **converts to Christianity**, augmenting Shylock's desire for **revenge against Christians**. Portia and Bassanio get married, but shortly afterwards they hear that Antonio's **ships** are **reported lost at sea**, so Antonio has **forfeited the bond to Shylock**. Shylock seeks Antonio out to claim his pound of flesh. Bassanio fears for his friend's life but then Portia, with her maid, **Nerissa**, comes up with a plan. Appearing in a court as a **male legal expert**, Portia frees Antonio from his bond on a **legal technicality** that while Shylock is entitled to the flesh, **he is not entitled to the blood**. She also informs him that he is guilty **of conspiring against the life of a Venetian citizen**. However, Shylock is spared death so long as he **converts to Christianity** and makes a will **leaving his estate to his daughter** and Lorenzo.

The Merry Wives of Windsor (1599–1600)

Sir John Falstaff is low on cash so plans to court **two wealthy married women**. He writes love letters to them, but his servants **refuse to send them** and end up **telling the two husbands, Page** and **Ford**, of Falstaff's plan. Ford gets the **Master of the Garter** to introduce him as **Master Brook**, so he can extract information from Falstaff without arousing suspicion. Meanwhile, three men are wooing Page's daughter, **Mistress Anne**. She wants to marry Master **Fenton**, but her father favours Master **Slender**, and her **mother** favours **Doctor Caius**. **Hugh Evans**, a parson, wants to help his friend Slender, so recruits the doctor's servant **Mistress Quickly**. However, Caius discovers this and challenges Evans to a duel, but their plan to fight is scuppered by the Master of the Garter who gives them both a **different meeting place**. Mistresses Ford and Page find Falstaff's letters and decide to have some fun at his expense. They convince Falstaff to conceal himself in a **laundry basket** full of dirty clothes, which is then **thrown into the river**. Falstaff continues his plan unabated. This time, the merry wives convince Falstaff to disguise himself as **Mistress Page's aunt**. Master Ford returns home and proceeds to **kick the loathed aunt out of the house**. The wives contrive to play a **final joke on Falstaff** and let their husbands in on the fun. This time, Falstaff is persuaded to dress up as a **famous ghost** and travel to Windsor Forest, where he is **attacked by local children dressed up as fairies**. Page has told Slender to steal Anne away and marry her during the ensuing chaos, while Mistress Page has told Doctor Caius to steal Anne away. This seems to go to plan and they disappear with the people they think are their respective partners, while the others come clean to Falstaff. Falstaff acknowledges that **he got what was coming to him**. Slender and Doctor Caius return upon discovering that their 'partners' are actually **boys in disguise**. Meanwhile, **Fenton and Anne** are happily **married**. The group, including Falstaff, leaves in **high spirits**.

A Midsummer Night's Dream (1595–6)

Hot-headed **Hermia** refuses to obey her father's wishes to marry **Demetrius**. Meanwhile, **Oberon** and **Titania**, **King and Queen of the Fairies**, arrive at the **forest** outside Athens, having quarreled about the ownership of an Indian changeling (a child secretly exchanged by fairies for another child). As a punishment, Oberon calls for his servant **Puck** to find and apply a **potion** to **Titania's eyes,** which will make her **fall in love with the first man she sees. Demetrius is in love with Hermia, but she is in love with Lysander; Helena is in love with Demetrius, but he does not return her feelings.** Oberon witnesses Demetrius's cruelty to Helena, so **he orders Puck to apply the love potion** to his eyes. Puck **mistakenly applies the potion to Lysander,** who wakes up to see Helena, and **falls in love with her.** Oberon sees Demetrius pursuing Hermia and becomes angry that Puck didn't do as he asked, so he sends **Puck to fetch Helena,** while **he administers the potion to Demetrius** to make him fall in love with her when he wakes. Puck and Oberon both apply the potions and now **both Demetrius and Lysander love Helena.** Helena is convinced that their love is mere **mockery,** but **Hermia is furious with her for stealing Lysander.** Meanwhile, a band of **amateur actors are rehearsing a play** to be performed at Theseus and Hippolyta's wedding. Their leader, **Nick Bottom,** is spotted by Puck, who transforms his head into that of a **donkey.** His friends run away in fear, and the commotion **awakens the enchanted Titania, who falls in love with him.** Taking advantage of her infatuation with Bottom, Oberon **takes the changeling from Titania** before releasing Titania from the enchantment. He also instructs Puck to restore Bottom's head, and to apply the potion to Lysander's eyes. When the four of them wake, **Lysander is in love with Hermia and Demetrius is in love with Helena.** Theseus and Hippolyta arrive, and Theseus calls for a group wedding.

Much Ado about Nothing (1598–9)

Leonato, governor of **Messina,** receives news that a Spanish prince (**Don Pedro**) and his two officers (**Claudio** and **Benedick**), are coming to visit him. Claudio has a history with Leonato's daughter, **Hero,** and **falls in love with her again.** Meanwhile, **Benedick** and **Beatrice,** Leonato's niece, who have known and fought with each other for a long time, continue bickering. Benedick **swears he will never get married,** incredulous of Claudio's love for Hero. At a ball, Don Pedro attempts to help Claudio by wooing Hero on his behalf, but his vindictive brother, **Don John,** uses the opportunity to tell Claudio that Don Pedro is after his girl. But the misunderstanding is resolved between Claudio and his friend, and **Claudio proposes to Hero.** Shortly afterwards, Benedick and Beatrice's friends **hatch a plan to get the two enemies to admit their love** for each other, as Hero puts it: **'Some Cupid kills with arrows, some with traps'.** Claudio and Don Pedro speak of Beatrice's love for Benedick when they know him to be **eavesdropping,** and the women do the same with Beatrice listening in. Each responds by **resolving to requite the other's love.** Meanwhile, Don John makes another attempt at sabotaging Claudio's happiness. He gets his friend to flirt with Hero's chambermaid as though she were Hero herself, while placing Claudio in a position to observe. Claudio, believing Hero to be unfaithful, **mocks**

and **disparages** her at their wedding. Leonato publically disowns his daughter on hearing of her supposed disgrace. Hero faints. Amid the tumult, Beatrice and Benedick **openly declare their love for each other**. The local friar, believing in Hero's innocence, gets her to **fake her own death** to ignite Claudio's remorse. Fortunately, it turns out that a **watchman overheard** Don John hatching his evil plan, **exonerating Hero** from any impropriety. Claudio, remorseful, declares he will marry a cousin of Hero's as recompense. The cousin at the wedding **turns out to be Hero herself**. Don John is captured and happiness wins the day.

Othello (1601–2)

Othello, the **Moorish** general of the **Venetian army** is respected for his valued service to the state. However, he is nonetheless subjected to **racial prejudice** and is accused by senator **Brabantio** of **practising witchcraft to seduce his daughter**, **Desdemona**. Othello tells the senate how his stories, not witchcraft, won her heart. Othello is soon ordered to Cyprus to combat the invading Turks. Bitter and jealous of Othello's success, **Iago**, his standard-bearer, **plots against Othello** while **pretending to be his confidant**. He makes clear his plan to use **Cassio** – who was promoted up the ranks over him – as bait to ruin Othello and persuades Desdemona's disappointed suitor, **Roderigo**, to **pick a fight with Cassio**. Othello comes to quell the ruckus and **strips Cassio of his rank**. Iago then tells Cassio **to appeal to Desdemona** to get her husband to reinstate him, meanwhile **suggesting to Othello that Cassio is having an affair with his wife**. Next, Iago's wife, **Emilia**, comes across Desdemona's **handkerchief**, which was Othello's first gift to her. Upon request, Emilia hands it to Iago **who plants it in Cassio's room**. Iago orchestrates a scene watched from a distance by Othello, in which **Bianca**, a prostitute romantically involved with Cassio, **discovers the handkerchief** and **accuses Cassio of having another lover. Iago persuades Othello that Desdemona is Cassio's lover** and that **she received the handkerchief as a present from him**. Worked into a fit of jealousy, **Othello resolves to kill her** and **orders Iago to slay Cassio**. He steals into her bedroom **to smother her**. Emilia is horrified when she discovers Desdemona's dead body and calls for help. Othello attempts to justify his actions by accusing his wife of **adultery**, mentioning the handkerchief. Emilia, who now realises Iago's **treachery, outs her husband**, who stabs her. Othello wounds Iago and demands to know the reason **'why he hath ensnared my soul and body?'**, but Iago replies: **'Demand me nothing; what you know, you know:/From this time forth I never will speak word'**. Othello kills himself before he can be taken away.

Pericles, Prince of Tyre (1607–8)

King **Antiochus** has offered the **hand of his beautiful daughter** to any man who can solve the riddle he has devised, but at the price of death for an incorrect answer. **Pericles, Prince of Tyre**, manages to work out the answer but does not offer the solution because it would reveal the incestuous relationship between the king and his daughter and would, therefore, surely lead to Pericles' execution. He asks for more time to consider the puzzle, but **escapes back to Tyre**. However, certain of Antiochus's desire for revenge, he decides to leave Tyre until the threat has passed. His ship is **wrecked** in a **storm**, and Pericles is washed up in **Pentapolis**, where King **Simonides** is holding a tournament. Pericles wins, and marries his daughter, **Thaisa**, who has fallen in love with him. News arrives that **Antiochus has died**, and Pericles decides to sail for Tyre with his wife, Thaisa, who is **pregnant**. Another storm threatens his ship and **Thaisa apparently dies** while **giving birth to a daughter, Marina**. Thaisa's body is cast overboard in a **watertight coffin,** as the sailors believe it will calm the storm. Pericles stops at **Tarsus**, and leaves Marina in the care of **Cleon** and his wife, **Dionyza,** before returning to Tyre. Meanwhile, Thaisa's coffin washes ashore at **Ephesus** where **Lord Cerimon**, a physician, **revives her**. Thaisa becomes **a priestess in the temple of Diana**. Marina is now grown up and is so beautiful that Dionyza plots to have her killed, because she takes attention away from his birth daughter. However, before this happens, Marina is **kidnapped by pirates**, who then sell her to a **brothel** in **Mytilene**. While working there, she miraculously remains a **virgin**, preaching virtue to the clients. **Pericles returns to Tarsus** for Marina, but Cleon and his wife claim she has died. Grief-stricken, he once again sets sail and **arrives in Mytilene where he recognises Marina**. The goddess **Diana** then appears to him, instructing him to visit the temple at Ephesus, where he is **reunited with his long-lost wife**.

Richard II (1595)

The play opens on an argument: King Richard is hearing the case of his cousin, **Henry Bolingbroke**, who is in dispute with **Thomas Mowbray, Duke of Norfolk**. Bolingbroke accuses Mowbray of **squandering money** given to him by Richard to pay the King's soldiers, and also of murdering the **Duke of Gloucester**. The two challenge each other to a **duel**, which Richard reluctantly agrees to. However, Richard **disrupts the subsequent duel** and **banishes** both men from the country, Bolingbroke for only **six** years, but Mowbray for **life**. Then **John of Gaunt, Bolingbroke's father**, and **Richard's uncle**, dies, but not before using his last breath to criticise Richard's government and to praise the nation's virtues: '**This royal throne of kings, this scept'red isle/... This precious stone, set in a silver sea.**' As soon as Gaunt dies, Richard promptly **seizes all his money and property**, intending to finance the **Irish wars** with the proceeds. The nobles, Lord Ross, Lord Willoughby, and the Earl of Northumberland, are so angry at this action and at Richard's policy of heavily taxing the common people that they **plot to overthrow the king** and **return Bolingbroke from exile**. While Richard is away waging war on Ireland, **Bolingbroke returns, assembles an army and invades England**. On Richard's return, Bolingbroke claims not only the return of his property, but also the throne.

Richard is taken prisoner and, while in prison, bemoans his fate, but also reminds his subjects of his rightful position as king: **'Not all the water in the rough rude sea/Can wash the balm off from an anointed king.'** Richard advises his Queen, **Isabel**, to flee to France. A nobleman, Exton, murders Richard, having taken literally Henry's words **'Have I no friend will rid me of this living fear?'** Bolingbroke then crowns himself **King Henry IV** and vows to make a pilgrimage to Jerusalem to atone for Richard's death.

Richard III (1592–3)

The play opens with the deformed **hunchback Richard, Duke of Gloucester** and member of the **House of York**, enviously describing the accession of his brother, **Edward IV: 'Now is the winter of our discontent/Made glorious summer by this sun of York.'** Richard starts to plot his path to the throne. He stitches up his brother **Clarence** and has Edward send him to the **Tower**. Next, **Richard woos Anne Neville**, a member of the **House of Lancaster** and widow of the former Prince of Wales, and she eventually **agrees to marry him. King Edward IV suddenly falls ill and dies**, but because his **son Edward is too young to accede to the throne**, he names Richard **Lord Protector**. Richard pays a visit to the precocious **Edward** and his younger brother, the **Duke of York**, who outwit him, causing Richard to **fear the threat they might pose** in the future. He **persuades the two princes to stay in the Tower** for their protection. Richard then transforms himself into an **outwardly pious and humble** man to secure support. Richard and his cousin the **Duke of Buckingham start a rumour** that the **two young princes in the Tower are illegitimate** and, after some persuasion, the lords reluctantly accept Richard as king. He then has the **princes murdered. Buckingham falls out** with Richard over a promise of land and he joins **Henry, the Earl of Richmond and leader of the House of Lancaster**. Buckingham leads a **rebellion**, but he is **captured** and **executed**. Henry leads a **second rebellion** and his and Richard's armies meet at the **Battle of Bosworth**. Richard is **unhorsed** during the battle and cries out **'A horse, a horse, my kingdom for a horse!'** before he is **slain by Henry**, who is later crowned **Henry VII**. He marries **Elizabeth of York**, uniting the two royal houses.

Romeo and Juliet (1595–6)

The two great families of **Verona**, the **Montagues** and **Capulets**, are mortal enemies. **Count Paris** is looking to marry **Juliet Capulet**, and his wishes are supported by both of her parents. Meanwhile, **Romeo**, a Montague, is down on his luck in love so his cousin, **Benvolio**, and friend, **Mercutio**, persuade him to crash the **Capulet ball** with them. At the ball **Romeo and Juliet fall in love**. Later that night, Romeo creeps to the foot of **Juliet's balcony** and overhears her frustrations about their family ties: **'What's in a name? That which we call a rose/By any other word would smell as** sweet'. Romeo reveals himself and they both **declare their love.** They **secretly marry** the next day, with the help of **Friar Lawrence** who hopes to end the discord between the two families through their union. Juliet's cousin **Tybalt, challenges Romeo to a duel** to **protect the family honour** that Romeo has abused by sneaking into the ball. When Romeo refuses, Mercutio takes over, **attacks Tybalt** and is **fatally wounded. Romeo kills Tybalt** in revenge and is consequently **banished** from Verona. Before he leaves, he **spends the night with his bride.** Juliet's parents subsequently arrange for her to marry Paris, and in desperation, Juliet asks the Friar for help. His plan is to give her a **drug,** which will put her in a **deep, death-like sleep,** and to let Romeo know of this so that they can be **reunited** after she is given up for dead by her family. The plan goes wrong as **no message reaches Romeo,** and **he thinks his Juliet is truly dead.** Overcome by grief, **Romeo buys poison** from an **apothecary.** He enters the crypt where Juliet is buried and is attacked by Paris, who believes Romeo is a vandal. **Romeo kills Paris** and then **kills himself,** after kissing Juliet's lips. **Juliet wakes up** shortly afterwards, and finding Romeo dead, **she takes his dagger** and **kills herself.** The two feuding families, finding their young dead, **agree to end their enmity.**

The Taming of the Shrew (1590–1)

Katherina and **Bianca** are the daughters of **Baptista,** a Paduan lord. Katherina's temper is **fearsome,** which puts off all potential suitors. Bianca, meanwhile, is wooed by two men, **Hortensio** and **Gremio.** However, Baptista has vowed that **Bianca may not marry until Katherina does,** so Hortensio and Gremio **hatch a plan to marry off Katherina.** A new student at Padua, **Lucentio,** arrives and falls in love with Bianca. He eavesdrops on Baptista, finding out that he **requires a tutor** for Bianca. Lucentio gets his servant **Tranio to pretend to be him,** while Lucentio **dresses up as a Latin tutor** and calls himself **Cambio** so **he can woo Bianca without Baptista knowing.** Meanwhile, **Petruchio,** an old friend of Hortensio's, arrives in Padua to find a wife and is persuaded by his friend **to marry Katherina without meeting her.** Hortensio convinces Petruchio to **present a music tutor** named **Litio** (secretly Hortensio) to Baptista so **he can woo Bianca without Baptista knowing.** Petruchio meets Katherina and they have a **blazing war-of-words** before he tells Baptista, falsely, that Katherina has agreed to marry him. She does not fight this, so the **pair marry** and travel to Petruchio's country house. He begins to '**tame**' her employing **reverse psychology** to convince her that her fiery words are, in fact, sweet and gentle. Meanwhile, **Bianca falls in love with Lucentio** after hearing a Latin translation revealing his love for her. Tranio (as Lucentio) meets with Baptista and **wins his approval for Lucentio to marry his daughter,** by promising her a large dowry. Baptista insists that Lucentio's father **Vincentio** must confirm the amount, so Tranio and Lucentio find an old man to pretend to be him. Lucentio and Bianca subsequently **elope. Petruchio and Katherina** encounter the real **Vincentio**, who is **shocked to find Tranio pretending to be Lucentio**. Lucentio and Bianca arrive and after much confusion, the **sisters are forgiven by their father**. Hortensio has married a rich widow and, at the wedding banquet, **a contest is staged** to see who the most obedient wife is. **Katherina wins** and gives a speech encouraging wives to obey their husbands.

The Tempest (1610–1)

The **magician Prospero** is the rightful **Duke of Milan**, but has been **usurped** by his brother **Antonio** and abandoned on an island with his daughter **Miranda**. Prospero rescues the spirit **Ariel** from imprisonment by a witch but takes her as his servant, promising to eventually release her. Prospero adopts the witch's son **Caliban**, a hideous creature, and teaches him how to speak. Caliban later tries to rape Miranda and is **enslaved** by Prospero. Prospero discovers that his brother Antonio is sailing close to the island and **conjures a terrible storm, or tempest**, to wreck the ship. A number of passengers survive, including Antonio's friend **King Alonso of Naples**, Alonso's brother, **Sebastian**, Alonso's son, **Ferdinand,** and the servant **Gonzalo**. Caliban falls in love with both the steward **Stephano** and the jester **Trincolo**, and the three of them **plan a rebellion** against Prospero. Prospero acts as matchmaker between **Miranda and Ferdinand**, and they fall in love, but Prospero worries that the fact that they fell in love so easily may **'make the prize light'**, so he makes Ferdinand his slave. **Antonio and Sebastian plot to kill Alonso and Gonzalo, so Sebastian will replace his brother as King of Naples**, but **Ariel intervenes**, transforming into a terrifying harpy and lambasting them for their evil ways. All of the shipwreck survivors are brought before Prospero and Miranda, the latter of whom exclaims **'How beauteous mankind is! O brave new world/That has such people in't!'** Prospero **forgives** Alonso, Antonio, Sebastian and Caliban for their respective transgressions. He agrees to the **marriage of Ferdinand and Miranda** and commands Ariel to guide Alonso's ship to Naples, after which he promises her **freedom**. Prospero **snaps his magic staff**, finally pleading with the audience to release him from the island through their applause: **'As you from crimes would pardon'd be/Let your indulgence set me free.'**

Timon of Athens (1607–8)

Timon is a wealthy citizen of **Athens**, generous to his friends and surrounded by **flatterers** and **sycophants**. He gives a lavish banquet and makes a speech on the value of friendship. Everyone professes to be his friend, except the canny and **cynical** philosopher, **Apemanthus**, who warns him about his reckless extravagance and his false friends. Gradually, Timon **gives all his wealth away**, at which point his faithful steward, **Flavius**, voices his concerns to his master about his abusive and exploitative so-called friends. Timon's creditors soon appear demanding money that he now cannot pay. Flavius explains to them that there is no money left, adding

'We have seen better days.' Apemanthus goes a step further and attacks the greedy creditors whom he despises. Timon then sends his servants out to **beg his closest friends for funds**, but they are **refused**. In the face of this, Timon plans his **revenge**. He gives a small dinner for the people who have betrayed him. Under the covered dishes, the guests find only **rocks and lukewarm water**, the latter of which **Timon throws in their faces**. Timon **flees Athens** in disgust, and makes his home in a **cave in the woods**. While digging for roots to eat, he discovers a hoard of **gold**. News of this discovery spreads and he is soon visited by Apemanthus, Alcibiades, and two prostitutes. Timon decides to give money to Alcibiades, so that he can **attack Athens in revenge**, and to the prostitutes, so that they can spread more **disease**. Flavius arrives and begs Timon to return to Athens but he refuses: he has had enough of society and has become a bitter **misanthrope**. He does at least recognise Flavius as **'one honest man'**, but then orders him to leave. Timon dies in the wilderness leaving an epitaph cursing humanity: **'Here lie I, Timon, who alive, all living men did hate,/Pass by, and curse thy fill, but pass and stay not here thy gait.'**

Titus Andronicus (1593)

Saturnius and **Bassianus** are arguing over who will succeed their father as **Emperor**. The people's choice, **Titus Andronicus**, arrives, with the captured **Queen of the Goths, Tamora**, her three sons **Alarbus, Demetrius** and **Chiron**, and her secret lover **Aaron, a moor**. Titus **kills Alarbus** in recompense for the loss of his sons during the war. Titus does not want to become Emperor, and **supports Saturnius**, who becomes Emperor. Saturnius plans to marry Titus's daughter **Lavinia** in spite of the fact that **she is engaged to Bassianus**. Bassianus is furious and is backed up by Titus's sons, **Quintus, Martius** and **Mutius. Titus accuses them all of treason** and, in an ensuing melee, **he kills Mutius**. Saturnius denounces the Andronici and **marries Tamora instead**. Meanwhile, Aaron convinces Demetrius and Chiron to **kill Bassianus** and to rape Lavinia. They do so and cut off her tongue and hands to prevent her from disclosing the truth. **Aaron stitches up Titus's sons Martius and Quintus** by forging a letter and the Emperor condemns them to die. Aaron visits Titus and **concocts a story** that **Saturnius will allow Martius and Quintus to live if one of Titus or his three sons cuts off their own hand** and sends it to the Emperor. Titus allows Aaron to cut off his own hand but, shortly afterwards, he receives the **severed heads of his two sons**. Titus orders his remaining son **Lucius** to flee Rome and **raise an army**. Meanwhile, **Tamora gives birth to a mixed-race baby**, which Aaron takes and flees. Lucius **captures Aaron** and forces him to disclose the plot. Tamora's sons and Tamora **dress up as the spirits of Revenge, Murder and Rape** to convince Titus to make Lucius **call off the impending invasion**. Tamora (as Revenge) leaves and **Titus then kills Chiron** and **Demetrius**. The following day, Titus asks Saturnius if a father should kill his daughter if she has been raped and he says yes. **Titus kills Lavinia** and tells

Saturnius about the rape. When the Emperor sends for Chiron and Demetrius, Titus reveals that they are **baked in the pie Tamora is eating. Titus kills Tamora,** and is **then slain by Saturnius,** who is in turn killed by Lucius. **Lucius is proclaimed Emperor,** and Aaron is buried chest-deep, **left to die of thirst.**

Troilus and Cressida (1601)

This play takes place during the **Trojan War,** which started when Paris, son of King Priam of Troy took Helen from her husband Menelaus, the King of Sparta, and brought her to Troy. The play opens with the Trojan prince **Troilus** falling in love with **Cressida,** the daughter of a **Trojan priest** who has **joined the Greeks.** Meanwhile, the commander of the Greeks, **Agamemnon,** is perplexed as to why his troops seem so troubled. **Odysseus, King of Ithaca,** advises him that the disrespectful behaviour of Achilles, who refuses to fight, is causing this discord. A message from **Hector, Prince of Troy,** arrives at the Greek camp, inviting their champion to **single combat** the following day. Odysseus plans to send **Ajax,** a strong but impetuous hero, with the hope that **Achilles' pride will be affected** by this snub and he will take up arms again. The Trojans deliberate over whether to continue fighting, or whether to deliver Helen back to the Greeks, thus ending the war. Hector wants to sue for peace, but **Troilus convinces the Trojans to continue fighting.** That night, **Troilus and Cressida vow to stay together forever.** Meanwhile, Cressida's father negotiates the **exchange of a Trojan prisoner for Cressida,** and a Greek lord named **Diomedes** then leads her out of Troy. The next day, **Ajax and Hector fight,** but the honours are even. **Odysseus sneaks Troilus in to Cressida's father's tent,** where he witnesses Diomedes **persuading Cressida to become his lover.** The following day, Hector and the furious Troilus **drive the Greeks from the city walls.** Achilles's best friend **Patroclus,** wearing **Achilles's armour,** is **killed by Hector,** who believes he has slain Achilles. Beside himself with grief and anger, Achilles joins the battle, but **cannot defeat Hector in single combat,** instead **surrounding the now unarmed Hector with Greek warriors and killing him.** He attaches Hector's body to the back of his chariot and **drags him around the walls of Troy.** The Trojan citizens mourn their hero.

Twelfth Night (1601)

Viola and her twin brother, **Sebastian,** are separated during a shipwreck on the shores of **Illyria.** Viola believes that her brother is dead and decides to **disguise herself as a boy called Cesario.** Cesario (Viola) soon takes a job as a servant to the **Duke Orsino. Cesario (Viola) falls in love with the Duke** but he is in love with **Lady Olivia.** Olivia does not reciprocate Orsino's feelings, but when he sends his young page Cesario (Viola) to deliver messages of love, Olivia is captivated by the youth's way with words and declares that **'Love sought is good, but giv'n unsought is better'.** In the comic subplot, Olivia's mischievous uncle, **Sir Toby Belch,** along with his fellow conspirators, plays a trick on Olivia's pompous and conceited steward, **Malvolio** to make him believe that his mistress wants to marry him. Malvolio comes upon a **letter** which looks as though it is in Olivia's handwriting. The letter advises **'be not afraid of greatness: some are born great, some achieve greatness, and some have greatness thrust upon 'em'** and asks him to appear before his mistress in **yellow stockings**. Olivia, bemused that her charms have failed to win over Ceasrio (Viola), is shocked by Malvolio's strange appearance and behaviour: **'this is very midsummer madness'**. Taken as mad, **Malvolio is locked up** and mocked for his foolery by the others who, he now realises, had faked the letter. When Viola's lost twin Sebastian emerges on the scene, the confusion escalates. Olivia, confusing him for his twin, Cesario (Viola), and in a burst of passion, **asks him to marry her**. After some confusion, **Sebastian accepts**. **Viola and Sebastian are reunited** and they appear before Orsino and Olivia. Viola reveals that she is **actually female** and that Sebastian is her twin brother. The Duke **declares his love for Viola** and **asks her to marry him**. Malvolio is released from prison.

Two Gentlemen of Verona (1592–3)

Valentine departs his home town of **Verona**, and says goodbye to his best friend **Proteus**, who refuses to join him on account of his love for **Julia**. Julia's maid, Lucetta, tells Julia that she suspects Proteus likes her; although Julia returns his feelings, she is embarrassed to admit it. **Lucetta produces a letter from Proteus**, but Julia **rashly tears it up** before trying to piece it back together. Proteus's father sends **Proteus to join Valentine in Milan**, but not before Julia **and Proteus declare their love for each other and exchange rings**. Meanwhile, **Valentine has fallen in love with Silvia**, the Duke's daughter. When **Proteus joins the court, he also falls in love with her**. He finds out Valentine's secret plans to elope with Silvia and reveals this to the Duke, who then **banishes Valentine**. Back in Verona, **Julia disguises herself** as a man named **Sebastian**, and travels to find Proteus. However, she discovers him wooing Silvia. Meanwhile, Valentine is accosted by a **group of outlaws** in a forest. They insist that **he becomes their leader** and will kill him if he declines. Sebastian (Julia) becomes Proteus's page and is sent to Silvia bearing a present from Proteus – **the ring that he received from Julia in Verona**. Silvia, however, is unimpressed, and refuses to believe Proteus's claim that Valentine is rumoured to be dead. She enlists the help of her friend Sir Eglamour to find Valentine. They travel into the forest but are apprehended by the outlaws. Meanwhile, the Duke has sent out a **search party** to find Silvia. **Proteus frees Silvia** from her captors, secretly watched by Valentine. Proteus tells her that he loves her and implies that he will rape her, but **Valentine saves her**. Proteus is filled with **contrition**. Sebastian (Julia) faints, which **reveals his true identity**. Upon seeing Julia, **Proteus remembers his feelings for her**. The Duke enters and allows Valentine his daughter's hand in marriage. **The two couples marry** and the Duke pardons the outlaws.

The Two Noble Kinsmen (1613–4)

On the day planned for **Duke Theseus's** wedding to **Hippolyta**, he is visited by **three queens** who petition him to go to war against **King Creon of Thebes** to **avenge the deaths of their respective husbands**. Theseus agrees to their request and wages war on Creon. In Thebes, two cousins, **Palamon** and **Arcite**, are disgusted with Creon's behavior, but are honour-bound to fight for him. In the ensuing **battle** between Creon's and Theseus's forces, Palamon and Arcite **fight valiantly**, but Theseus wins the day and the two of them are imprisoned in Athens. They glimpse Hippolyta's sister, **Emilia**, and both fall in love with her. **Arcite is released** from prison, but chooses to disguise himself rather than return home. **Palamon escapes** with the help of the jailer's daughter, who has fallen in love with him, but he does not return her feelings. When Palamon and Arcite meet again, they agree to **mortal combat**, but Theseus intervenes and orders their executions. However, Hippolyta and Emilia **persuade Theseus** to decree that, rather than fighting, a **tournament** shall decide which of them **wins the right to marry Emilia** and which of them will be **executed**. Stricken by unrequited love, the jailer's daughter loses her mind. Her father seeks the help of a doctor, who advises him to fetch her former suitor and get him to pretend to be Palamon. Before the tournament, Arcite prays to **Mars** to help him win the battle, while Palamon prays to **Venus** that he may marry Emilia. Emilia prays to **Diana** to deliver victory to the cousin who loves her the most. **Arcite triumphs**, but is **thrown from his horse and dies**, bequeathing Emilia to Palamon before he dies.

The Winter's Tale (1611)

Polixenes, the **King of Bohemia**, has been visiting his old friend **Leontes, King of Sicilia**, but grows homesick. Leontes sends his **pregnant wife, Hermione**, to plead with him to stay. **She manages to convince him**, but Leontes's initial joy is replaced with **paranoia** that his wife and Polixenes are having an **affair**, and that **the baby she is carrying, is actually Polixenes'**. Leontes commands his loyal retainer **Camillo** to **poison Polixenes**. Camillo, instead, warns Polixenes, and they both **flee to Bohemia**. Leontes has Hermione **arrested for adultery**. She **gives birth to a girl** in prison, and her friend **Paulina** takes the child to Leontes to convince him that he is the father. However, this plan doesn't work and Leontes accuses Paulina and her husband **Antigonus** of **conspiring against him**. Leontes orders Antigonus to **abandon the child** on the coast of Bohemia. Hermione is **tried for treason** and, despite a stirring speech and word from the **Oracle** corroborating her innocence, Leontes is unmoved. However, a messenger delivers news that **their son is dead**, **fulfilling an earlier prophecy from the Oracle**. Hermione **faints**, and is assumed to have died of shock. Leontes suddenly realises how foolish he has been. Meanwhile, Antigonus, has arrived on the coast of Bohemia carrying the newborn, which he names **Perdita**. He is **chased by a bear and eaten**, while the child is found by a shepherd. **Sixteen years** pass and, in Bohemia, Polixenes's son Florizel has **fallen in love** with Perdita. Unaware of her history, Polixenes objects to their plans to marry and the couple **flee to Sicilia**. The shepherd follows them and is taken into custody, where he **reveals Perdita's heritage**. Leontes is **amazed to see Polixenes,** and the two **reconcile,** joyfully **agreeing to the marriage** between their children. The party decides to visit Paulina and her **statue of Hermione,** whereupon Leontes is overcome by grief. The **statue suddenly comes to life** and **she, Leontes and their daughter are reunited.**

PLOT SUMMARIES OF GREAT NOVELS

Frankenstein by Mary Shelley

Captain Robert Walton travels to the **North Pole**, where his ship becomes trapped by **ice**. He makes out a **large figure** in the distance, and, several hours later, the crew find a **half-dead man**. Aboard the ship, the man tells the captain his story. His name is **Victor Frankenstein**, a **Swiss scientist** who discovered how to **give life to inanimate bodies**. He had planned to create a **beautiful creature**, but what he produced was a **horrifying monster**. Appalled with what he had done, Victor fled, hoping to forget his terrifying creation. Some years later, news of **his brother's death** reached Victor, and he returned home, where he caught sight of the creature again. **He became convinced that the creature was responsible for his brother's death,** but a young woman was suspected and subsequently **tried and executed** for the murder. Victor **fled** to the **mountains**, with the weight of **two deaths on his conscience,** but the creature found him, and begged Victor **to create a companion for him** to cure him of his loneliness. Victor eventually agreed and travelled to the **Orkney Islands** with his friend **Henry Clerval** to create his **second creature**. However, Victor found the monster **staring at him through a window** and became terrified by the implications of his work, so **he destroyed it**. The **creature vowed to exact revenge** on the day of Victor's upcoming **wedding night**. The monster **murdered Clerval** shortly afterwards, and Victor was **wrongly imprisoned** for the crime. He was acquitted and soon afterwards married his **childhood love Elizabeth**. On the wedding day, he left her while he **hunted for the creature**. However, the **creature found Elizabeth and killed her**. Grief-stricken at **her death** and the **subsequent death of his father,** Victor vowed to kill the monster, pursuing it to the **North Pole**. **Victor dies** several days after his rescue on the ship, and the captain finds the **monster crying over Victor's body**. He tells the captain of his **suffering** and believes that he will be **free** now that his creator has died. The monster **drifts away** on an ice sheet and **disappears into the distance**.

Great Expectations by Charles Dickens

Great Expectations is a story about the grief that love and obsession bring, as well as the wounds time heals. **Pip**, an **orphan**, is being brought up by his sister and her husband, **Joe**. When out on the marsh, he is accosted by a **fleeing convict** who tells him to get him food and a file to rid him of his chains. Pip dutifully brings these things, asking no questions. The convict is captured the following day. Shortly after, Pip is sent for by **Miss Havisham** of Satis house. Miss Havisham, who cannot get over **being jilted at the altar**, has her **wedding breakfast still in place**, and continues to wear her **wedding dress**. She introduces Pip to the beautiful but cold **Estella**. Just as Pip begins to foster ideas of bettering himself to be worthy of Estella, Miss Havisham breaks off their meetings and sponsors Pip to be a **blacksmith** under Joe's tutelage. After his sister is attacked by Joe's labourer, **Orlick**, Pip's hatred of him deepens. One day, **Jaggers**, a lawyer, appears telling Pip that **he has a benefactor who wants him to become a gentleman**. Jaggers tells Pip: 'he has great expectations'. Pip journeys to London where he meets childhood acquaintance **Herbert Pocket**, who swiftly becomes his friend. The two fall into debt just as Pip's hopes of marrying Estella are renewed. **Pip's sister dies** and, when the convict appears at his home in London, he discovers it was **he and not Miss Havisham who is his benefactor**. He learns that the convict's name is **Abel Magwitch**. Pip, initially horrified, grows to love Magwitch, **seeing much good in the convict**. He also discovers that **Estella** is **Magwitch's daughter**, and that his partner in crime, **Compeyson**, is the **cad who jilted Miss Havisham**. Miss Havisham later **sets herself alight but survives**, deformed, and asks for Pip's forgiveness which he gives, reflecting: '**And could I look upon her without compassion, seeing her punishment in the ruin she was**'. **Pip and Herbert help Magwitch escape** but he is caught by the police who have been tipped off by Compeyson. The two criminals have it out and **Compeyson dies**. **Magwitch is sentenced to death**. Pip falls ill and Joe comes to take care of him, the two reunited after Pip's initial rejection of his family. After some years away, Pip returns to Satis house and **here comes across Estella**. Having lived with her abusive husband, who is now dead, Estella's coldness has dissipated and the **two leave the ruins together**.

Middlemarch by George Eliot

In the small country town of Middlemarch, **Dorothea Brooke**, a well-meaning young woman, astonishes her sister, **Celia**, by rejecting the wealthy landowner, **Sir James Chettam**, and instead marrying **Edward Casaubon**, a cold, middle-aged scholar in poor health. She is devoted to helping him in his work. '**Of course I submitted to him, because it was my duty**', insists Dorothea to Celia. Through her husband, Dorothea is introduced to the handsome **Will Ladislaw**, Casaubon's young cousin. **Tertius Lydgate**, an enthusiastic young doctor, arrives in Middlemarch. While working at the hospital, he meets the unscrupulous financier,

Mr Bulstrode, and his niece, **Rosamund Vincy**, a pretty, but empty-headed young woman. **Lydgate falls for Rosamund**, and marries her but, through her profligacy, he is soon in debt, and their marriage becomes strained. **He is forced to borrow money from Bulstrode**, and becomes associated with the financier's shady dealings. Rosamund's equally empty-headed brother, **Fred Vincy**, has a sensible girlfriend, **Mary Garth**, who will not marry him until he gives up his ideas of going into the Church. Fred loses money gambling and is forced to borrow money from Mary's father, Caleb Garth, which humiliates him and prompts him to re-evaluate his life. He decides to train to be a **land agent** under Mary's father, and, as this is deemed to be a suitable career, **he wins the hand of Mary**. **Casaubon dies** and Dorothea learns that **she will be disinherited** from her husband's estate if **she marries Ladislaw**. Nevertheless, she has become attracted to Will. Meanwhile, Will has **secretly been in love** with her since their first meeting. **They marry**, once again to the disapproval of her sister, Celia, who is by now contentedly **married to Sir James Chettam**. Dorothea donates a large amount of money to Lydgate and to the hospital and helps to clear his name from the business dealings of Bulstrode.

Nineteen-Eighty-Four by George Orwell

Nineteen-Eighty-Four is a **dystopian** novel about a **totalitarian** regime. The book is set mostly in **London**, now part of the super-state **Oceania**, which is in a state of perpetual war with two competing super-states. Society is controlled by the ruling **Party**, led by the omnipresent leader **Big Brother**, whose image is emblazoned across thousands of **telescreens** that watch everything people do. **Individuality, free thought** and **emotion** is **outlawed**; order is maintained through the **Thought Police**, a network of spies who detect anyone even thinking of challenging the power of the Party. The novel's principal character is **Winston Smith**, a member of the **Outer Party**, who works in the **Ministry of Truth**. He is **growing increasingly frustrated** with Party's oppressiveness and starts to keep a diary of his negative thoughts, a crime punishable by death. He starts to become **paranoid**, and suspects that a dark-haired female co-worker, who keeps looking at him, is an informant for the Thought Police. One day, she hands him a note that reads 'I love you' and reveals that her name is **Julia**. They begin an affair and rent a room in a district occupied by **Proles**, the lowest stratum in Oceania's hierarchy. His bitterness towards the regime intensifies. Winston is soon approached by **O'Brien**, a member of the **Inner Party**, whom Winston suspects is a member of the secret revolutionary organisation known as the **Brotherhood**. Winston and Julia travel to meet him and he confirms Winston's suspicions, claiming to be a member of the Brotherhood. He gives Winston a book by the Brotherhood's leader revealing truths about the Party. Later, **Julia and Winston meet in their room but are arrested by the Thought Police**. Winston is **interrogated, tortured** and **brainwashed** by O'Brien who reveals himself as a Party spy. He is condemned to **Room 101**, the dreaded place where prisoners face their deepest fears. Faced with the prospect of having rats eat him alive, **Winston finally betrays Julia,** and after accepting the doctrine of the party, **he is sent back into society.** Meanwhile, **Julia has also betrayed Winston.** One day, the pair meets by chance in a park, but they feel nothing for each other anymore.

Pride and Prejudice by Jane Austen

Pride and Prejudice is a story of **love, status** and **society. Elizabeth Bennett** is from a family of a modest income. Her mother, a foolish and frivolous woman who wants to **marry off her five daughters** as soon as possible, is thrilled to hear that a **rich, handsome young man – Mr Bingley** – is renting a nearby property. At a local ball, Bingley and Jane hit it off but Bingley's friend, the extremely **wealthy and proud Mr Darcy,** avoids dancing with Elizabeth. Elizabeth is affronted and a deep **dislike of Darcy sets in.** Meanwhile, Elizabeth's youngest and most flirtatious sister, **Lydia,** takes a shine to **Mr Wickham,** a **charming militia officer.** Wickham and Elizabeth are chatting amiably, when he reveals that Darcy's father was his guardian and that **Darcy has wrongfully denied him a promised inheritance.** Elizabeth's dislike of Darcy grows, but, conversely, Darcy develops an admiration for Elizabeth's independence and intelligence. After much thought, Darcy proposes to Elizabeth, **'against his better judgement',** since **such a marriage is beneath him. She angrily refuses him,** insulted and prejudiced by what she has heard from Wickham and suspicious that he was responsible for separating Bingley and Jane: **'I had not known you a month before I felt that you were the last man in the world whom I could ever be prevailed on to marry'.** In an effort to clear his name, Darcy denies Wickham's accusations against him and reveals how **Wickham seduced his own younger sister.** Soon after, **Lydia elopes with Mr Wickham** and the veracity of Darcy's claim seems to be confirmed. During a visit to Darcy's estate, Elizabeth, who assumes he is away, bumps into him, finding Darcy much more **affable** than before. Her dislike of Darcy begins to fade, and learning that he **negotiated a marriage between Lydia and Wickham at great cost to himself,** her affection grows. Bingley and Jane get engaged, after which Darcy proposes to Elizabeth a second time and she accepts.

Tess of the D'Urbervilles by Thomas Hardy

As the novel opens, Tess's father, the uneducated **John Durbeyfield,** hears that he is related to the noble **D'Urberville** family who live nearby. But the Durbeyfields are wretchedly poor, so Tess visits the wealthy **Mrs D'Urberville, claiming kinship,** and asking for work. However, Tess finds instead her son, **Alec,** who secures her a job at the **family poultry farm.** Tess instinctively distrusts Alec, and does all she can to repel his advances, but he is determined and, one night, **rapes her.** Tess returns to her family, where she gives birth to a baby, whom she baptises **'Sorrow'** before he dies, burying him in a marmalade box. Some two years later, Tess has recovered, and finds work as a dairymaid at Talbothays Dairy. There she meets **Angel Clare**. Angel and Tess fall in love, but Tess is reluctant to marry as she is aware of her shame at not being a virgin. She decides to write a letter of confession to Angel but, too late, discovers that he has never received the letter. When, on their wedding night, Angel confesses to a previous affair, so Tess does the same, begging: **'Forgive me as you are forgiven.'** But Angel is horrified, saying: **'You were one person: now you are another'.** He goes off to Brazil to begin a new life. Tess, once again, returns to her parents and encounters Alec, who is as determined as ever to have her. **He insists that her husband will never return to her.** Eventually, seeing no other way to save her destitute family, **she unhappily becomes Alec's mistress.** Meanwhile, Angel returns, having at long last forgiven her. Driven to desperation at the return of her much-loved husband, **Tess murders Alec**, explaining later to Angel: **'He has come between us and ruined us, and now he can never do it any more.'** The two escape to an empty house where they spend a **few blissful days together**. When they are discovered, they escape again, only to reach **Stonehenge**, where the police come for Tess. She begs Angel to marry her sister, **Liza-Lu**, after her inevitable death by execution.

To Kill a Mockingbird by Harper Lee

To Kill A Mockingbird is a story about a girl growing up in small-town America and the effect of victimisation and prejudice on innocence. It is told through the eyes of **Jean-Louise Finch (Scout)** as she looks back on her life with her father, **Atticus Finch**, a lawyer of **Maycomb county**, her brother, **Jem**, and their maid, Calpurnia. When they are young, Scout and Jem fear their neighbour, **Arthur Radley (Boo Radley)**, who they refer to as a **'malevolent phantom'.** Boo has not emerged from his house for as long as anyone can remember and is the subject of much superstition. After some time has passed, it emerges that **Mayella Ewell**, a part of a family considered 'trash' by the rest of Maycomb society, has accused **Tom Robinson**, **a black man**, of **rape**. **Atticus**, who **knows Tom to be innocent**, decides to defend him in court, but knows that he can't win given the town's deeply ingrained racial prejudice. He later explains to Scout, **'Courage is not a man with a gun in his hand. It's knowing you're licked before you begin but you begin anyway'.** In court, it emerges that Mayella is afraid of her alcoholic father, Bob Ewell, and that Mayella actually made advances towards Tom, but was caught by her father and beaten. Despite this evidence, Tom is convicted and sentenced to death, but is later killed trying to escape prison. Meanwhile, Bob, resentful that Atticus has exposed him, **attacks Jem and Scout** on their way back from a school play. A stranger saves Jem's life and carries him home, whereupon Scout realises that the stranger is **Boo Radley**. It emerges that Bob was killed in the struggle. Atticus, believing Jem to have killed Bob, tells the sheriff that he needs to report him. But the sheriff, not wanting either Jem or Boo to be exposed, insists that Bob fell on his knife. The mockingbird is used at various points in the novel as a symbol of innocence, in particular by Atticus, when he tells Jem and Scout that **'it's a sin to kill a mockingbird'**. Scout realises the significance of this symbol and compares putting Boo on trial to **'sort of like shootin' a mockingbird'**, demonstrating her understanding and maturity.

Ulysses by James Joyce

Ulysses is set on the day of **16 June 1904**. The episodes are loosely structured on Homer's *Odyssey*. The initial episodes focus on **Stephen Dedalus** as he distances himself from his friend, **Buck Mulligan**, and **Haines**, the Englishman staying with them. Stephen resents Haines' presence. After teaching a class, Stephen collects his wages from the headmaster, an English loyalist who asks Stephen to deliver a letter to the newspaper office. Stephen says: **'History is a nightmare from which I am trying to awake'**. Alone on a beach, he reflects on the world around him and the **'ineluctable modality of the visible'**. The novel shifts to **Leopold Bloom**, an advertising canvasser, who at 8am fixes his breakfast which he **'ate with relish'**. **Where Stephen is more of a thinker, Bloom is in tune with his bodily functions**. He takes breakfast in bed to his wife, **Molly**, an opera singer, whom he suspects is having an affair with her manager, **Blazes Boylan**. At 11pm, Bloom rides with the other Dubliners, including Stephen's father, Simon Dedalus, to his friend **Paddy Dignam's** funeral. As a Jewish Irishman, Bloom is both an **insider and outsider**. He sits apart from the others at the church. At midday we see Bloom negotiating an ad with the **editor of the Freeman newspaper**, **Myles Crawford**. Bloom leaves the office and Stephen arrives with the headmaster's letter. Later, at the National Library, Stephen gives his theory on *Hamlet* to a poet and librarians. Bloom passes Stephen on his way into the library. While having dinner with an attorney at the Ormond hotel, **Bloom keeps on eye on Blazes**, also in the hotel. Later in the day, Bloom arrives at the pub, only to be berated by an anti-semitic and xenophobic character known only as the 'Citizen'. They have a dispute until Bloom is whisked away by **Martin Cunningham**, with whom he is helping sort out the Dignams' financial affairs. On **Sandymount Strand**, a young woman, **Gerty MacDowell**, notices a strange man looking at her. She enjoys being looked at and reveals a little more of herself. The man – it turns out to be Bloom – masturbates. Gerty leaves and as she walks away, Bloom notices that she is lame. **At 10pm**, Bloom **arrives at the hospital where Mina Purefoy is in labour**. Stephen is getting drunk with his medical friends and soon decides to go to **Nighttown**, the red light district of Dublin. Feeling protective of Stephen, Bloom follows him and his friend. He locates them at **Bella Cohen's brothel** and a scene mixing dream, reality and nightmare ensues. After creating a ruckus, **Stephen gets knocked out by a British soldier** and is helped by Bloom who takes him back to his house. Before Stephen leaves, they have a heart-to-heart. Bloom goes to bed and next to him, **Molly lays awake thinking of the day behind her, the sex she had with Blazes** and the moment of intimacy she last shared with Bloom.

War and Peace by Leo Tolstoy

The novel is set during the **1812 French invasion of Russia**, led by **Napoleon Bonaparte**. It begins with a soirée in which we meet the **St Petersburg aristocracy**, among them the illegitimate son of a wealthy count, **Pierre Bezukhov**, an honest but awkward man, and his friend, **Prince Andrei**, who is disenchanted with society and married life. In Moscow are the less-well-off **Rostovs** with their four children, including the young **Natasha** described as 'This black-eyed, wide-mouthed girl, not pretty but full of life'. In his search for fulfilment, Prince Andrei departs for war, leaving his wife, **Lise**, with his father and sister, **Maria Bolkonskaya**. In book two, some years later, Natasha has turned into a beautiful young woman. Pierre has received his inheritance upon his father's death and has become a highly eligible bachelor. He falls for **Princess Elena (Hélène)** and proposes **marriage**. However, Hélène cheats on Pierre and he leaves her. He becomes spiritually bereft and in his search for meaning, joins the **Freemasons**. Meanwhile, **Andrei has been wounded in battle and is on the brink of death**; he realises that his ambitions for greatness are meaningless: '**Gazing into Napoleon's eyes, Prince Andrei mused on the unimportance of greatness ... and the still greater unimportance of death**'. He recovers from his wounds to find his **wife dying in childbirth**; he is torn apart by **guilt**. Meanwhile, Hélène begs Pierre to take her back, which he does. Andrei falls in love with the effervescent Natasha and proposes marriage. But their union is delayed for a year at the request of Andrei's father. Andrei departs and Hélène's brother, **Anatol**, seduces her. Natasha breaks her engagement with Andrei but her plan to elope with Anatol is foiled. **She attempts to kill herself**. In book three, the Battle of **Borodino** takes place, in which the Russians defeat the French. This section provides insight into Napoleon not only as a leader, but also as a petty man. Despite the Russian army's valiant effort, the French are left to advance on **Moscow**. During the final book, Pierre, witnessing the deaths caused by war, sees it as his mission to **assassinate Napoleon**. He fails and is taken captive, where he meets **Karataev**, a person of great integrity whose conversation provides Pierre with a renewed sense of the meaning of life. Fleeing Moscow, the Rostovs, on Natasha's advice, help transport the wounded. Andrei, who is among them, **forgives Natasha before dying**. **Hélène also dies**, and Pierre, fully aware of his love for Natasha, **proposes to her**. The epilogue sees the wedding of **Pierre and Natasha**, as well as **Nikolai Rostov's marriage** to **Maria Bolkonsyaka**, whose great wealth helps relieve the Rostov family of their debts.

Wuthering Heights by Emily Brontë

Wuthering Heights centres on the all-consuming and ultimately doomed love between Catherine and Heathcliff. **Nelly Dean**, long-time housekeeper of the Wuthering Heights estate, tells the story of Catherine and Heathcliff to **Mr Lockwood**, tenant at **Thrushcross Grange**. Thirty years ago, **Mr Earnshaw** of

Wuthering Heights brought back a **gypsy boy whom he adopted as his son**. Although Heathcliff and Mr Earnshaw's daughter, Catherine, became as thick as thieves, Earnshaw's son, **Hindley, was deeply jealous** of Heathcliff. After a leave of absence, **Hindley returns a married man** to Wuthering Heights. His father now dead, **Hindley reduces Heathcliff to the status of servant**. One day, Catherine and Heathcliff spy on the **Linton family** at Thrushcross Grange. However, Catherine gets attacked by a dog and has to stay at the Grange to recover. After some time, **she returns to the Heights a lady**, and disdains Heathcliff's slovenliness. Hindley and his wife have a son, **Hareton**. Catherine tells Nelly that she is going to accept **Edgar's** (one of the Linton children) **offer of marriage**, even though she loves Heathcliff: 'It **would degrade me to marry Heathcliff now; so he shall never know how I love him'**. Heathcliff, hearing only how Catherine would scorn to marry him, **takes flight**, before hearing her proclaim: 'Nelly, I am Heathcliff!' After some time, recovering from the stress induced by Heathcliff's departure, **Catherine and Edgar marry**. Heathcliff returns three years later a gentleman. Edgar's sister, **Isabella, falls in love with him** and Heathcliff, hating her, nonetheless encourages her love, seeing it as an opportunity for **vengeance on Edgar**. Catherine falls ill and **Heathcliff elopes with Isabella**, returning to steal into **Catherine's room before she dies after giving birth to a daughter, Cathy**. Upon her death, Heathcliff cries: 'I **cannot live without my life! I cannot live without my soul!'** Isabella gives birth to Heathcliff's son, **Linton**. Hindley dies and **Heathcliff becomes master of Wuthering Heights** and the guardian of Hindley's son, **Hareton**. Over a decade later, Heathcliff nurtures plans for his son, **Linton, to be married to Cathy**, which would make him master of Thrushcross Grange. Heathcliff traps Cathy at Wuthering Heights and **marries her to Linton**, but she **escapes to see her dying father**. However, she has to return to the Heights and, soon after, **Linton dies**. Lockwood returns after leaving the Grange and discovers that **Heathcliff has died**. He is **buried next to Catherine. Cathy** and **Hareton** now plan to marry.

SUMMARIES OF GREAT POEMS

Anthem for Doomed Youth by Wilfred Owen

This famous sonnet was written in 1917 while Owen was recovering from shell shock at a hospital in Edinburgh. An anthem suggests a song of religion, celebration or patriotism, but in this poem its connotations are tainted with irony. As the title suggests, the poem asks what kind of send-off can be given to soldiers who 'die as cattle', and it illustrates how death on the battlefield cannot be made meaningful by religious ritual. Thus 'Only the stuttering rifles' rapid rattle/Can patter out their hasty orisons'. The alliteration of 't' and 'r' create an onomatopoeic, 'stuttering' effect and portrays the fear of soldiers trying to say their prayers amid the rifles' 'rattle'. The image poignantly merges the battle-scene with man's experience of it. Further, the poetic speaker urges that there be no **'voice of mourning save the choirs, –/The shrill, demented choirs of wailing shells'**. The position of choirs at the end of the line leads us to hang in suspension as the poet then reveals these are not religious choirs to commemorate the dead but rather, ironically, the choirs of the pitiful sounds of war. The blank verse meter and rhyming pattern create a mournful, tolling effect. Towards the end of the sonnet, the poet moves to those who are left behind: **'The pallor of girls' brows shall be their pall'**. A tone of critical irony is established through the metaphor; the soldiers will have not have a coffin, only their girls' bereavement. The final, heroic couplet unites **'patient minds'** and **'drawing-down of blinds'** to illustrate how soldiers dying on the open battlefield will not have blinds drawn down as a sign of respect for their death, rather they will wait patiently for the emergence of dusk.

The Charge of the Light Brigade by Alfred, Lord Tennyson

Written in 1854, this poem tells the story of a doomed English cavalry charge during the Crimean War. As a result of miscommunication, a lightly armed cavalry brigade is ordered to charge through a narrow valley to attack Russian artillery. The poem starts suddenly, the metre conjuring a sense of frenzied momentum that mirrors the imagery of the galloping horses. The soldiers knew that there had been a terrible mistake and that they would ride to certain death, but they were proud and fearless: **'Was there a man dismay'd?/Not tho' the soldiers knew/Someone had blundered'** and trained to obey orders: **'Theirs not to reason why,/Theirs but to do and die'**. Tennyson uses repetition: **'Half a league, half a league ...'** to emphasize the fearful and interminable nature of the charge; while **'cannon to the left of them/cannon to the right of them ...'** highlights the unrelenting nature of the bombardment. Against all odds they reach the Russian artillery and wreak havoc: **'Right thro' the line they broke; Cossack and Russian/Reel'd from the sabre-stroke'** but sustained heavy losses. Tennyson uses stark imagery to evoke the horrors of war, describing the few survivors' ride back **'... thro' the jaws of death/Back from the mouth of hell'**. Despite the disastrous number of casualties, their heroic advance will be immortalised: **'When can their glory fade?/O the wild charge they made!'**.

Kubla Khan by Samuel Taylor Coleridge

Based on an opium-induced dream, *Kubla Khan* is seen as an archetype of Romantic poetry. The poetic speaker describes Mongol leader Kubla Khan's pleasure dome and its surrounds in Xanadu. The perfection of Xanadu is contained by walls, beyond which nature continues indefinitely. The poetic speaker draws attention to a dark chasm in Xanadu which is described in ambiguous terms: **'But oh! that deep romantic chasm which slanted/Down the green hill/... A savage place! as holy**

SUMMARIES OF GREAT POEMS

and enchanted/As e'er beneath a waning moon was haunted'. The chasm is described antithetically as both 'savage' and 'holy', presenting the idea of the sublime (simultaneously terrifying and awe-inspiring) in the poetic speaker's vision. A fountain is depicted as springing from the chasm, forming the river Alph. The fountain illuminates the ethereality of the life of man: **'Then reached the caverns measureless to man,/And sank in tumult to a lifeless ocean'.** The river, both 'measureless' and 'lifeless' as it moves into the ocean, transcends man. If the fountain and river it forms are symbolic of man's creative energy and life force, then these are portrayed as only fleeting phenomena. The pleasure dome, which is framed by nature and the lifeless ocean, is seen as miraculous: **'It was a miracle of rare device,/A sunny pleasure-dome with caves of ice!'** The caves of ice in the sun illuminate the fantastical, dream-like and richly creative quality of the poet's vision. The last passages of the poem refer to an Abyssinian maid who sings of Mount Abora. Her song prompts the poetic speaker's desire to imitate the actions of Kubla Khan through poetry: **'I would build that dome in air'.** He cautions others to 'beware' of his vision which transcends the individual and contains prophetic power, for he has **'drunk the milk of Paradise'.**

Ode to a Nightingale by John Keats

Ode to a Nightingale celebrates the nightingale's song, which is recreated through iambic pentameters, as a momentary escape from human care and mortality: **'My heart aches, and a drowsy numbness pains/My sense'.** Seeking to escape from the suffering that comes with being human, the poetic speaker aspires to the heights of nightingale's song, the self-contained happiness it signifies, and ponders different ways of achieving this. The speaker thinks about wine as an escape from his human condition: **'O for a beaker full of the warm South!'** Through use of the metonym 'warm South' Keats highlights the transformative effect of poetry, which echoes that of wine; wine is transformative because it induces forgetfulness: **'Where but to think is to be full of sorrow/And leaden-eyed despairs'.** But he rejects wine and chooses poetic writing as the means of escape and flight. Earth is unlike the heavens, **'here there is no light',** so the speaker will rely on his imagination. Nonetheless, the speaker's imaginative flight through poetry cannot last for long: **'Forlorn! the very word is like a bell/To toll me back from thee to my sole self!'** As he comes back to himself, the speaker recognizes his inability to fully escape the mortal condition through poetry, and, as the nightingale flies away, the speaker is left disorientated by the potency of his vision.

Paradise Lost by John Milton

Written in blank verse, *Paradise Lost* tells the biblical story of Adam and Eve when, tempted by Satan, they fall from God's grace. Satan, having been thrown out of heaven into hell, uses rhetoric to rally his troops. In an act of vengeance, he states that he will brave the abyss to get into the Garden of Eden and bring about the ruin of mankind. Milton describes Satan's arduous journey: **'Into this wilde Abyss,/The Womb of nature and perhaps her Grave . . ./He had to cross'.** Disguised as a cherub, Satan steals into the Garden of Eden. Adam and Even look after the Garden, taking care to obey God's request not to eat from the Tree of Knowledge. As a toad, Satan speaks into Eve's ear, urging her to eat from the forbidden tree. God sends Raphael to protect his creations by warning them of Satan's evil. Raphael tells Adam and Eve of Satan's envy of God's son, and the war between Heaven and the rebellious angels. Satan then takes the form of a serpent and finds Eve alone. Satan, complimenting Eve on her beauty, persuades her to eat from the tree. Once Adam realises what she has done, he decides that since they are of one flesh, he must fall with Eve, so he also eats the forbidden fruit. Their love turns to lust and soon they experience guilt and shame. Suggesting that they repent, Adam says: **'What better can we do, than to place/Repairing where he judg'd us, prostrate fall/Before him reverent, and there confess/Humbly our faults, and pardon beg'.** Although God grants them grace, they are banished from Paradise. Just before they leave, the angel Michael shows Adam the future sins of mankind which culminate in the Great Flood. Distraught by this vision, Adam is also told of the sacrifice of God's son to redeem mankind from original sin. Adam and Eve are the led out from Paradise into a new world.

The Prelude by William Wordsworth

The Prelude is an autobiographical poem split into 14 sections. It is written in blank verse and charts the poet's development from early reflections in youth, to his experiences in France and London and the development of his aesthetic philosophy in later life. Leaving London and the artificiality of society, the poet feels relief at being back with nature: **'Escaped/From the vast city, where I long had pined/. . . now free,/Free as a bird to settle where I will'.** He remembers stealing a boat in his youth and journeying across a lake; the looming mountains seem to come alive as he rows: **'the grim shape/Towered up between me and the stars, and still,/. . . with purpose of its own/. . . Strode after me'.** After musing on his early development and communion with nature, the poet reflects on his time at Cambridge, encountering great architecture and pondering 'sweet Spencer'. Describing his time traversing the Alps mid-way in the epic poem, the poet comes across a narrow chasm and beholds nature: **'woods decaying, never to be decayed . . ./The torrents shooting from the clear blue sky . . ./The unfettered clouds and region of the Heavens . . ./Were all like workings of one mind'.** This encapsulates the Romantic vision of surrounding nature, perfectly in harmony with the poetic mind. The literal journey of crossing the Alps is a metaphor for the poet's quest for his philosophy of art and aesthetic vision. The latter half of the poem recounts the poet's time in France in the wake of revolution, soaking up the atmosphere of liberty and optimism. The ending the of the poem follows the poet's ascent of Mount Snowdon and the epiphany he encounters there: 'as I looked up .../The Moon hung naked in a firmament/... and at my feet/Rested a silent sea of hoary mist .../far beyond, the solid vapours stretched .../Into the main Atlantic, that appeared/To dwindle, and give up his majesty'.

The Raven by Edgar Allan Poe

Published in 1845, Edgar Allan Poe's *The Raven* is one of the most famous pieces of American literature. The poem begins at midnight on a cold December evening and introduces the narrator's fragile mental state: **'Once upon a midnight dreary, while I pondered weak and weary . . .'** The narrator sits by the dying fire lamenting the loss of his love, Lenore, when he hears something tapping at the door. He opens the door to the bedroom, but there is nothing there. After the tapping continues, he opens the shutters to reveal a **'stately raven'**, who steps in to his bedroom and flies up to perch on a bust above the door. He asks the raven its name: **'Ghastly grim and ancient raven wandering from the nightly shore – Tell me what they lordly name is on the Night's Plutonian shore!'** The raven replies: **'Nevermore'**. The narrator deduces that it is the only word the raven knows, but continues to ask it questions, despite the inevitability of the raven's answer. This cycle of deliberate self-flagellation transports him from sorrow to despair and then finally madness, as the raven seems to prophesize that he will never be reunited with Lenore in heaven. The poem ends with the narrator's realization that his soul is stuck beneath the raven's shadow and it will never be lifted. The poem is known for its musical nature, achieved through the pattern of stressed and unstressed syllables as well as the use of internal rhyme.

The Rime of the Ancient Mariner by Samuel Taylor Coleridge

The Rime of the Ancient Mariner is an epic poem about the sanctity of nature and is usually interpreted as a Christian allegory. It is about a sailor who recounts the story of a fateful voyage, where his ship is blown off course and into a **'land of mist and snow'** with colossal icebergs. An albatross suddenly appears, the ice breaks and the wind picks up, leading the ship out. The mariner impulsively shoots the bird and the crew are enraged with him. But the ship sails into warmer, clearer waters and the crew praises the mariner's actions. However, the wind later dies down and they run out of water, **'Water, water everywhere/And not a drop to drink'** and sea creatures start to emerge from the depths. The crew blame the mariner and hang the dead albatross around his neck like a cross. A ship appears in the distance and they think they've been saved. But it is a spectral ship commanded by Death and Life-in-Death, who are playing dice for the souls of the sailors. The ghostly ship vanishes and the sailors drop dead, cursing the mariner, who remains alive. For seven days he is surrounded by corpses and the **'slimy things'**. However, he begins to appreciate the creatures and blesses them, causing the albatross to fall from his neck. The crew rise from the dead, possessed by benign spirits and steer the ship homeward, where it sinks into a whirlpool, leaving the mariner, who is rescued. His guilt forces him to wander the world telling people his story and preaching: **'He prayeth best, who loveth best/All things both great and small/For the dear God who loveth us/He made and loveth all.'**

The Tyger by William Blake

The poetic speaker asks a series of rhetorical questions asking what deity could have produced such a magnificent creature. The questions serve to show how the tiger, a symbol for the passion, beauty and mystery in nature – **'burning bright/in the forests of the night'** – cannot either be satisfactorily depicted in art and cannot be tamed by the modern world. The regular meter (trochaic tetrameter), rhyming couplets and equal stanza length all suggest the formal constraints the poem is putting in place, which echo the constraints placed on the tiger. Nonetheless, the fiery, awe-inspiring attributes of the tiger – its **'fearful symmetry'** and **'fire of thine eyes'** – suggest the tiger's transcendence of any constraint. As the poem progresses, the more sinister and destructive connotations of the tiger emerge. Blake speaks of artistic creation in terms of **'hammer'**, **'chain'**, **'furnace'** and **'anvil'**, which cannot tame that which has been created by nature. Blake also suggests the way in which the mystery and passion that the tiger symbolises signifies a threat against conventional religion: **'When the stars threw down their spears, And watered heaven with their tears'**. The tiger coexists with the lamb, symbolic of innocence, and Blake questions how good and evil (the lamb and the tiger) can exist on the same plane. This implies a questioning of the benevolent nature of god.

The Waste Land by T.S Eliot

The five-section poem partly explores a land which has been laid waste by industrialism and the effects of war, but also a culture so rich with the detritus of knowledge that meaning is lost. Importantly, the poem is very dense in trans-cultural and inter-textual allusion. The poem draws on different myths, the central one being that of the Fisher King whose impotency made his land a dry waste land. The first section, Burial of the Dead, explores the idea of infertility and death. It subverts traditional images of renewal: **'April is the cruellest month'**. This section suggests that in the modern world, the regeneration April signifies is stunted, **'feeding/a little life with dried tubers'**. This episode also offers an insight into the poetic speaker's alienation from modern life: **'Son of man, You cannot say, or guess, for you know only/A heap of broken images'**. The second episode, A Game of Chess, represents two social classes and two kinds of women: the first, the high-society woman surrounding herself with **'strange synthetic perfumes'**, and the second, working-class women in the pub, whose idle chit-chat the poetic speaker disdains: **'Good night, ladies, good night, sweet ladies, good night, good night'**. The third section, The Fire Sermon, depicts Tiresias who, **'throbbing between two** lives', sees a typist clumsily seduced by a clerk, whose caresses **'are unreproved, if undesired.'** This encounter underscores the sense of apathy which pervades the poem. The fourth section, Death by Water, suggests other literary forms such as parables (biblical stories layered with instructive principles). The message of this episode, however, is the finality of death and the lack of renewal it signifies. The final section, What the Thunder Said, is split into two distinct sections. The first draws on biblical imagery associated with the quest for the Holy Grail. The drought plaguing the land finally ends with the rains, but this renewal has arrived by chance rather than through someone claiming the Grail. The second half is set by the River Ganges, where thunder is rumbling. Borrowing from Hindu fables, Eliot reflects on the three components of the thunder's power, namely that it 'gives', 'sympathises' and 'controls' through its rumbling, or speech. These reflections elicit a sense of finality, embodied by the Fisher-King sitting on the shore, putting his kingdom in order. The poem concludes with the Sanskrit **'Shantih, shantih, shantih'**, which Eliot translates as 'the peace that passeth understanding'.

GREAT HISTORICAL FIGURES

Alexander the Great
'Remember upon the conduct of each depends the fate of all'.

Born in **356 BC**, **Alexander III** was a king of **Macedon**, a state in ancient Greece. He is considered one of history's great military commanders, **winning every single battle he ever fought in**, despite often being outnumbered. He died aged **32**, believed to be as a result of contracting a high fever, but by this time his empire extended over **5,200,000 km²** (**2,000,000 sq. miles**). In his short lifetime, he conquered the whole of the Persian Empire, decisively defeating **Darius III** at the **Battle of Issus** in **333 BC** and **Gaugamela** in **331 BC**. He invaded the Indian subcontinent in **326 BC**, and scored a convincing victory against **King Porus**, a ruler of part of the Punjab. Shortly after this battle, at the **Hyphasis River**, Alexander's **exhausted army**, faced with a punishing crossing and the prospect of meeting an opposing army on the river's eastern bank, **mutinied**. One of his generals, **Coenus**, begged Alexander to march back, imploring him to see that the men **'longed to again see their parents, their wives and children, their homeland'**. His closest friend **Hephaestion** died in 324 BC, possibly by poisoning, leaving Alexander devastated. He planned to invade Arabia, but died before the campaign started. Soon after Alexander's death, war broke out between his rival successors and the empire was split into four. Alexander was responsible for spreading Greek influence and civilisation to the east, establishing trade routes and influencing countless military leaders and statesmen.

Amazing fact: Alexander's father, Philip II, arranged for the Greek philosopher Aristotle to tutor Alexander in exchange for Philip rebuilding Aristotle's hometown of Stageira.

Augustus

'I found a Rome of bricks; I leave to you one of marble'.

Born in 63 BC, **Gaius Octavius Thurinus** was the great-nephew of **Julius Caesar**. Caesar had no legitimate children, so he named Octavius as his principal heir. The year after his great-uncle's **assassination**, Octavius formed a political alliance with **Mark Antony** and **Marcus Aemilius Lepidus**, which became known as the **Second Triumvirate**. Octavius emerged as the **sole triumvir** after forcing Lepidus into exile and defeating Antony in a civil war, but faced a public wary of accepting a dictator as their leader. He was elected as **Consul**, along with Marcus Agrippa, and in 27 BC, returned power to the Roman Senate. That same year, the Senate awarded him the title **Augustus** (the illustrious one) and **Princeps** (first citizen). Although never officially regarded as an emperor, Augustus' financial, military and political power gave him unprecedented **control over the Senate and the empire**. During his reign, the Roman Empire expanded significantly after conquering northern **Hispania** (modern-day Spain and Portugal) **Egypt**, **Raetia** and **Noricum** (modern-day Switzerland, southern Germany, Austria and Slovenia), **Illyricum** and **Pannonia** (modern-day Albania, Croatia, Hungary and Serbia) and **parts of Africa**. He also acquired **Syria** and **Galatia** (modern-day Turkey) without conflict. Despite the military acquisitions at Rome's frontiers, Augustus's rule **ushered in a period of peace** in the Mediterranean area, known as the *Pax Romana* which lasted for over 200 years. Augustus largely rebuilt the city of Rome, and introduced the first **police** and **fire-fighting forces** to Rome as well as an official courier system. He also established the fabled **Praetorian Guard**, the elite bodyguard utilised by Roman emperors. Augustus died in AD 14 and was **declared a god by the Senate**. The **eighth month of the Roman calendar,** until then known as Sextilis, was re-named in his honour.

Christopher Columbus

'Gold is a treasure, and he who possesses it does all he wishes to in this world, and succeeds in helping souls into paradise'.

Columbus was a great explorer born in **1451** in the then Republic of **Genoa**. After unsuccessful pleas to many royal European courts, he was sponsored by the crown of **Castille** to sail westward to the **Orient**, unaware that this was impossible via the route he planned. He set sail from **Palos de la Frontera** in southern Spain and made for the Canary Islands to replenish his provisions, before embarking on what ended up being a **five-week voyage** across the Atlantic. The first land they sighted was the present-day **Bahamas**; they also travelled to present-day **Cuba** and **Hispaniola**. Columbus was convinced that the lands he had discovered were part of the East Indies, and thus named the native peoples **'Indians'**. He went on three more voyages across the Atlantic, in which he travelled to other islands in the Greater and Lesser Antilles, and to the **coast of Colombia**, **Venezuela** and **central America**, claiming them for the Spanish Empire and beginning the process of Spanish **colonisation**. He was **arrested** during his third voyage for **torturing natives** and was also accused of **incompetence** and **mismanagement**, but his extraordinary expeditions heralded an unprecedented wave of European voyages to the **'New World'**, changing the world forever.

Mohandas Gandhi

'An eye for an eye only ends up making the whole world blind'.

Born in 1869, Mohandas Gandhi was the leader of the **Indian nationalist movement** during the **British Raj** and is regarded as **the father of his nation**. His campaign of **peaceful civil disobedience** has been the inspiration for many similar campaigns across the world. Gandhi trained as a barrister in London and took a job for an Indian legal firm in South Africa. Keen to obtain basic rights for immigrant Indians in South Africa, Gandhi helped found the **Natal Indian Congress** in 1894. The African government granted many of Gandhi's demands in 1914. Gandhi subsequently established the *satyagraha* (devotion to truth), a form of non-violent protest. He soon became a leading political figure advocating freedom for India. Bolstered by Hindu and Muslim support, Gandhi initiated **peaceful demonstrations** and **boycotts of British products and institutions** and was subsequently **imprisoned** in 1922. In 1930, he led the famous **Dandi Salt March** as a protest against the British salt tax. During the Second World War, Gandhi intensified his campaign for Indian independence and was again imprisoned in 1942. Upon his release in 1944, the political scene was dramatically different. The Muslim League leader, **Muhammad Al Jinnah**, wanted a **fully independent Pakistan but Gandhi was opposed to the partition**. India and Pakistan became separate countries in 1947, with months of bloodshed preceding and following the partition. Many believe that without Gandhi's input, this would have been much bloodier and more protracted. Just a few months later, on 30 January 1948, Gandhi was **shot dead** by a Hindu fanatic.

Amazing fact: Gandhi was thought to have been given the honorific name Mahatma, which is taken from the Sanskrit words *maha* and *atma* (translating as 'Great Soul') by the poet Rabindranath Tagore.

Genghis Khan

'Conquering the world on horseback is easy; it is dismounting and governing that is hard'.

Genghis Khan was a name given to **Temujin**, the military and political leader who founded the Mongol Empire. He was born around **1162**, and rose to power by **uniting many tribes in northeast Asia**. He defeated the neighbouring **Western Xia Dynasty** in **1209** before annihilating the **Jin Dynasty** at the **Battle of Badger Pass** and capturing their capital, **Yanjing** (which subsequently became Beijing) in **1215**. He sent a small army to defeat the **Kara-Khitan Khanate**, which was completed in **1218** with the execution of their khan, **Kuchlug**. Genghis Khan's next move was to establish a trade route using the **Silk Road** with the **Khwarezmian Empire**, but his caravan was **attacked by** Khwarezmian forces. Khan sent three ambassadors to the **Shah**, but **one was executed** and the others had their heads shaved; Khan reacted by launching a **colossal invasion force**, which faced limited resistance from the piecemeal brigades commanded by the Shah. Khan's troops **massacred thousands of people, destroyed hundreds of buildings** and **enslaved** the population. **Khan had defeated this vast empire in just three years**. After this conquest, he **split his army in two**. One half invaded **Afghanistan** and **northern India**, while the other force pushed into Russia, **conquering Georgia** and much of **Armenia** and **Azerbaijan**. The Mongols won a decisive victory at the **Battle of Kalka Ridge** against a larger **Kievan** force. **Transoxiana** and **Persia** fell soon afterwards before Khan's armies returned to Mongolia. Khan died in **1227**, having established a vast empire stretching from the **Caspian Sea** to the **Sea of Japan**.

Amazing fact: The governor of Otrar, Inalchuq, who attacked Genghis Khan's trade caravan, was eventually captured alive by Mongol forces. He is thought to have been executed by having molten silver poured into his eyes and ears.

George Washington

'The first in war, first in peace, and first in the hearts of his countrymen'.

George Washington was a **military** and **political leader** of the **late 18th century** and is regarded as the **'father' of the United States of America**. He became the **commander-in-chief of the Continental Army** during the **American Revolutionary War** against **Great Britain** and won renown for his valour, leadership, military strategy and commitment to organising and training his troops. After success driving the British from **Boston** in **1775**, he was defeated trying to recapture **New York City**. He regrouped his forces and **defeated British forces twice** before forcing the surrender of two British armies, at **Saratoga in 1777** and **Yorktown in 1781**. The loss of Yorktown was catastrophic for the British and ultimately led to the signing of the **Treaty of Paris in 1783**. Washington presided over the **Constitutional Convention**, which led to the drafting of the **United States Constitution**. He was unanimously elected **President** in **1789** – the only President in history to receive **100 per cent** of the electoral-college votes – and served in the post for nearly **8 years**. Some of the unique features of Washington's presidency, such as the **inaugural address** and his **development of the cabinet system of government**, have been in place ever since. He appears on the **$1 bill**, the most numerous banknote in the USA, and is one of the **four presidents** to be immortalised in the **Mount Rushmore** national memorial.

Amazing fact: Washington freed all of his slaves in his will of 1799, the first of the Founding Fathers to do so.

Hannibal
'I will either find a way, or make one'.

Hannibal was a **Carthaginian** military leader and is widely regarded as one of the finest commanders in history. He was made **commander-in-chief of the army in 221 BC** and set off to finish his father's conquest of **Hispania**. **The Roman Empire grew wary of him** and cemented an alliance with the city of **Saguntum**. However, Hannibal perceived this action as a **violation of a treaty**, and so he captured the city. Rome demanded justice but the only thing they received was a declaration of war. Hannibal's forces marched across the **Pyrenees** and **into Gaul** with around **50,000 men and a number of war elephants**, before travelling through northern Italy and making a **legendary crossing of the Alps**. His army was finally intercepted by a Roman army, but Hannibal led his troops to major victory in the ensuing **Battle of the Trebia in 218 BC**. The Romans anticipated a subsequent attack on Rome, but because he did not possess siege engines, **Hannibal marched to central Italy instead, hoping to encourage a revolt against the Romans**. Pursued by a Roman army, he laid a famous ambush which wiped out the Roman force at the **Battle of Lake Trasimene**. He was attacked by another Roman army at the **Battle of Cannae in 216 BC**, but a shrewd battle plan led to another decisive victory. After this battle, the Romans were reluctant to fight Hannibal in a pitched battle, and the war turned into one of attrition. However, the war began to turn against the Carthaginians and **Hannibal's brother's army**, transporting much-needed siege equipment, **was comprehensively beaten at Metaurus**. An attack on **Carthaginian soil in 203 BC** by Roman general **Scipio Africanus** prompted the **return of Hannibal to his homeland**. The two forces met at the **Battle of Zama**, which, although closely fought, ended in Hannibal's defeat, and led to the Carthaginian surrender. After a period in political office, Hannibal went into exile, but was eventually hunted down by the Romans, finally **committing suicide *c.*183 BC**.

Joan of Arc

'Of the love or hatred God has for the English, I know nothing, but I do know that they will all be thrown out of France, except those who die there'.

Joan of Arc was born around **1412** and claimed to have divine visions that started from the age of **12**, instructing her to retake the French homeland. At this time, the French and English were locked in the **Hundred Years' War**, and the **English had the upper hand, occupying much of France**. After making an astonishing prediction about a military reversal near **Orléans**, she was allowed to visit the **French court**, where she **impressed King Charles VII**. However, the king's advisers were concerned that she might be a **heretic** or a **sorceress**, so she was **subjected to a theological examination**, which declared her a **'good Christian ... of irreproachable life'**. Joan arrived at the **Siege of Orléans** in **May 1429**, seven months into the siege, and **led an attack that crushed the English stronghold**. She was **wounded in the neck** during the battle. She then led the French to victories at **Jargeau**, **Meung-sur-Loire**, **Beaugency** and the decisive **Battle of Patay**. Under her leadership, the French also retook the **Burgundian**-held city of **Auxerre**, as well as **Troyes** and **Reims**. Joan was **wounded in the leg by a crossbow bolt** during the attempted recapture of Paris, but continued to marshal the French troops, until Charles ordered them to withdraw. Joan travelled to Compiègne to bolster the city's defences against an English and Burgundian siege but was **captured and subsequently bought by the English**. She was **convicted of heresy at Rouen on 9 January 1431** and after a sham trial, during which she showed remarkable intelligence and courage, Joan was **burned at the stake on 30 May 1431**. **Twenty-five years after her death**, the **Pope declared her** a **martyr**. She was canonised in 1920 in Rome in a ceremony attended by over 30,000 people.

Napoleon Bonaparte

'To do all that one is able to do, is to be a man; to do all that one would like to do, is to be a god'.

Napoleon Bonaparte was a military and political leader in the early 19th century. He is remembered as a **great reformer** and **military commander**, winning major battles against numerically superior forces. Born in Corsica in **1769** to an affluent family, he was admitted to the elite *École Militaire* in **1784**, graduating in **1785**. He won fame commanding Republican forces during the **French revolution**. He was given command of the army of Italy and became increasingly influential in French politics, eventually staging a **coup d'etat** in **1799** and becoming **First Consul**. He won **decisive victories** against Austrian forces at the **Battle of Marengo (1800)**, against Austrian and Russian forces at the **Battle of Austerlitz (1805)** and against Prussia and Saxony at the **Battle of Jena-Auerstedt (1806)**, but he suffered a major defeat at the **Battle of Leipzig** in **1813**. **Paris was captured** and he was forced into exile on **Elba**. He escaped and returned to France, rallying an army of **200,000** men but the European powers readied armies to thwart him. He was finally defeated at the **Battle of Waterloo (1815)**, but came very close to victory. He was imprisoned and sent to the island of **St Helena** where he died in 1821. Among his political achievements were the introduction of the **metric system (1799)**, the establishment of the *Banque de France* and the introduction of a number of civil laws, known subsequently as the **Napoleonic Code**.

Ramesses the Great

'King of Kings *am I, Osymandias. If anyone would know how great I am and where I lie, let him surpass one of my works'.*

Ramesses the Great is possibly the most celebrated of all the **Egyptian Pharaohs**. Born around **1300 BC**, he lived until the extraordinary age of **90**, and during his long life, he instigated an unprecedented **building campaign**, as well as **re-establishing Egypt's influence over Syria**. He led a number of campaigns against the **Hittites**, culminating in the **Battle of Kadesh** (1274 BC), during which he gained a reputation for **valour**, after a brave counter-attack following an ambush. However, the battle was inconclusive; the Egyptians did retreat but this was principally due to their over-stretched supply chain. Subsequent campaigns in Syria against the Hittites were more successful, and eventually, Ramesses decided to **negotiate peace**. The **peace treaty** he signed with the Hittite king Hattusili III **survives as a stone tablet** and is believed to be the **oldest peace treaty in existence**. Among his building achievements were the city of **Pi-Ramesses**, a substantial temple complex, now known as **Ramasseum**, the colossal rock temples of **Abu Simbel** and the **tomb of his favourite consort, Queen Nefertari**. By the time of his death, he had outlived many of his children and wives. He was buried in the **Valley of the Kings** and his sarcophagus is now on display in the **Cairo Museum**.

Amazing fact: Scientific analysis has revealed that Ramesses was a redhead, a fact which, according to Egyptian custom, meant that he would have been associated with the God Seth.

Saladin

'Have no fear. It is not the custom of kings to kill kings'.

Born in 1137, Saladin was a Kurdish Muslim who was responsible for **uniting and leading the Muslim world** in the 12th century. He became the emir of **Egypt in 1171**, conquered **Yemen in 1174** and **Syria** in **1183** and **as well as parts of Mesopotamia**. He successfully **freed Palestine from the Crusaders**, after annihilating them at the **Battle of Hattin** in **1187** during which he proved his **strategic cunning** by preventing the Crusader army from accessing **fresh water**. He retook Jerusalem soon afterwards. This led to **Pope Gregory VIII** ordering the **Third Crusade** and **Henry II's** introduction of the *Saladin tithe* in England in **1188** to raise funds for the crusade. Despite the crusade's success, **Richard the Lionheart's** armies failed to retake Jerusalem. Reduced by Saladin's forces to an army of around **2,000** soldiers in **1192**, and with no hope of capturing Jerusalem, **Richard** and **Saladin** negotiated the **Treaty of Ramla**, the terms of which **secured Jerusalem as a Muslim city**, but allowed unarmed Christian pilgrims to visit. Saladin was renowned for his **chivalry** and **honour**, which won him the **respect of many adversaries**. He died of a fever soon after Richard returned to Europe and was buried in a **simple wooden coffin** in a **mausoleum** in **Damascus**, having **donated much of his wealth to the poor**.

Amazing fact: Saladin is said to have supplied Richard with two horses after he lost his at the Battle of Arsuf and sent him iced water when he was suffering from a fever.

FAMOUS BATTLES

Battle of Austerlitz

Considered one of Napoleon Bonaparte's **greatest victories**, the Battle of Austerlitz was fought on **2 December 1805** between the **French Empire** and an allied **Austrian and Russian force**. The French force numbered approximately **70,000** and the allies around **85,000**. Napoleon hoped that the allies would attack and **tactically weakened his right flank** to encourage an assault, while **concealing his main force** in dead ground behind a sloping hill. **Predicting that he would need reinforcements** to bolster the weak right flank, he summoned a corps to immediately march from Vienna – a distance of **110km (68 miles)**. **The battle started** with the allies **taking Napoleon's bait** and attacking the French right. Aided by the mist, the French force launched a **surprise attack** down the centre and forced the allies to retreat. The allies countered by sending in the elite **Russian Imperial Guard** who drove the French back. Napoleon reacted by ordering forward his **Imperial Guard**, accompanied by **horse artillery**, who wreaked havoc on the Russian force. Meanwhile, in the northern extreme of the battlefield, the French prevailed after a **long and bloody fight**. In the south of the battlefield, the French launched a **two-pronged attack**, breaking the enemy lines. **The allied force fled**, many heading south towards an area of frozen lakes. The ice broke under heavy bombardment and many soldiers **perished in the icy waters**. In total, the allies lost **27,000** men to the **9,000** lost by the French. In his victory speech, Napoleon famously said: **'Soldiers, I am pleased with you'**. The battle paved the way for France's domination of Europe over the next decade.

Battle of Bannockburn

The English-held castle of **Stirling** was besieged by Scottish forces in the spring of **1314**, so the English king, **Edward II**, sent an army of around **18,000** men to annihilate them. The Scottish king, **Robert the Bruce**, had been preparing for this since May, and had formed his army of between **6,000** and **9,000** men in a heavily wooded area to conceal their movements and to afford cover for a retreat. Bruce had also **dug holes in the main road** to prevent a charge from the **heavy cavalry**. On the first day of battle, **Henry de Bohun**, the nephew of the **Earl of Hereford**, spotted the Scottish king and impetuously charged him with his lance. Bruce, wearing **no armour**, met the charge, avoided the lance and delivered an **almighty axe blow** to his adversary's head, **instantly killing him**. Spurred on, the Scottish king charged the English lines. Meanwhile, the English cavalry, keen to prevent a Scottish retreat, tried to **outflank** the Scots but were surprised by **spearmen appearing from the wood**. With no support from archers, the English cavalry were forced back. The following day, Edward II made a **catastrophic decision to cross the Bannockburn River to the east**, leading his large and unwieldy army into a **restricted space**. Bruce's infantry charged them, eventually causing the English army to break. The English archers could not fire for fear of hitting their own men so moved further away from the battle, only to be met by Scottish cavalry. They fled and the English infantry soon followed. Many of the English **drowned** trying to cross the Bannockburn and the Forth, and by the end of the battle, the English had sustained **heavy casualties**. Although a treaty recognising Scotland's independence wasn't signed until **1328**, this battle was a **decisive contributing factor**, also **consolidating Bruce's kingship** and leading to the **release of his family from captivity**.

Battle of Britain

The Battle of Britain was fought between **10 July** and **31 October 1940** and was the **first** significant campaign to take place entirely in the air. Hitler sought to **establish air superiority** over Britain by **knocking out their air defences** and **annihilating their fighter aircraft**, but they never achieved this, and therefore never launched the planned invasion, codenamed **Operation Sea Lion**. The Battle of Britain can be categorised into **four phases**: **the Channel battles**, which inflicted **heavy losses** on **British merchant shipping** at the hands of **Stuka** dive bombers; the second phase targeted **radar stations** and witnessed heavy casualties on both sides; the **third phase** sought to nullify RAF Fighter Command by **decimating British airfields**, but **failed to deliver a fatal blow**. The **fourth phase** marked a shift in strategy, turning attention to **British cities** with the intention of **demoralising the people** and **disrupting production lines**. This continued through to **May 1941**, after the threat of invasion had realistically passed. By the middle of October 1940, **Hitler cancelled the proposed invasion indefinitely** and the Germans suffered their first serious defeat of the war. The Germans had **1,887 of their aircraft** destroyed with the loss of **2,698 aircrew** and a further **967** captured by the British. Britain suffered the loss of nearly **20,000 civilian lives** during the battle in addition to **544 aircrew** and the destruction of **1,547 aircraft**. Britain **rebuilt its military forces,** and in securing Britain, provided the **platform** from which to launch the **liberation of Western Europe three years later.**

Battle of Gettysburg

Fought between **1–3 July 1863,** the Battle of Gettysburg was a pivotal conflict in the **American Civil War.** The **Union army,** led by **Major General George Gordon Meade,** defeated **Robert E. Lee's Confederate army,** in what would be the last strategic offensive launched by the Confederate forces. Lee had engineered a victory at **Chancellorsville** two months earlier and his army were in high spirits. He sought to engage the Union army and on 1 July, a **brief skirmish** broke out which saw a Union force retreat. The following day, the Union army assembled in a **defensive fish-hook formation** ready for the inevitable onslaught. In the afternoon, Lee ordered a heavy assault on **Meade's left flank,** while simultaneously feigning an attack on the right flank. These feints evolved into full-scale attacks on the Union right, but their lines **stood firm** despite sustaining **heavy casualties.** The following day, hostilities resumed at **Culp's Hill** in the north of the battlefield, but this was overshadowed by a **dramatic assault** on **Cemetery Ridge,** the Union's centre, by **12,500** Confederate soldiers. **Meade had predicted** such an ambitious assault and repelled the attack with **artillery and rifle fire,** leading to a hasty Confederate retreat after suffering heavy casualties. This effectively **ended the battle and Lee's campaign in Pennsylvania.** Both sides had lost around **20,000** men each, but **Union forces now had the initiative.**

Battle of Hastings

Fought on **14 October 1066,** the Battle of Hastings **changed the course of English history.** **Harold Godwinson,** son of the Earl of Wessex, claimed the throne after the death of **Edward the Confessor. William, the Duke of Normandy** and cousin to Edward, received news of Harold's coronation, and, believing that the throne should be rightfully his, **prepared an invasion force.** Harold had anticipated such a move, but was **forced to confront an invading army** commanded by the **King of Norway, Harald Hardrada. Harold won a decisive victory** but his triumph was shortlived, as **William had landed** at **Pevensey** in Kent. The English army rushed to meet them, forming a defensive line on a hill northwest of Hastings. Harold's army comprised **only infantry,** while William had **archers, infantry** and **cavalry** at his disposal. William ordered his archers to fire volleys of arrows, but the English were protected by their shield wall. When the Normans met the English front line in hand-to-hand combat, the **defensive line held firm. William sent in his cavalry,** but faced with spears and shields, many of them fled. After an hour of fighting, the

Norman left flank broke, and soon most of **William's army retreated.** The **English then committed a terrible error, abandoning their defensive position,** and pursuing the fleeing Normans, but **William counter-attacked,** exploiting the weakness in the English line. He ordered his archers to fire over the shield wall and into the lines behind, before attacking again. **The English line began to fragment** and his **knights struck down the English king,** after which most of the army were routed. After the battle, William marched on London and was **crowned on Christmas Day.**

Battle of Marathon

Fought in 490 BC, the Battle of Marathon was the **first Greek victory** over Persian forces during the **First Persian Invasion of Greece** and led to the Persian withdrawal to Asia. The Persians, under **Darius I,** had originally invaded in response to the Greek involvement in the **Ionian revolt,** a series of rebellions in parts of **Asia Minor against Persian rule.** The Greeks **captured and burnt** the ancient Persian city of **Sardis,** and Darius sought **retribution.** After a successful campaign in the Aegean, Darius's fleet docked close to the town of **Marathon.** The Greek force, comprising almost **every Athenian soldier** and a small force of **Plataeans,** successfully sealed the exits from the plain of Marathon. After five days of waiting, the Greeks attacked, **concentrating their forces on the Persian flanks,** while a thin line moved towards the Persian centre. The **thick armour** of the Greek hoplites offered them significant protection from the hail of arrows that rained down on them as they charged. In their **phalanx formation,** in which a rectangular mass of closely packed infantry locked their shields together with several lines of spears pointing at the enemy, the **Greeks swiftly routed the Persian flanks** and moved towards the Persian centre. After sustaining heavy casualties, the Persian centre fled towards their ships, the vast majority launching successfully. Aware that **Athens was undefended,** the Greek army marched there quickly to intercept the Persian ships before they were able to land. The Greeks made it back in time and the **Persians retreated back to Asia**.

Amazing fact: According to the Greek historian Herodotus, an Athenian runner named Pheidippides had been sent to Sparta before the battle to summon reinforcements, and he managed to complete the 140-mile journey in a little over a day. This story became conflated with the Greek army's 25-mile march back to Athens after the battle, creating the legendary but erroneous story that Pheidippides had ran the 25 miles back to Athens after the battle to proclaim that the Greeks had won the battle.

Battle of Stalingrad

Among the **bloodiest battles** in the history of warfare, Stalingrad was fought between **23 August 1942** and **2 February 1943** in the city of Stalingrad in **south-west Russia**. It is considered to be a **turning point in World War II** due to the heavy casualties sustained by the Germans. The battle started with an intensive **bombing campaign** by the **Luftwaffe**, which turned the city to **rubble**. Fierce **building-to-building fighting** continued for months, and even though at one point the German army occupied roughly **90 per cent** of the city, the Soviets managed to **hold their remaining positions** on the west bank of the **Volga** river. The Soviet soldiers were galvanised by the 'Not a Step Back' direct order from Stalin, decreeing that unauthorised retreat would lead to a military tribunal. In November 1942, the Soviets launched a massive offensive, codenamed **Operation Uranus**. The plan was to **encircle the German 6th army by simultaneously attacking its flanks**, comprising weaker Romanian, Italian and Hungarian forces. **The plan succeeded** and the **German army was cut off**, left to survive the **harsh Russian winter without supplies** and under **constant bombardment**. By **early February 1943**, German **resistance was over**. They had suffered nearly **850,000** casualties, while the Russians had sustained over **1.1 million**, including **40,000 civilians**.

Battle of Thermopylae

This legendary battle in 480 BC is one of history's most renowned **last stands**. Having been defeated by the Greeks at the Battle of Marathon in 490 BC, King **Xerxes I** amassed a **Persian army** numbering between **100,000 and 300,000** to conquer all of Greece. Their path was blocked by a small Greek army of around **7,000** men guarding the pass of Thermopylae. **King Leonidas of Sparta** with his elite **300 Spartan warriors** commanded the Greek army. On the first day of fighting, Xerxes ordered **5,000** archers to fire arrows at the Greek lines, but their bronze armour and shields protected them. Xerxes sent **10,000** infantrymen forward, but the Greek force, spanning the width of the narrow pass in **phalanx formation**, and armed with **long spears** and **tall shields**, repelled **wave upon wave of attack**, killing thousands for only a handful of casualties. Exasperated, the following day Xerxes sent in his elite troops, the **Immortals**, but they suffered the same fate. The Greeks were finally undone by a traitor named **Ephialtes**, who offered to show Xerxes **a hidden pass** that would enable the Persians to **encircle the Greeks**. Realising that they had been betrayed, many Greeks left the battle, but **Leonidas's 300 Spartans, 700 Thespians and 400 Thebans remained**. Xerxes ordered 10,000 Persians to charge the Greek front line, while a force of Immortals entered from the rear. The Greeks ran to meet the onrushing Persians and were eventually overwhelmed, although the Persians sustained **heavy casualties**, including the death of **two of Xerxes's brothers**. The Persians then **rained down arrows** until **every last Greek soldier was dead**.

Battle of Waterloo

Fought on the **18th June 1815** in present-day Belgium, the Battle of Waterloo pitted **Napoleon Bonaparte** against a coalition force led by the **Duke of Wellington** with a Prussian contingent commanded by **Gebhard von Blücher**. Napoleon met and defeated Blücher's Prussian army at the Battle of **Ligny** two days before Waterloo, but the Prussians had regrouped. Aware of the threat of Wellington's and Blücher's armies joining forces, **Napoleon sought to destroy one and then turn his attention the other**. Anticipating a French attack, Wellington formed a **strong defensive line** across a **long ridge**, hoping to hold it until Blücher's reinforcements arrived. Wellington also garrisoned the chateau of **Hougoumont**, the farmhouse of **La Haye Sainte** and the hamlet of **Papelotte**, which lay in front of the ridge. The battle started at **10am** with a heavy assault on Hougoumont. Napoleon also sent forward a **large infantry attack** towards La Haye Sainte, which succeeded in cutting off the farmhouse. The hard-pressed allied infantry were reinforced by a **British heavy cavalry charge**, but they **overreached themselves** and were **largely destroyed by the French lancers** (light cavalry equipped with lances). **Marshal Ney** launched a counter attack with his cavalry, **hoping to break Wellington's centre**. However, **with no infantry support**, the allies were able to form defensive squares and repel the attack. Ney finally ordered his infantry forward and again overwhelmed La Haye Sainte, but he **desperately needed more troops** to break the allied position on the ridge. However, Napoleon had committed reserves to repel the **Prussians who had arrived on their right flank**. He succeeded in driving them back, and then took a gamble, sending his as yet undefeated **Imperial Guard** to break through the allied centre. However, **Wellington had regrouped** and the **Guard were repulsed**. Compounded by the Prussians sending the French right flank into retreat, the **French army fled the field**. By the end of the day, Napoleon had lost around **25,000 men**, Blücher **7,000** and Wellington **15,000**. Napoleon later surrendered to the British and Europe experienced a period of relative peace and stability that lasted for 50 years.

Battle of Zama

Occurring in **202 BC**, the Battle of Zama was the final conflict of the **Second Punic War**, fought between **Rome** and **Carthage**. The Roman army was led by Publius Cornelius **Scipio** and the Carthaginian force was commanded by the legendary leader **Hannibal**. Hannibal had **already defeated several Roman armies**, so the Romans elected to **attack Carthage directly**, hoping that Hannibal would **abandon the Italian peninsula** to **meet the invading army** on his home soil. The two armies met at Zama Regia in present-day Tunisia. Hannibal's army comprised **45,000 infantry, 6,000 cavalry** and **80 war elephants**, while Scipio led a force of around **35,000 infantry** and **6,000 cavalry**. The battle commenced with Hannibal's fearsome **war elephants** charging towards the Roman lines, but Scipio had prepared for such a move and ordered his men to **blow loud horns** to frighten the animals. This succeeded and some of the **elephants broke away**, charging **at the Carthaginian left flank and causing much damage**. Scipio had also organised his infantry so that **empty channels appeared in his lines**, which he hoped the elephants would make for instead of charging through the massed soldiers. **His plan worked** and he largely nullified the threat from the elephants. The Roman cavalry on both flanks **charged the Carthaginian cavalry and routed them**, but Hannibal had expected this, hoping to lure the Roman cavalry away from the battlefield. Scipio ordered his centre forward and a **furious struggle** took place. The inexperienced **Roman first lines sustained heavy casualties**, but were reinforced by the more experienced second line, **which drove the Carthaginians back**. The battle raged on with no side winning superiority until the Roman cavalry returned, charging into the **Carthaginian rear and annihilating it. Hannibal escaped with a few thousand men** but **20,000 of his men were killed** and around the same number taken prisoner. Scipio only lost around **2,500 men**. Carthage **sued for peace** shortly afterwards, with **humiliating terms** imposed upon them, and **never recovered from this decisive defeat**.

MAJOR REVOLUTIONS

Name of Conflict	Date	Location	Combatants	Outcome
American War of Independence	1775–83	Mainly Eastern North America	Great Britain; 13 British colonies in North America	American independence; Britain loses land south of Great Lakes and east of the Mississippi
French Revolution	1789–99	France	Supporters of the French monarchy; opponents of the monarchy/nobility	Execution of King Louis XVI; formation of a secular republic
Glorious Revolution	1868	Spain	Republican and liberal uprising led by General Juan Prim against Spanish monarchy	Queen Isabella II deposed and a provisional government formed

Name of Conflict	Date	Location	Combatants	Outcome
Mexican Revolution	1910–20	Mexico	Forces loyal to President Porfirio Díaz; revolutionary forces loyal to Francisco I. Madero	Díaz removed from power and exiled; Mexican Constitution of 1917 enacted
Russian Revolution	1917	Russia	Bolshevik Red Army; anti-Bolshevik White Army	Bolshevik victory saw the destruction of the Tsarist regime; formation of the Soviet Union
Chinese Revolution	1949	China	Forces loyal to the Chinese Nationalist Party; forces of the Communist Party of China (People's Liberation Army)	Communist revolutionary Mao Zedong proclaims establishment of People's Republic of China
Egyptian Revolution	1952	Egypt	Pro-independence, anti-monarchy force (Free Officers Movement) led by Gamal Abdel Nasser	Deposed King Faruq and set up Muhammad Naguib as President of the new Republic
Cuban Revolution	1953–9	Cuba	Forces loyal to dictator Fulgencio Batista; revolutionary forces led by Fidel Castro	Collapse of the Batista regime; establishment of Castro's revolutionary government
Iranian Revolution	1979	Iran	Forces against the Shah Mohammad Reza Pahlavi led by Ayatollah Ruhollah Khomeini	Deposition of the Shah and the establishment of the Islamic republic under Ayatollah Ruhollah Khomeini

MAJOR CIVIL WARS

Name of Conflict	Date	Location	Combatants	Outcome
War of the Roses	1455–87	England, Wales, Calais	House of Lancaster; House of York	Unification of the two houses; beginning of Tudor dynasty
English Civil War	1642–9	England	Royalists under Charles I; Parliamentarians under Oliver Cromwell	Parliamentarian victory; execution of Charles I
American Civil War	1861–5	Southern, northwestern and western United States	Union States; Confederate States	Union victory; Reconstruction Era in the Southern United States; abolition of slavery
Spanish Civil War	1936–9	Continental Spain; Spanish empire in Africa	Republican forces aided by Soviet Union and Mexico; National forces under Francisco Franco aided by Germany/Italy	Nationalist victory; collapse of the Spanish Second Republic; beginning of Franco's dictatorship
Palestinian Civil War	1947–8	Palestine	Jewish community who supported UN partition plan; Arab community against the partition plan	Termination of the British Mandate for Palestine; establishment of the State of Israel; the 1948 Arab-Israeli war

Name of Conflict	Date	Location	Combatants	Outcome
Korean War	1950–3	Korea	Communist North Korea (or the Democratic People's Republic of Korea); non-communist South Korea (or the Republic of Korea)	Armistice signed and the Korean Demilitarised Zone dividing North and South established
Vietnam War	1955–75	Vietnam, Laos and Cambodia	Communist North Vietnam (or the Democratic Republic of Vietnam); non-communist South Vietnam (or the Republic of Vietnam)	South Vietnam surrendered to North Vietnam; Vietnam reunited as a communist country, the Socialist Republic of Vietnam
Bosnian War	1992–5	Bosnia and Herzegovina	Bosnian Serbs; Bosnian Croats and Muslims	War ended with the signing of the peace agreement, the Dayton Accords

A SPORTING GUIDE

ASSOCIATION FOOTBALL

The Basics

In the game of association football, the winner is decided by which team has scored the most goals by the end of a match. If both teams have scored the same amount of goals, or neither team has managed to score, the game ends in a draw. In elimination competitions such as the FA Cup or the World Cup final, a 30-minute **extra time** period is played if the scoreline is still level at 90 minutes. If there is still no clear winner by the end of this period, **penalty kicks** decide the game, with each team taking five penalties. If neither team has scored more penalties than the opposition after five penalties, it is decided by **sudden-death**, where if one team's player scores his/her penalty and the other team's player misses their penalty, the team that scored win the match.

The classic formation of an **11-a-side** team is **one** goalkeeper, **four defenders**, **four midfielders** and **two attackers** (see diagram). In modern football, a team is usually allowed to name seven possible substitutes and conventionally allowed to make **three substitutions** during a match.

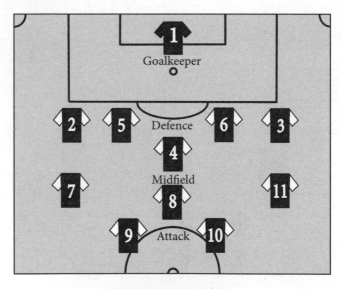

The goalkeeper is the only player allowed to use his hands to control the ball, although he may only do so inside his own penalty area.

If a foul is committed by a player, the opposition team will be awarded a **free-kick**, or a **penalty** if the incident happened inside the guilty player's own penalty area.

Players will be **sent off** from the field of play if they receive a **red card** or **two yellow cards** (which equate to a red card). This may happen for a number of reasons including **professional fouls**, **unprofessional conduct**, **handballs**, or cheating (such as diving to simulate a foul). A red card is typically shown to a player who has committed serious misconduct, while a yellow card, or 'booking' indicates a warning. A team with a player sent off continues for the remainder of the game with 10 players.

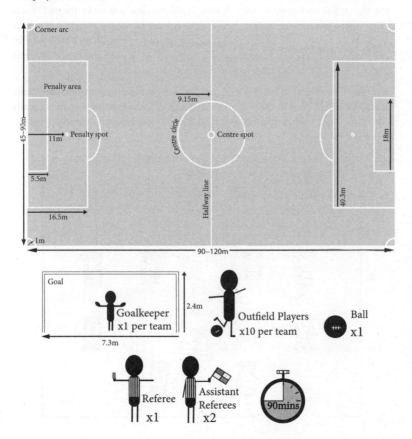

Corner kicks occur when the ball has gone out of play behind the goal line if the ball last touched a player who was defending that goal line. If the ball has gone out of play behind the goal line last touching a player attacking that goal, a **goal kick**

will be awarded to the defending team. **Throw-ins** occur when the ball has gone out of play over the touchline and is awarded to the opposing team of the player which the ball last touched before going out of play.

Glossary

12th man: Fans of a team whose support inspires confidence and belief in their players.

Away goals rule: Used in two-legged fixtures, if at the end of the second match the score is level, the team who has scored more goals in their away-leg win.

Back-pass rule: If a player intentionally kicks the ball back to their own goalkeeper, the goalkeeper is not allowed to handle the ball. To do so results in an indirect free-kick from where the offence occurred.

Ball to hand: Describes an incident when the ball hits a player's arm unintentionally. Conversely, 'handball' refers to a player deliberately using his hand or arm to control the ball.

Cap: When a player is selected for a national team. School caps were originally presented to players chosen to play for England.

Captain: Also known as the 'skipper', the captain is the leader of his or her team on the pitch and typically wears an armband to signify their responsibility.

Dribble: A player moving with control of the ball close to their feet.

Dummy: Performed by a player who looks as if to connect with a ball but does not, therefore confusing the opposition.

Foul: An unfair act by a player which is penalised by the referee.

Free-kick: An unobstructed kick of a stationary ball after an opponent has committed a foul or has been penalised for being offside.

Hat-trick: The achievement of a player scoring three goals in the same match.

Nutmeg: A skill when the ball is played between an opposition player's legs. This term arose in the 1870s from the nutmeg trade between America and England. As nutmeg was a valuable commodity, American exporters mixed wooden replicas of nutmegs into sacks of the spice being shipped to England. The English who were fooled by this trick were said to be 'nutmegged'.

Offside: A player is in an 'offside' position if, when the ball is played forward by a team-mate, there are fewer than two opposing players between the attacking player and the goal line. A player can only be offside in the opponents' half (*Fig. 1*).

Park the bus: Used as a negative allusion to a team with an extremely defensive formation who have metaphorically parked their team bus in front of their goal.

Penalty: A one-on-one situation in which the ball is placed on the penalty spot and a player is allowed one kick to score against the opposition goalkeeper. This is caused by an infringement in the penalty box by the defending team.

Tiki-taka: Spanish in origin, this is a term used to describe short pass-and-move tactics by a team.

Total Football: A Dutch term which gained prominence in the 1970s used to describe tactics where outfield players constantly switch roles to join attacks while maintaining the same formation.

Fig.1 The Offside Rule

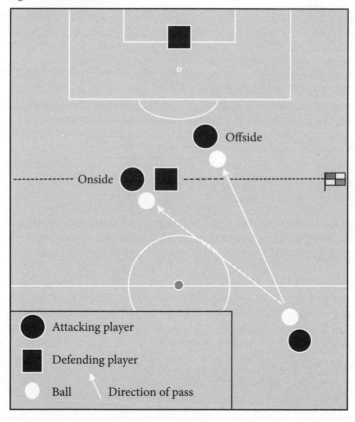

Football Heroes

EDSON ARANTES DO NASCIMENTO (PELÉ)

'I was born for soccer, just as Beethoven was born for music.'

Brazilian Striker Pelé is quite rightly considered by many as the greatest footballer of all time. A winner of three World Cups and the youngest scorer in a World Cup at just 17-years-old, Pelé was a magician who dazzled fans with football that had never been seen before. In his glittering career, he scored a remarkable 1,281 goals in 1,363 games, including Brazil's 100th World Cup goal. In 2000, his career was crowned with the award of FIFA Player of the Century.

Greatest Moment: Winning the 1958 World Cup in Sweden at 17-years-old after scoring two goals in the final. He was triumphantly carried off the field in tears of joy.

BOBBY MOORE

'Without him England would never have won the World Cup.' Sir Alf Ramsey

The only England captain to lead his team to World Cup success, Moore remains an iconic figure. Almost 50 years on from the 1966 World Cup final against West Germany, Moore is still considered one of the greatest defenders in the history of the game. Referred to by Pelé as 'the greatest defender I ever played against', Moore is remembered for his ability to read the game and his composure in the tackle and on the ball. A 20ft bronze statue of Moore now stands outside Wembley Stadium, the scene of his and England's greatest triumph.

Greatest Moment: Undoubtedly captaining England in the 1966 World Cup, beating West Germany 4-2 in the final at Wembley and collecting the Jules Rimet trophy from Queen Elizabeth II.

DIEGO MARADONA

'A little with the head of Maradona and a little with the hand of God.'

With even a religion based around him – *The Church of Maradona* – 'El Diego' remains a notorious figure in the world of football. From the sublime to the scandalous, the little Argentine maestro has never been out of the headlines. Maradona was the star of the 1986 Mexico World Cup, thrilling the world with his technical skills but causing controversy with his hand-balled goal against England in the quarter final – an incident branded the 'Hand of God'. Maradona inspired his club teams too, especially Napoli where he won Italy's Serie A league title twice, becoming a club legend.

Greatest Moment: His stunning goal against England just minutes after the 'Hand of God' goal, dribbling round six England players before scoring; it was later voted FIFA Goal of the Century.

ZINEDINE ZIDANE
'I've known skilful players before, but Zizou was different. I could have spent the whole night watching him.' Rolland Courbis, Zidane's manager at Bordeaux

Zizou's two goals at the Stade de France in the 1998 World Cup final made him a household name across the world. Before retiring in 2006 in dramatic circumstances, Zidane achieved great things with his country, his clubs and as an individual. In addition to the '98 final, the pinnacle of his career was a spectacular volleyed goal in the 2002 UEFA Champions League final. His extraordinary career was punctuated by a poor disciplinary record, and in the 2006 World Cup Final, he was sent off for a headbutt on Italian defender Marco Materazzi, his final act in football. With three World Player of the Year Awards and even a film made about him, Zidane is regarded as one of the most magnificentand mercurial players of all time.

Greatest Moment: The two goals in the final of France 98 against favourites Brazil to win his country the World Cup.

LIONEL MESSI
'It is clear that Messi is on a level above all others. Those who do not see that are blind.'
Xavi Hernández

Messi is already considered one of the greatest players in history and the finest of his generation. The Argentinian forward, who suffered a growth-hormone deficiency as a child, has amassed an incredible array of Spanish League titles, UEFA Champions Leagues and Club World Cups for his club Barcelona. Messi has been named by FIFA as the best player in the world for three consecutive years – an unprecedented achievement in men's football. In May 2012, he surpassed Gerd Müller's European scoring record of 67 goals in one season, completing the season with an incredible 73 goals.

Greatest Moment: In March 2012 at the age of 24, Messi became Barcelona's all-time leading goal scorer, eclipsing the record of 232 goals scored by César Rodríguez.

TENNIS

Tennis is a racquet sport played either between two players (singles) or four players (doubles) on a court divided by a raised net.

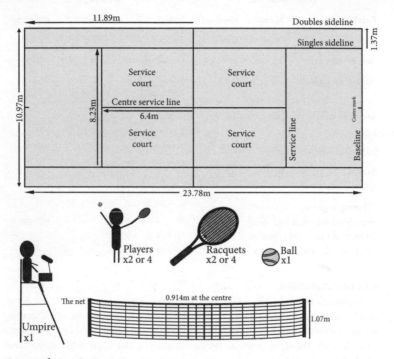

Layout of a tennis court
Tennis is played on a rectangular court divided by a net. Singles is played up to the singles sidelines, whereas doubles occupies the entire court.

A Match Explained

A match is split into individual **'games'** and **'sets'**. The winner of a match is the player who wins the most sets from a pre-determined amount. Usually, matches are played in a **best-of-three** sets or **best-of-five** sets format. A player normally needs to **win four points to win a 'game'** and must win the game by two clear points. Players **take it in turns to serve**; one serves a game while the other receives, and vice versa. Both players start each game at 0 (known as 'love'). Each player (or team in doubles) accumulates points in the format **15, 30, 40** and **'game'** (i.e. the first point a player scores is denoted by '15', the second point '30' etc). However, if both players are tied at 40-all (known as 'deuce'), one of them must win two consecutive points to win the game *(see table below)*.

Game example			Advantage Rule		
Point	**Server**	**Receiver**	**Point**	**Server**	**Receiver**
Love	0	0	Deuce	40	40
Server wins point	15	0	Server wins point	A	40
Server wins point	30	0	Server wins point and game	Game	40
Receiver wins point	30	15	**Deuce and Advantage**		
Server wins point	40	15	Both players have won three points each, so the score is 40-all, commonly known as **'deuce'**. Whichever player wins the next point has their score at **'advantage'** (A). If they win the next point they win the game. However, if their opponent wins that point, the score is reverted back to 'deuce'.		
Server wins point and the game	Game	15			
Winning a game					
The server has won four points and is more than two points clear of his opponent, so wins the game.					

A Point Explained*

Each point in tennis begins with one player serving to their opponent. The server stands behind the **baseline**, to the right or left of the **centre mark**. In each game, the server first serves from the right side of the centre mark and then alternates sides for each point. The server must hit the ball into the **service court** of their opponent, situated **diagonally** from the side of the court they are serving from. If the ball does not land in this zone, by **hitting the net**, or **bouncing outside the zone**, then the serve is a '**fault**'. If this happens twice during one point, it is a '**double fault**' and the receiver wins the point.

The receiver must allow the ball to **bounce** once if it does land in the service court, before returning the ball. **It is not legal to return a serve by volleying the ball** but either player is allowed to volley the ball after the serve has been returned. Each player is only allowed **one touch** of the ball each time it is in their half of the court. If a player **returns the ball into the net** or if their shot **lands outside their opponent's court, they lose the point**. If a returned ball lands in the court but bounces twice before the player can reach it, that player loses the point.

* Example is for a singles match

A Set Explained

The winner of a set is usually the first player to win six games. However, to win a set, the player must be at least two clear games ahead of their opponent eg 6–4, 6–3 etc. A player can also win a set 7–5 if the game score plays out at 5–5, 6–5, 7–5. If a set goes to 6–6, a tiebreak is played in which the winner of the set is usually the first player to win seven points; again this must be by at least two points. However, if both players are on 6 points each, the tiebreak continues until one player is two clear points ahead eg 8–6, 11–9 etc.

In the eventuality that a deciding set is played, there is no tiebreak if the final set reaches 6–6. The players continue until one player is two games ahead of their opponent, at which point they have won the match eg 8–6, 15–13 etc. This method is used in every Grand Slam except the US Open where a final-set tiebreak is played.

Glossary

Ace: A serve where the ball is not touched by the receiver. The fastest recorded ace is 155mph, shared by Andy Roddick and Milos Raonic.

Bagel: When a player has lost a set without winning a game, as the '0' resembles a bagel.

Ball Boy/Girl: Person who retrieves balls that have gone out of play and supplies the server with balls.

Break: To win a game as the receiving player, thus 'breaking' the opponent's serve.

Deuce: When a game is tied at 40–40.

Grand Slam: The four main annual tournaments. They are, in calendar order: the Australian Open, the French Open, Wimbledon and the US Open.

Groundstroke: A shot that is played after the ball has bounced.

Hawk-Eye: Computer system used to determine the path and bounce off the ball. Typically used for challenges by players who believe the ball to have landed in or out of the court.

Let: Occurs when a serve hits the top of the net and bounces into the correct service area; this can happen on the first or second serve and means that the serve is taken again.

Line-Judge: Assistant who is positioned in line with the court boundary lines to observe if the ball has landed in or out of the court.

Love: Term for a player who is on 0 points eg 'fifteen-love'. Possibly derived from the French *l'oeuf* ('the egg') due to its similarity in shape to a zero.

Rally: The sequence of shots during an individual point.

Serve and volley: Tactic usually utilised by a big server to move forward after their serve and volley their opponent's return.

Umpire: Person who oversees a match; sits on a raised chair beside the net.

Tennis Heroes

BJORN BORG

'We're playing tennis, he's playing something else.' Ilie Nastase

The distinctive Swede, sporting his trademark headband and mane of blonde hair, won 11 Grand Slam titles between 1974 and 1981, including five consecutive Wimbledon titles. Known as 'Ice Borg' for his composure on the court, the Scandinavian was the first player to earn $1m in a season. He famously won both the French Open and Wimbledon three seasons in a row, renowned as the most difficult 'double' in the sport. His fabled rivalry with the hot-headed John McEnroe included one of the greatest matches of all time, the 1980 Wimbledon Final, which Borg won 8–6 in the fifth set. Borg shocked the world when he retired at just 26.

PETE SAMPRAS

'Just when you think he's dying, that's when he kills you.' Jim Courier

The big-serving American is well remembered for his dominance of Wimbledon where he won seven singles title in the 1990s. In 1990, aged only 19, Sampras became the youngest winner of the US Open. That was to be the first of his 14 Grand Slam titles as he succeeded in winning every Slam besides the French Open. He won his last one in 2002 where he had won his first, defeating his great rival Andre Agassi in the US Open final. Known for his powerful and accurate serve and his exceptional running-forehand, Sampras was world number one for a record 286 weeks, making him one of the all-time greats.

ROGER FEDERER

'Federer is the best player in history, no other player has ever had such quality.' Rafael Nadal

The stylish and graceful Swiss player is talked of by many players, pundits and fans, as the greatest player of all time. However, he has not just won praise for his artistic style of tennis – which has lead him to more Grand Slam singles titles than any other male player – but also for his humble approach to the game, whether in victory or defeat. In a 2011 poll, Federer was named second only to former South Africa president Nelson Mandela in a study of the most reputable public figures. His devastating forehand was famously described by John McEnroe as 'the greatest shot in our sport'.

MARGARET COURT

'I have always been a champion and always loved what I do.'

Nicknamed the 'Aussie Amazon' due to her commitment to weights and strength training, Court was a powerhouse of tennis during the 1960s. She was renowned for her big serve as well as her agility at the net. Court won a remarkable 24 singles' Grand Slams in her career, including seven consecutive Australian Open titles. Court is the only player to have achieved the Career 'boxed set' (winning the singles, doubles and mixed doubles titles at all four Grand Slams) twice. She retired with an unparalleled 62 Grand Slam titles and the highest win percentage (91.74) in the open era.

MARTINA NAVRATILOVA

'I hope, when I stop, people will think that somehow I mattered.'

It is impossible to speak of Navratilova's career without citing statistics. In a long professional career, sustained by fitness and a love of the sport, the Czech-American won 59 Grand Slam titles, including 18 singles, 31 doubles and 10 mixed doubles titles. She won her first Grand Slam title in the mixed doubles at the French Open in 1974 and her last an incredible 32 years later. Navratilova enjoyed an immensely successful doubles partnership with Pam Shriver, famously winning all four women's doubles Slams in 1984 as part of a 109-match winning streak. Her 15-year rivalry with Chris Evert was one of the greatest in tennis history.

STEFFI GRAF

'Steffi is definitely the greatest women's tennis player of all time.' Billie Jean King

Ranked as the number one female player for an unprecedented 377 weeks, Graf's place at the pinnacle of the sport is indisputable. Her 22 Grand Slam singles titles are second only to Margaret Court's total of 24. The German is the only player, male or female, to win the Calendar Year Golden Slam, when in 1988 she won all four Slams plus the Olympic gold medal in Seoul. Known on the circuit as *'Fräulein Forehand'* in reference to her powerful forehand drive, Graf boasts a singles win-loss record of 900–115. Graf retired in 1999 stating 'I have done everything I wanted to do in tennis. I feel I have nothing left to accomplish'. She married fellow professional Andre Agassi in 2001.

BASKETBALL

The Basics

One of the most popular sports in the world, basketball is a game contested between two team of **five** players each, with the objective being to shoot a ball through a **horizontally-positioned basket**. Played on a **28 metres** x **15 metres** court with a basket at each end, the winning team is the team that scores the most points at the end of the allotted four periods (or **'quarters'**, consisting of **12 minutes** each). The court itself is divided into various areas which dictate the scoring in the game: the two-point **'field goal'** area – 6.25 metres from the basket and a further 1.575 metres from the base of the court – is the most accessible area to score 'a bucket', and each basket scored from this area counts for two points; the three point zone begins after the **three-point line** (which is not part of the three-point goal area), and each basket scored from this area counts for three points. The ball can be advanced on the court by bouncing it while walking or running (commonly known as **'dribbling'**), or throwing (passing) to a teammate. A **'free throw'** is awarded when a shooting player is fouled. They are taken from the **free-throw line** and range in number from **one** to **three** depending on the severity of the foul. They are worth one point each. Players can also **'rebound'** the ball by gaining possession of the ball after the opposition team misses a free throw or field goal attempt. Additional overtime is played if the game ends in a draw.

The National Basketball Association (**NBA**) is the professional basketball league in the USA and also functions as the sport's governing body in the USA. It comprises **30** teams (**29** in the USA and **one** in Canada). The teams are split into the **Eastern** and **Western** Conference, each containing **three divisions** containing **five** teams each. At the end of the season, the top **sixteen** teams (eight from each Conference) make it to the **NBA Playoffs**, a best-of-seven-games elimination tournament which decides the four teams who make it to the **NBA Conference Finals**. Separate from this, the **NBA All-Star Game** is an annual event pitting the best players of the Eastern Conference against the best of the Western Conference.

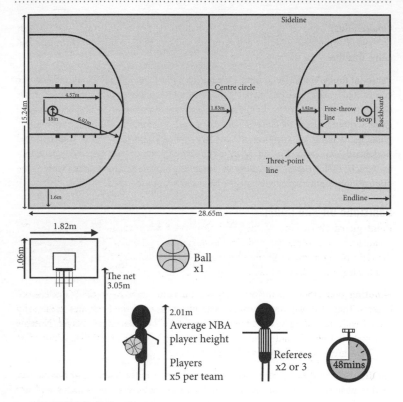

Layout of a basketball court

Basketball is played on a rectangular wooden court with two raised hoops at each end attached to a rectangular backboard.

There are various violations that can be committed during the game, many of which result in a loss of possession or free throws for the opposing team:

Travelling: When a player moves with one or both of his/her feet illegally without dribbling the ball.

Double dribble: When a player dribbles the ball, clearly holds on to it with a combination of one or two hands, and then dribbles again without attempting to shoot a basket or make a pass.

Carrying the ball: A player cannot place a hand under the ball during a dribble; doing so results in a foul.

Back-court violation: Once a team advances the ball beyond the halfway line they cannot retreat back into their own half.

Goaltending: A player cannot touch the ball on its downward trajectory towards the basket or interfere with the ball's contact with the hoop; doing so results in a foul and a free throw for the opposing team.

Personal fouls: The most common type of foul in basketball, 'personal fouls' can be committed by offensive or defensive players and normally result in two free throws (taken from the free-throw line) for the opposing team. In the original rules of the game written in 1891 by James Naismith, a foul is defined as 'shouldering, holding, pushing, striking or tripping in any way of an opponent'. The International Basketball Association has since refined the rules to focus on the 'cylinder principle' in which each player occupies an imaginary protected 'cylinder' which the opposition cannot infringe (by any of Naismith's aforesaid methods).

Positions On The Court

Point guard (PG): One of the most important positions in the game, the PG organizes the team's offense, and dictates the tempo of the play by playing the ball to the right player at the right time. Notable PGs include Steve Nash (Phoenix Suns) and the legendary Earvin 'Magic' Johnson (Los Angeles Lakers).

Shooting guard (SG): As the title suggests, the main objective of the SG is to score baskets. They also play important roles as 'playmakers' in the team and are usually tasked with defending against the opposing side's best perimeter player. Notable SGs include Kobe Bryant (Los Angeles Lakers), Vince Carter (Dallas Mavericks) and NBA-great Michael Jordan (Chicago Bulls).

Small forward (SF): The SF is the most active player in the team. Players who play in this position are usually smaller and quicker than their teammates and are regularly tasked with scoring points, keeping the ball moving and intercepting rebounds. Notable SFs include LeBron James (Miami Heat), Luol Deng (Chicago Bulls) and Scottie Pippen (Los Angeles Lakers).

Power forward (PF): PF is one of the more disciplined roles on the basketball court. A player assigned this role normally plays with their back to the basket and acts as a pivot for an offensive player; defensively they stand under the basket and are tasked with gathering both offensive and defensive rebounds. Notable PFs include Paul Gasol (Los Angeles Lakers), Chris Bosh (Miami Heat) and Karl Malone (Utah Jazz).

Center (C): Similar to the PF, the center is invariably the tallest member of the team, and is tasked with scoring and defending in close proximity to the basket. Centers are commonly used for the 'jump-ball' at the start of the game. Notable Cs include Shaquille O'Neal (Los Angeles Lakers), Yao Ming (Houston Rockets) and NBA legend Wilt Chamberlain (Philadelphia 76ers and Los Angeles Lakers).

Basketball Heroes

MICHAEL JORDAN

Michael Jordan is officially considered by the NBA as 'the greatest basketball player of all time'. A combination of skill, power and raw, unbridled talent led Jordan to superstardom as he inspired the Chicago Bulls to league titles in 1991, 1992 and 1993. His leaping ability and sheer audacity earned him the nickname 'Air Jordan' and he is quite rightly seen as one of the greatest athletes of his generation. In his astonishing career, during which he played as both Shooting guard and Small forward, he was a six-time NBA Champion, picked up 14 NBA All-star selections and holds the record for the highest average points per game in NBA history.

Greatest moment: Winning the 1990–1 Most Valuable Player (MVP) award. A tearful Jordan picked up the award after an amazing season which was topped off by an incredible lay-up in game two of the finals, avoiding Sam Perkins' block to tip the ball gracefully into the basket.

EARVIN 'MAGIC' JOHNSON

Magic by name and magic by nature, Earvin Johnson burst on to the NBA scene after winning titles at both high-school and college levels. He went on to become one of the darlings of the NBA and his rivalry with Boston Celtic's Larry Bird was one of the most entertaining in basketball history. Flamboyant and incredibly popular both on and off the court, Johnson was honoured as one of the 'greatest players in NBA history' in 1996 and holds the record for average assists per game – a massive 11.2. He played as both Point guard and Power forward during his career, winning five NBA championships and receiving 12 NBA All-star selections. Johnson was also a member of the 'Dream Team', the USA basketball team that won the gold medal at the Barcelona Olympics in 1992.

Greatest moment: Becoming the only rookie in NBA history to pick up the MVP award, which he did in 1980.

LARRY BIRD

A Boston Celtics legend, Larry Bird is the only person in NBA history to be named MVP, Coach of the Year and Executive of the Year, a record that sums up his extraordinary contribution to basketball. In his playing career he excelled as both a Small forward and Power forward, winning three NBA Championships and 12 NBA All-star selections. He also received three consecutive MVP awards between 1984–6, a feat only matched by fellow basketball greats Bill Russell and Wilt Chamberlain.

Greatest moment: Picking up the first of three championships with the Boston Celtics in only his second season.

KAREEM ABDUL-JABBAR

Born Ferdinand Lewis Alcindor, Jr in 1947, Jabbar showed his talent from an early age, leading his all-Catholic boys school team to three straight New York City championships during the early 1960s. As a member of UCLA Bruins, he participated in the sport's so-called 'game of the century' – an enthralling match between the Bruins and the Houston Cougars – and the first of its kind to be shown on live television. He went on to further greatness during his time in the NBA, representing both the Milwaukee Bucks and the Los Angeles Lakers, during which he won six NBA championships, picked up 19 NBA All-star selections and collected the NBA MVP award six times. If this wasn't enough, he is also the NBA's all-time leading scorer, amassing an unbelievable 38,387 points.

Greatest moment: Pioneering the legendary 'sky-hook', in which he would bend his whole body in one fluid motion to perform a shot which was nigh-on impossible to defend. This signature shot earned him the nickname 'Captain Skyhook'.

CHARLES BARKLEY

A dominating power-forward, Barkley was as controversial as he was talented, and his time both on and off the pitch was always a source of interest for the basketball press. He had stints at the 76ers, the Phoenix Suns and the Houston Rockets and was renowned for his versatility and tactical nous when many of his peers lacked such discipline. He picked up 11 NBA All-star selections and was voted the MVP in 1993. Affectionately known as Charles 'Round Mound for the Rebound' Barkley, he was also a member of the gold-medal-winning 'Dream Team' at the 1992 and 1996 Olympics. Barkley is now a pundit for the NBA and his insight and knowledge of the game is valued the world over.

Greatest moment: Amassing the highest points tally and points average amongst the galaxy of stars in the USA 'Dream Team' on the way to Olympic gold in 1992.

CRICKET

The Basics

A cricket match is a bat-and-ball game contested between two teams of **11** players on a rectangular **22-yard pitch**, surrounded by an **outer oval-shaped** field of play which is bounded by a **rope**. At each end of the pitch is a **wicket** – wooden sticks (**stumps**) with two smaller pieces of wood (**bails**) sitting on top of them. In a match, one team bats, trying to score as many points (**runs**) as they can, while the other team '**fields**', trying to **dismiss the batsmen** one of the **ten** ways listed below. The captain of the fielding team chooses a bowler to bowl an **over** (six balls) to the batsmen from one end of the pitch, and then chooses another bowler to bowl from the other end; the fielders change position accordingly. The **wicket-keeper** is a member of the fielding team situated **directly behind the wicket** that the bowler is bowling towards, and it is his/her job to **catch the ball** if the batsman does not connect with the ball. He is also able to catch the ball if the batsman connects with it or stump the batsman (see below). **The batting team always have two batsmen on the pitch**, one facing the bowler's delivery and one standing at the opposite end of the pitch. When **ten** batsmen have been dismissed, the batting team's performance (**innings**) is over and the other team bats. There are **ten** different ways that the batsman can be given 'out' by one of the two umpires.

A Cricket Pitch

Batsmen x2

Fielders x11

Umpires x2

Cricket Bat

Cricket Ball

Bails

Stumps 71.1cm above ground level

22.86cm

1.22m

Popping crease

2.64m

Cricket Pitch

Bowling crease

Stumps

20.12m

A Cricket Ground With Fielding Positions

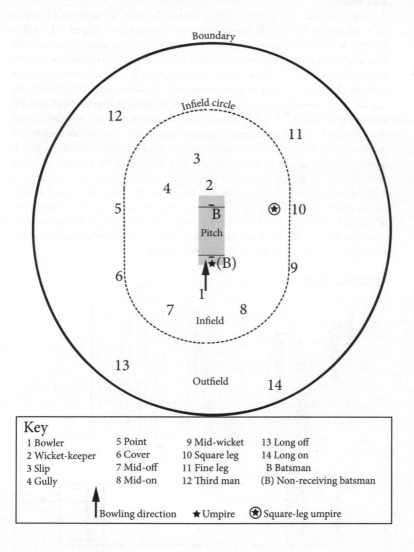

Boundary

Infield circle

12

11

3

4   2

5   B   ⊛ 10

Pitch

6   ★(B)

9

1

7   8

Infield

13

Outfield   14

Key			
1 Bowler	5 Point	9 Mid-wicket	13 Long off
2 Wicket-keeper	6 Cover	10 Square leg	14 Long on
3 Slip	7 Mid-off	11 Fine leg	B Batsman
4 Gully	8 Mid-on	12 Third man	(B) Non-receiving batsman

↑ Bowling direction   ★ Umpire   ⊛ Square-leg umpire

The Ways A Batsman Can Be Given Out

Type of dismissal	How the dismissal happens
Bowled	The bowler hits the stumps, knocking the bails off, with a delivery.
Caught	The batsman hits the ball in the air and one of the fielding team catch it before the ball bounces.
Leg Before Wicket (LBW) [See diagram below]	The bowler's delivery hits the batsman's body when it would have actually gone on to hit the stumps. In order for the batsman to be given out by the umpire, the bowler needs to appeal, which he does by shouting 'Howzat' (How is that?).
Run out	If the fielding team knock the bails off a wicket that the batsman is attempting to run to before he makes it to the popping crease.
Stumped	Similar to being run out, stumping occurs when the wicketkeeper knocks the bails off a wicket when the batsman has moved forward, away from his crease, in order to hit the ball.
Hit wicket (Infrequent)	The batsman being bowled to accidentally hits his wicket, knocking the bails off.
Hitting the ball twice (Infrequent)	Introduced as a law to protect close fielders, the batsman is given out if he makes contact with the ball twice unless he is protecting his wicket.
Obstructing the field (Infrequent)	If the batsman deliberately gets in the way of a fielder.
Handled the ball (Infrequent)	If the batsman deliberately touches the ball with his hand, eg to protect his wicket.
Timed out (Infrequent)	If the next batsman fails to arrive at the crease within three minutes of the previous batsman being given out.

The LBW Law

Example **1**: **Not out** because the ball hits the batsman outside the line of the stumps

Example **2**: Although the ball pitched outside the line of the stumps, it would have gone on to hit the stumps. However, the umpire can only give the batsman **out** if the batsman makes no attempt to hit the ball

Example **3**: **Out** if the umpire believes that the ball would go on to hit the stumps

Example **4**: **Out** as the ball pitched in the line of leg stump and would have gone on to hit the stumps

Example **5**: **Not Out** as the ball pitched outside the line of leg stump

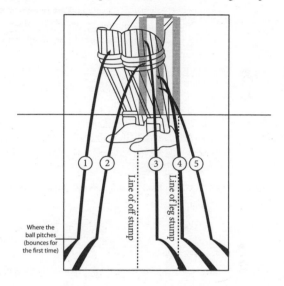

Glossary

Beamer: A delivery that reaches the batsman at head-height (illegal ball).

Corridor of uncertainty: Situated in an imaginary channel just outside the batsman's off stump, if a ball is pitched here, the batsman will often be unsure of whether to leave the ball or play it.

Declaration: A captain's decision to end the innings, usually performed when the batting team have accumulated enough runs to be sure to avoid defeat.

Duck: A term used if a batsman is dismissed without scoring a run.

Extras: Additional runs awarded to the batting team through errors committed by the fielding team, including wides, no balls, byes and leg byes (see table below).

Full-toss: A delivery reaching the batsman before it has bounced.

Googly: A disguised delivery bowled by a leg-spin bowler that spins to the off-side rather than the leg-side.

Leg-side: The half of the cricket ground behind the batsman as he stands at the crease (the batsman stands side-on to receive the ball).

Maiden: An over bowled without concession of a run.

Off-side: The half of the cricket ground in front of the batsman as he stands at the crease.

One-day match: A short form of cricket where each team bats only once and faces limited overs (often 50).

Popping crease: A white line that a bowler must not put his foot over when he releases the ball; it is also the line that the batsman must ground his bat past in order to score a run and to avoid being run out.

Run: If the batsman hits the ball, he can attempt a run; in order to score a run both batsmen have to run to the opposite popping crease before either one is 'run out'. A batsman can score four runs if he hits a shot that bounces before crossing the boundary rope, and six runs if the ball crosses the rope without bouncing.

Sledging: Verbal abuse meted out by the fielding team to distract the batsmen.

Slog: A firmly hit shot intended to go for six and struck with little finesse.

Swing: A type of bowling that is performed by polishing the ball on one side only so that the air flows over it quicker and causes the ball to move laterally in the air.

Tail-ender: A batsman who comes in towards the end of an innings, usually a specialist bowler with limited batting skill.

Test match: An international match played over five days with unlimited overs; each team bats twice and fields twice.

Twenty20: A fast-paced form of the game where each team only faces 20 overs and bats once.

Yorker: A delivery that pitches underneath the batsman's bat; often difficult to play.

Type of extra	Description
Wide	An additional run added to the batting team's score if the bowler's delivery is so wayward that it is outside of the batsman's reach.
No Ball	An additional run awarded to the batting team's score if the bowler either oversteps the crease or uses an illegal arm action; the bowler has to bowl the ball again.
Bye	Extras awarded if the batsman does not connect with the ball and the wicketkeeper misses the bowler's delivery; the batsman run as they would do normally and the number they run is added to the extras tally.
Leg Bye	Extras awarded if the bowler makes contact with the bowler's body and then runs away from fielders, allowing the batsman to run.

Cricket Heroes

SACHIN TENDULKAR

'It is hard to imagine any player in the history of the game who combines classical technique with raw aggression like the little champion does.' Sunil Gavaskar

The diminutive Indian batsman, affectionately known as the 'Little Master' is among the finest batsmen to have ever graced a cricket pitch. He is the leading run scorer of all time, and is the only cricketer to have scored 100 centuries in international cricket, a milestone he achieved in March 2012. He is ranked the second on the list of batsmen by *Wisden*, with only Sir Donald Bradman above him. Among his other achievements are being the first batsman to score a double century in a one-day international and the first player to make over 15,000 runs in his career. He is an inspirational figure in India and was made a member of India's upper house of parliament in April 2012 after a nomination from the president.

Greatest moment: Reaching the unprecedented milestone of 100 first-class centuries, which he achieved with 114 against Bangladesh on 16 March 2012.

SIR DONALD BRADMAN

'The greatest phenomenon in the history of cricket, indeed in the history of all ball games.' Wisden Cricketers' Almanack

Born in 1908, Bradman is rated by *Wisden* as the greatest batsman of all time. His batting average of 99.94 is considered one of the most extraordinary achievements, not only in cricket, but sport itself. His batting prowess led to the creation of a controversial style of bowling – Bodyline – by the England team in the 1932-33 Ashes series to try and dismiss him. In 1948, Bradman captained the Australian side that earned the nickname 'The Invincibles' for completing a tour of England without losing a single match. Regarded as a national icon, Bradman was described by former prime minister John Howard as 'the greatest living Australian' – a testament to his remarkable life.

Greatest moment: Passing 300 in a single day's play on the way to a then world-record score of 334 against England at Headingley in 1930.

SHANE WARNE
'It was said of Augustus that he found Rome brick and left it marble: the same is true of Warne and spin bowling.' Gideon Haigh, Australian sports journalist

The charismatic Australian spin-bowler is considered one of the greatest bowlers of all time. He took 708 wickets in his Test career, a record that was only surpassed by Muttiah Muralitharan in 2007. His ability to generate a remarkable amount of spin, his repertoire of deliveries and his capacity to disguise the type of delivery he would bowl revolutionised spin bowling. Warne was also extremely skilled at employing psychological tactics to unnerve batsmen. Indeed, he is thought to have terrorised well-known South African batsman Daryl Cullinan to the point that he sought the help of a therapist. Warne's flamboyant, gung-ho batting style also earned him a batting record – he is the highest-averaging batsman never to have scored a century.

Greatest moment: His first ball in his first Ashes Test generated such inexplicable spin that it completely fooled Mike Gatting and clipped his off-stump. Thereafter, it was known as the 'Ball of the Century'.

MUTTIAH MURALITHARAN
'The Don Bradman of bowling.' Steve Waugh

The highest wicket-taker of all time, Murali as he is commonly known, is a prodigious Sri Lankan spin bowler. His bowling action has courted controversy over the years, in particular for his 'doosra' (a delivery that spins in the opposite direction to his normal delivery), which many considered to be breaching rules with regard to elbow extension. However, several scientific studies have proved that his technique is legal. He achieved the remarkable and unprecedented milestone of 800 Test wickets in 2010, and he holds several world records, including the most five-wicket hauls in a match (67) and the highest number of one-day dismissals.

Greatest moment: His 800th wicket, which came in the final ball of his final over in Test cricket.

BRIAN LARA

'Did I entertain?' – The question Brian Lara asked to the crowd after his final dismissal in 2007.

Known as 'The Prince', Brian Lara is a West Indian batsman who can count Sachin Tendulkar as his only rival for the accolade of best batsman of the last twenty years. He holds the record for highest individual score in first-class cricket with an unprecedented 501 not out, which he achieved for county side Warwickshire in 1994. He also holds the record for highest score in a test match with his 400 not out against England in 2004. Lara is well-known for his astonishing natural talent and his flamboyant strokes. He holds the record for highest runs scored (28) in a single over in Test cricket and was hailed by Muttiah Muralitharan as the toughest opponent he has ever bowled against.

Greatest moment: Surpassing Hanif Mohammed's 1958 record score of 499 on his way to 501 not out.

SIR GARFIELD SOBERS

'The greatest all-round cricketer the world has seen.' Richie Benaud

Garfield Sobers is regarded as one of the finest all-rounders in cricketing history and was proclaimed 'King Cricket' by the media after captaining the West Indies to an impressive victory over England in 1966. In 1958, at only 21 years old, he broke the highest individual innings record in Test match, recording 365 not out. This record stood for over 25 years until Brian Lara surpassed it in 1994. In 1968, Sobers became the first person to score six sixes in a single over. Sobers was also an outstanding bowler, and one of the few able to bowl both spin and, later, pace to a high standard. He notched up 235 wickets in his Test career and over 1,000 in his entire first-class career.

Greatest moment: Breaking England legend Len Hutton's world record score on his way to 365 not out.

FORMULA ONE

The Basics

Formula One is the highest class of **single-seater** motor car racing sanctioned by the Fédération Internationale de l'Automobile (**FIA**). 'Formula' refers to a set of rules which must be complied with. There are commonly **24** drivers in a Formula One season competing in **12** constructor teams. Each series of races known in Formula One are known as **Grands Prix** (Grand Prize in English) and there are **20** in a season. Results of races determine **two annual prizes**, one for best driver and one for best constructor.

The **starting grid** is determined by a **qualifying** session. The faster the driver completes a single lap of a circuit, the higher they begin on the grid (see diagram below). The first place on the grid is known as **pole position**.

Drivers usually make around three **pit stops** throughout a race where they enter a **pit lane** and have their cars serviced by their team to **refuel** and **repair damage**. There are **six** different types of tyre that are employed according to the temperature, humidity and presence of rain. The first three drivers to finish the race are invited to the **podium** where the **national anthems** of both the winning driver and the winning constructor are played.

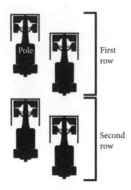

Pole Position

The quickest driver in qualifying starts in pole position, while the second-quickest is positioned a fraction further back and to the right. Third-quickest is situated behind pole position with fourth located behind second. Each pairing is known as a 'row', with the first two referred to as the 'front row'.

Flags

Flags are used in Formula One by marshals to relay important messages to drivers.

Black
Also displaying a car number, the driver is told to return to the pit, usually meaning he has been eliminated from the race.

Black with orange circle
Also displaying a car number, the driver is warned of a mechanical problem and must return to the pit.

Green
The driver is clear to proceed as normal and the yellow flag warnings are lifted.

Half Black, Half White
Also displaying a car number, the driver is warned of unsporting behaviour. If ignored, the driver may be shown a black flag.

Red
The session has been stopped, usually due to an accident or poor conditions.

Blue
Tells a driver he is about to be lapped and to let the faster car overtake. Failure to comply after passing three blue flags may result in a punishment.

Chequered
The session has ended. During a race it is shown to the winner and to every car that crosses the line thereafter.

White
Warns of a slow-moving vehicle on the track, such as the safety car.

Yellow
Indicates danger. A single yellow flag warns drivers to slow down. Two yellow flags tells the drivers to be prepared to stop. Overtaking is illegal at this point

Yellow and red striped
Warns of a slippery track, usually due to oil or water.

Formula One Circuits 2012–13

UAE – Abu Dhabi

Laps: 55
Circuit length: 3.45 miles
Race length: 189.73 miles

Australia – Melbourne

Laps: 58
Circuit length: 3.29 miles
Race length: 191.07 miles

Bahrain

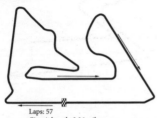

Laps: 57
Circuit length: 3.36 miles
Race length: 191.53 miles

Belgium – Spa

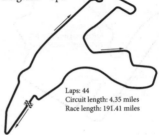

Laps: 44
Circuit length: 4.35 miles
Race length: 191.41 miles

Brazil – São Paulo

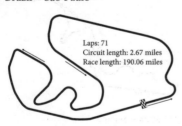

Laps: 71
Circuit length: 2.67 miles
Race length: 190.06 miles

Britain – Silverstone

Laps: 52
Circuit length: 3.66 miles
Race length: 190.26 miles

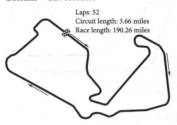

Canada – Montreal

Laps: 70
Circuit length: 2.70 miles
Race length: 189.65 miles

China – Shanghai

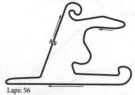

Laps: 56
Circuit Length: 3.38 miles
Race length 189.55 miles

Europe – Valencia, Spain

Laps: 57
Circuit Length: 3.36 miles
Race length 191.93 miles

Germany – Hockenheim

Laps: 67
Circuit length: 2.84 miles
Race length: 190.42 miles

Hungary – Budapest

Laps: 70
Circuit length: 2.72 miles
Race length: 190.53 miles

India – Greater Noida

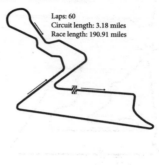

Laps: 60
Circuit length: 3.18 miles
Race length: 190.91 miles

Italy – Monza

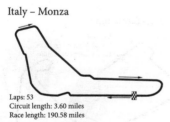

Laps: 53
Circuit length: 3.60 miles
Race length: 190.58 miles

Japan – Suzuka

Laps: 53
Circuit length: 3.60 miles
Race length: 191.05 miles

Korea – Yeongam

Laps: 55
Circuit length: 3.48 miles
Race length: 191.77 miles

Malaysia – Sepang

Laps: 56
Circuit length: 3.44 miles
Race length: 192.87 miles

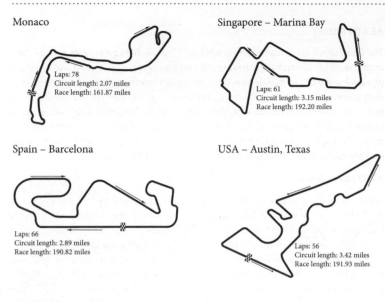

Monaco

Laps: 78
Circuit length: 2.07 miles
Race length: 161.87 miles

Singapore – Marina Bay

Laps: 61
Circuit length: 3.15 miles
Race length: 192.20 miles

Spain – Barcelona

Laps: 66
Circuit length: 2.89 miles
Race length: 190.82 miles

USA – Austin, Texas

Laps: 56
Circuit length: 3.42 miles
Race length: 191.93 miles

Formula One Heroes

JUAN MANUEL FANGIO

The Argentinian driver Juan Manuel Fangio dominated Formula One during the sport's infancy in the 1950s. Like many other drivers of his generation, the Argentinian possessed courage and nerves of steel in a sport which was intensely dangerous and without the safety precautions of modern racing. 'The Maestro' holds the record for the highest percentage of wins at 47% and his record five World Drivers' championships stood for 46 years before being broken by Michael Schumacher. Fangio's legacy is enhanced by his affable personality, epitomised after a kidnapping by Cuban rebels who were charmed by the driver and released him unharmed.

SIR JACKIE STEWART

With his trademark sunglasses and sideburns, Jackie Stewart was the first superstar of Formula One. As a three-time World Champion, 'The Flying Scot' is remembered for his courageous driving, typified by his victory at the 1968 German Grand Prix despite suffering a broken wrist, but his legacy to the sport goes further. After a crash in the 1966 Belgian Grand Prix at the perilous Spa circuit, Stewart began a crusade to implement safer conditions for drivers including seatbelts and full-face helmets.

ALAIN PROST

The first French driver to be crowned World Champion, Prost's career was far more erratic than his conservative driving style might suggest. It is almost impossible to discuss Prost without mentioning his rival Ayrton Senna (see below) as they pushed each other to limits unseen before in Formula One, whether on the same team or not. In the 1990 Japan Grand Prix, the rivalry reached a dramatic finale when Senna crashed into Prost's Ferrari, handing the Brazilian the title and leaving Prost to declare 'What he did was disgusting'. Nicknamed 'The Professor' for his careful and sensible racing style, Prost won the World Championship four times.

AYRTON SENNA

Voted the greatest driver in Formula One history in a poll by 217 drivers, Senna thrilled spectators with his fast and audacious driving style. He won three World Championships, in 1988, 1990 and 1991 and holds the record for most Monaco Grands Prix victories, with six. He also held the record, until 2006, for most pole positions. Senna is also renowned for his compelling performances at post-race press conferences. His life ended in tragic circumstances at the San Marino Grand Prix in 1994 when his Williams car hit a concrete wall at 135mph (217kph). This devastating accident came only a day after the Austrian driver Roland Ratzenburger was killed in an accident on the same circuit.

MICHAEL SCHUMACHER

Statistically the best driver in Formula One history with a record seven titles, Schumacher dominated the sport at the beginning of the 21st century driving for Ferrari. The first German World Champion, Schumacher also holds the record for most Grand Prix wins (91). In 2002 'Schumi' finished on the podium in all 17 races. With an undying passion for the sport, Schumacher was blessed with a natural talent for racing which he combined with his ambition and determination to succeed. After retiring in 2006, Schumacher made a return to Formula One in 2010. Although no longer dominating the field, his love of the sport remains there for all to see.

THE OLYMPIC GAMES

The Olympic Games originated in **Olympia**, Greece in the **8th century BC** and is now a major international sporting event in which athletes from all around the globe compete in multiple disciplines including running, cycling, fencing, swimming, shooting, wrestling and many more. Victorious athletes in each discipline are awarded with **gold** medals. **Silver** and **bronze** medals are awarded to second- and third-placed athletes respectively. A gold medal is composed of 550g of silver, with only 6g of pure gold and is thought to be worth **$494 (£307)**. A silver medal is composed of 550g of silver and is worth approximately **$260 (£162)**, while a bronze medal is made of copper, tin and zinc and is worth only about **$3 (£1.86)**.

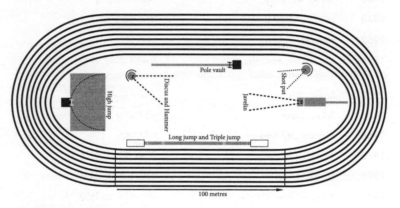

Olympics Track and Field
This illustration shows the oval running track and location of the 'field' events at the Olympic Games.

Host Cities

In 1896, Athens hosted the first modern Olympic Games and the summer games have been held in a host city every four years since, apart from 1916, 1940 and 1944, due to the First and Second World Wars.

Year	Host City	Nation with most gold medals
1896	Athens, Greece	USA (11)
1900	Paris, France	France (27)
1904	St. Louis, USA	USA (80)

Year	Host City	Nation with most gold medals
1908	London, Great Britain	Great Britain (56)
1912	Stockholm, Sweden	USA (25)
1920	Antwerp, Belgium	USA (41)
1924	Paris, France	USA (45)
1928	Amsterdam, Netherlands	USA (22)
1932	Los Angeles, USA	USA (41)
1936	Berlin, Germany	Germany (33)
1948	London, Great Britain	USA (38)
1952	Helsinki, Finland	USA (40)
1956	Melbourne, Australia and Stockholm, Sweden	Soviet Union (37)
1960	Rome, Italy	Soviet Union (43)
1964	Tokyo, Japan	USA (36)
1968	Mexico City, Mexico	USA (45)
1972	Munich, Germany	Soviet Union (50)
1976	Montreal, Canada	Soviet Union (49)
1980	Moscow, Soviet Union	Soviet Union (80)
1984	Los Angeles, USA	USA (83)
1988	Seoul, South Korea	Soviet Union (55)
1992	Barcelona, Spain	Unified Team* (45)
1996	Atlanta, USA	USA (44)
2000	Sydney, Australia	USA (40)
2004	Athens, Greece	USA (35)
2008	Beijing, China	China (51)
2012	London, Great Britain	
2016	Rio de Janeiro, Brazil	

* Or CIS (Commonwealth of Independent States). 12 states of the former Soviet Union

Olympic Heroes

JESSE OWENS
'For a time, at least, I was the most famous person in the entire world.'

James Cleveland Owens was the first American track and field athlete to win four gold medals at a single Olympiad. This was achieved in 1936, when the Olympic Games were hosted in Nazi Germany and used as an excuse for promotion of the 'Aryan' race. As an African-American, Owens discredited Adolf Hitler's hopes of showcasing German athletic supremacy, gaining international fame by proving that individual ability and determination, as opposed to race, enable a person to succeed.

Medals: Gold × 4 (100m, 200m, 4 × 100 relay, long jump) at the 1936 Olympics.

NADIA COMANECI
'Everybody was surprised to see a 14-year-old being able to do the level of gymnastics that I did, but even I didn't know that I was extraordinary at the time.'

When she was just 14-years-old, the Romanian teenager Nadia Comaneci became the first female gymnast to receive a perfect score of 10.0. In fact, the scoreboards were unable to display the digits correctly due to the unforeseen circumstance and Comaneci's score was displayed as 1.00! Comaneci was competing at the 1976 Olympic Games in Montreal when her routine on the uneven bars made Olympic history. Comaneci went on to receive six additional perfect scores in gymnastic events in Montreal. She eventually won nine Olympic medals and is still one of the best-known gymnasts in the world. Comaneci is the only athlete to be awarded the Olympic Order – the highest award of the Olympic Movement – twice.

Medals: Gold × 5 (All-around, Uneven bars and Balance beam in 1976; Balance beam and Floor in 1980); Silver × 3 (Team in 1976; All-around and Team in 1980); Bronze × 1 (Floor in 1976)

SIR STEVE REDGRAVE
'This is the stuff of dreams.'

Heralded as Great Britain's greatest Olympian, rower Sir Steve Redgrave won a gold medal at five consecutive Olympic Games between 1984 and 2000. Throughout much of his career, Redgrave suffered with serious illnesses including type 2 diabetes but his passion for rowing, his fitness and his determination to succeed made him a national hero. Following his victory in the 1996 Olympic Games, Redgrave famously stated that anyone who saw him near a rowing boat again could shoot him. However, he went on to win one final gold at the 2000 Sydney Olympic Games. Sir Matthew Pinsent deserves an honourable mention for partnering

Redgrave to three Olympic victories and winning one further gold in 2004 after Redgrave's retirement.

Medals: Gold × 5 (Coxed Four in 1984 and 2000; Coxless Pair in 1988, 1992 and 1996); Bronze × 1 (Coxless Pair in 1988)

MICHAEL PHELPS

'He's maybe the greatest athlete of all time. He's the greatest racer who ever walked the planet.' Mark Spitz

The American swimmer won 16 Olympic medals during two Olympiads including a clean-sweep of eight gold medals at the 2008 Beijing Olympic Games – the record for the most gold medals won at a single Olympics. This surpassed Mark Spitz's record set in the 1972 Olympics in Munich in which Spitz swam to seven gold medals, setting seven world records. Prior to the 2012 London Olympic Games, Phelps was the second most successful Olympian of all time in terms of number of medals won after Soviet gymnast Larisa Latynina who won 18 medals. Phelps possesses physical attributes that are ideal for swimming: over six feet in height; an arm span of two metres; flexible ankles which act as fins; and a long torso which provides Phelps with low drag. Phelps is a certainty to be remembered as one of the greatest Olympians in history.

Medals*: Gold × 14 (100m butterfly in 2004 and 2008; 200m butterfly in 2004 and 2008; 200m medley in 2004 and 2008; 400m medley in 2004 and 2008; 4 × 200 freestyle in 2004 and 2008; 4 × 100m medley in 2004 and 2008; 200m freestyle in 2008; 4 × 100, freestyle in 2008); Bronze × 2 (200m freestyle and 4 × 100m freestyle in 2004)

USAIN BOLT

'I wasn't bragging. When I thought I had the field covered I was celebrating. I was happy.'

At the 2008 Beijing Olympic Games, Usain Bolt became the first man in history to win the 100m, 200m and 4 × 100m gold medals all in world record times. In the 100m final, the Jamaican had the audacity to slow down and celebrate 15 metres from the finish line, such was his lead over the chasing finalists. In doing so, the 'fastest man on earth' set a new world record of 9.69 seconds, beating his own previous world record. Bolt smashed this new record a year later at the 2009 World Championships, recording a time of 9.58 seconds. He has additionally bettered his 200m and 4 × 100m world records since competing in Beijing. Similarly to Phelps, the 'Lightning Bolt' has a perfect physique for the sport he dominates; he stands six

---

*   Before London 2012 Olympic Games

feet and five inches tall and sprints with great strides due to his long legs. Bolt is a favourite of athletics fans and arguably the greatest sprinter of all time.

Medals*: Gold × 3 (100m, 200m and 4 × 100m relay) at the 2008 Olympics

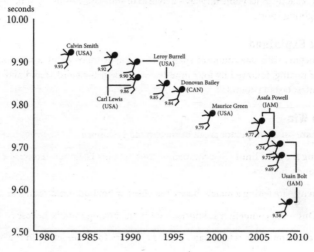

100m Men's World Record Progression

* Before London 2012 Olympic Games

UNUSUAL SPORTS

CHESSBOXING

Chessboxing is a relatively new sport which hosted its first World Championship in 2003. It is exactly as its name implies – a hybrid of the classic thinking sport and the classic fighting sport.

A Fight Explained

A fight begins with one round of speed chess. This is followed by a three-minute round of boxing, followed by four minutes of chess in the third round and so on. Each contest lasts 11 rounds.

How to Win

Checkmate - if a competitor is put in checkmate, he loses.

Exceeding the time limit – if a competitor runs over his 12 minute allowance in the chess rounds, he loses.

Retirement – forfeiting a match during the chess or boxing round results in a loss.

Knock Out – If a competitor is knocked out in the boxing rounds, he loses.

Referee decision – The referee can award the victory to a competitor in the boxing rounds.

If the chess game ends in a stalemate, the competitor with the highest score in boxing wins the fight. If there is an equal score in boxing, the competitor with the black chess pieces wins.

TIDDLYWINKS

The classic game in which you can play a squop, crud and even a John Lennon memorial shot began as a parlour game in Victorian England. There are two basic aims in tiddlywinks: to get your 'winks' into a pot, and to cover opponent's winks with your own. Players use 'squidgers' to propel winks by pressing down on a wink to flick it into the air. The winner is the first player to flick all their winks into the pot.

Glossary

Boondock: A squopped wink is freed by sending it away from the pot.

Brunch: To pot inadvertently when attempting to send a wink over the pot.

Crud: A shot played with force to separate a pile of winks.

John Lennon memorial shot: The combination of a boondock and squop.

Lunch: To pot an opponent's wink.

Nurdled: A wink resting beneath the rim of the pot.

Rabbit-bashing: Obtaining high scores by playing a weak opponent.

Squop: To flick a wink so it lands above another wink, leaving it squopped.

KABADDI

Kabaddi is a south Asian combative team-sport in which two teams compete against each other for higher scores by touching or capturing players of the opponent team. Each game consists of two 20-minute halves and is played on a court area measuring 12.5m x 10m. In each team there are a total of 12 players with seven competing on the court at any one time.

The teams alternate as the attacking or defending side. In each play, the attacking team sends a 'raider' into the opponent's half, with the raider chanting '*kabaddi-kabaddi*'. The raider's objective is to touch one or all of the opposition players and return to his court in one breath. The members of the opposition that the raider has touched are then out of the game. The defending team's aim is to hold the raider in their court until he runs out of breath, at which point, if he is no longer chanting '*kabaddi*', he is out of the game. The raider is also out of the game if he crosses the court boundary lines.

Each team obtains a point on every occasion that an opposition player is out. A team is awarded two bonus points if their entire opposition is out.

Although the game is predominantly Asian in origin and popularity, the sport has spread to Canada, the US and UK.

HIGHLAND GAMES

Scottish in tradition, culture and atmosphere, the Highland Games combine events such as tug-of-war, track and field and the renowned caber toss.

The biggest meeting of the Highland Games calendar is the Cowal Highland Gathering in Argyll, which combines sports including wrestling and athletics, with traditional music such as bagpipe bands, dance and local food. It attracts 20,000 spectators and approximately 3,000 competitors.

The Highland Games receive worldwide popularity, especially in the US. There are also events in Canada and Europe.

The Caber Toss

The most traditional sporting event at the Highland Games is the caber toss. A caber is a large wooden pole and the event is believed to have originated from the process of throwing logs across chasms in order to cross them. Cabers are around 19 feet tall and over 100 pounds in weight. The tosser's objective is to launch the caber to fall with the top end nearest the thrower at a 12 o'clock angle.

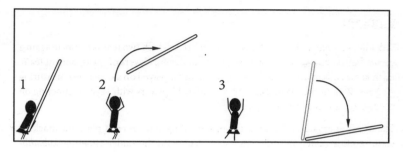

HOW TO SOUND
CLEVER

HOW TO SOUND CLEVER

THE 10 FILMS YOU SHOULD HAVE HEARD OF

Battleship Potemkin

Battleship Potemkin was made by legendary Russian director, Sergei Eisenstein, and released in 1925. A silent, propaganda film in which Eisenstein pioneered the use of montage, it recreates the crew's mutiny against the tsarist officers in 1905 after being served rotten meat in a soup. The ship pulls in to Odessa and finds that the local civilians are sympathetic to the mutineers, but the regime responds by executing hundreds on the Odessa steps, including women and children. The tsar's ships approach the *Potemkin*; the crew react by sending signals and lights, imploring the fleet to treat them as comrades in arms. The cannons are trained on *Potemkin* but it is finally allowed to pass through. The mutineers rejoice. The film was initially banned in West Germany, Britain and France for its violent scenes and revolutionary themes.

Amazing fact: Hitler's propaganda minister Joseph Goebbels described *Battleship Potemkin* as 'a marvellous film without equal in the cinema ... anyone who had no firm political conviction could become a Bolshevik after seeing the film'.

Citizen Kane

Written and directed by Orson Welles, *Citizen Kane* opens with the death of newspaper tycoon Charles Foster Kane, clutching a snow globe and uttering the word 'Rosebud'. Thompson, a reporter, is assigned the task of deciphering this word. As he investigates, the story unfolds through a number of flashbacks, and he discovers Kane's squalid upbringing, his abusive father, his questionable business successes, his egocentrism, his extramarital affair and the construction of his palatial home. Thompson also finds out that Kane's faults led to the loss of his fortune, friends and his cherished second wife. However, Thompson never finds out the significance of the word rosebud. The final shot sees workmen burning Kane's seemingly worthless possessions, including the sledge that he was riding the day that he was abandoned by his mother – the last day he was truly happy. On the side of the sledge is the word 'rosebud'.

Stars: Orson Welles, Joseph Cotten, Dorothy Comingore
Awards: Nominated for nine Academy Awards, winning one (Best Writing).
Amazing fact: *Citizen Kane* was based on William Randolph Hearst, a business mogul and head of a newspaper empire. Hearst did everything in his power to suppress the film's emergence into the public domain, including banning all his newspapers from reviewing it.

Once Upon a Time in the West

Directed by Sergio Leone, *Once Upon a Time in the West* is regarded as one of the greatest examples of the Western genre. The film centres on two story strands, the first involving a harmonica-playing stranger on a revenge mission against a cold-blooded murderer named Frank, and the second, a dispute over a vital patch of land containing the only water supply for 50 miles, which is crucial for the building of a railroad. The film features one of cinema's iconic opening scenes: three gunmen wait for a train to arrive, while a succession of mundane sounds penetrate the silence, building the tension superbly. The film ends in a duel between the man known as 'Harmonica' and Frank, before which we learn of Harmonica's motive in a flashback. Many years ago, Frank had strung up Harmonica's brother with a noose around his neck, forcing Harmonica to carry his brother's weight on his shoulders, before forcing a harmonica in his mouth. Harmonica finally collapsed from exhaustion, killing his brother. In the duel, Harmonica mortally wounds Frank. Frank asks his name, but Harmonica simply responds by placing a harmonica in Frank's mouth before he dies.

Stars: Henry Fonda, Charles Bronson, Claudia Cardinale

Amazing fact: Henry Fonda initially turned down the role of Frank. When he did accept the role, it was one of the first times in the western genre that the villain was played by the lead actor.

The Godfather

Considered the paradigmatic mob film and often topping lists of the greatest films of all time, *The Godfather* was based on a novel by Mario Puzo, and was directed by Francis Ford Coppola. It forms the first of a trilogy about an influential mafia family, the Corleones, and is set just after the Second World War. Vito Corleone (Marlon Brando) is the head of the family and is acknowledged as 'the Godfather'. His youngest son Michael (Al Pacino) has just returned after fighting for his country in the war and wants nothing to do with the family. The film charts Michael's progression from innocent outsider to ruthless crime-lord and ends with his coronation as Godfather following his father's death. The film's characterisation is one of its greatest strengths, with the assortment of villains portrayed with depth and insight, considered unusual in previous mob films.

Stars: Marlon Brando, Al Pacino, Diane Keaton

Awards: Three Academy Awards (Best Picture, Best Actor, Best Adapted Screenplay)

Amazing fact: Al Pacino boycotted the Academy Award ceremony because he was annoyed at being nominated for best supporting actor and not best actor. Pacino argued that he had more time on screen than his costar Marlon Brando (who won the Best Actor category that year) and therefore should have been nominated for the award.

Monty Python's Life of Brian

Life of Brian is a comic religious satire about an ordinary man who happens to have been born on the same day and next-door to the Messiah. It was considered controversial upon its release, condemned as blasphemous by religious groups and banned in various countries. The film charts the life of Brian, who loathes the Roman occupation and joins the independence movement the People's Front of Judea. After committing a series of crimes, he is pursued by Roman guards, but escapes them by joining a group of speakers who are addressing a crowd. He mumbles a series of truisms and ends up unintentionally inspiring a huge following, who proclaim him the Messiah. Brian's mum grows increasingly frustrated with the followers and rebukes them: 'He's not the Messiah, he's a very naughty boy!' Brian is eventually captured and crucified. One optimistic condemned man starts singing 'Always Look on the Bright Side of Life' and they all break into song.

Stars: John Cleese, Graham Chapman, Eric Idle, Michael Palin, Terry Jones, Terry Gilliam
Amazing fact: The original financial backers of the film pulled out at the eleventh hour due to concerns regarding the subject matter. Python fan George Harrison put up the money (which Eric Idle referred to as 'the world's most expensive cinema ticket') and appears in a cameo.

2001: A Space Odyssey

One of the most influential films in history, *2001: A Space Odyssey* was based on the Arthur C. Clarke science-fiction novel and was directed by Stanley Kubrick. The film is renowned for its exploration of artificial intelligence and unprecedented visual effects. It is split into several chapters, during which the appearance of a mysterious black monolith heralds a significant advancement in human understanding. The first chapter focuses on a community of man-like apes discovering how to use tools. The next section centres on scientists discovering a monolith on the moon which emits a high-pitched noise. The next chapter focuses on two scientists, David (Dave) Bowman and Frank Poole, and their supposedly infallible computer HAL. After discovering Dave and Frank's plan to deactivate HAL, the computer switches off the life-support functions of the crew members in suspended animation, severs Frank's oxygen hose and then tries to kill Dave. Dave manually disconnects HAL, who endeavours to stop him by employing different emotions as he talks. In the final chapter, Dave leaves the ship in a pod and is pulled into a tunnel of coloured light before ending up in a 18th-century bedroom, where he sees progressively older versions of himself until a monolith appears. He touches it and is transformed into a foetus encased in an orb of light floating beside the earth.

Stars: Keir Dullea, Douglas Rain
Awards: Nominated for four Academy Awards, winning one (Visual Effects)

Amazing fact: In Clarke's novel HAL stands for 'Heuristically programmed ALgorithmic computer. The fact that the letters of H-A-L are a one-letter shift from the initials of the computer company IBM is actually a coincidence.

La Dolce Vita

Directed by Frederico Fellini, *La Dolce Vita* is the story of a week in the life of gossip columnist Marcello Rubini. Marcello spends his time ingratiating himself with high society, embracing a shallow, materialistic lifestyle of sex and parties. The film opens with Marcello's news helicopter following another helicopter transporting a statue of Jesus with his arms open in benediction, but Marcello is more interested in the sunbathing young women below. This scene prompted an outcry from the Catholic Church and the film was subject to widespread censorship. Marcello's numerous affairs push his fiancée Emma to the verge of suicide, and he only discovers that she has overdosed when he comes in from a night of making love to an heiress. He is consumed by the actress Silvia and in one of cinema's iconic scenes, they cavort in the Trevi fountain. However, Marcello's salacious nights are interspersed with sombre days. The visit of his lonely, cuckolded father offers a tragic portrayal of Marcello's future. On the sixth day, he receives news that his intellectual friend Steiner has killed himself along with his two children. On the final day, Marcello comes across a bloated Leviathan-like creature washed up on the beach.

Stars: Marcello Mastroianni, Anita Ekberg
Awards: Nominated for four Academy Awards, winning one (Best Costume Design); Palme d'Or winner at Cannes
Amazing fact: *La Dolce Vita* introduced the term 'paparazzi' into the English language, as well as la dolce vita (translating as *the sweet life*) itself, used with irony to reference a shallow materialistic lifestyle.

Seven Samurai

Directed by legendary Japanese director Akira Kurosawa, *Seven Samurai* is about a group of farmers who convince seven lord-less samurai to protect them against bandits. The film subtly explores themes of class division and codes of honour in Japan in the late 16th century. The samurai make fortifications and begin to get along with the villagers. However, they discover that the farmers have murdered samurai in the past and are enraged. One of the samurai, Kikuchiyo, defends the farmers: 'But then who made them such beasts? You did! You burn their villages! ... Destroy their farms! Steal their food ... And kill them if they resist! So what should farmers do?' The samurai's anger turns to shame. Bandit scouts soon arrive, but one is captured by the samurai, and he reveals the location of the bandits' camp. The samurai launch a successful pre-emptive strike before returning to the village. The bandits attack the village in force but are slain by the samurai, who lose four men.

The bandit leader hides in a hut and dishonourably shoots two samurai, but is killed. After the battle, the samurai see the farmers planting their crops. The samurai leader, Kambei, reflects that 'The winners are those farmers, not us'.

Stars: Toshiro Mifune, Takashi Shimura

Amazing fact: Toho studios closed down production at least twice due to budget concerns; Kurosawa was confident that production would continue, as so much money had already been spent, so he spent the down-time fishing.

Double Indemnity

Double Indemnity is a classic film noir directed by Billy Wilder. The film opens with gravely wounded Walter Neff, a successful insurance salesman who is relaying his story into a dictaphone. Neff first came across femme fatale Phyllis Dietrichson while visiting her husband to renew his insurance policy. Phyllis asks Neff about the possibility of taking out a life insurance policy on her husband without his knowledge. Neff becomes suspicious, but despite his initial reluctance, they begin an affair, and hatch and successfully execute a plan to kill her husband, making use of the double indemnity clause which pays out twice in any case of accidental death. Keyes, the investigator who works with Neff, suspects foul play and pursues Phyllis and her accomplice, but has no reason to suspect Neff. The victim's daughter, Lola, suspects that Phyllis is responsible. So Phyllis starts an affair with Lola's boyfriend, Nino, with the intention of convincing him to murder Lola. Neff discovers this and tries to kill Phyllis but she shoots him first. He asks her to shoot again but she can't. He takes the gun from her and while she clings to him, he shoots her. Neff dictates his confession in his office for Keyes but Keyes overhears him. Neff tries to leave but collapses and dies.

Stars: Fred MacMurray, Barbara Stanwyck

Amazing Fact: It was only discovered 60 years after the film's release that co-screenplay writer Raymond Chandler appears in a cameo – the only known footage of him.

Apocalypse Now

Apocalypse Now is a Francis Ford Coppola film based on the novella *Heart of Darkness* by Joseph Conrad. Set during the Vietnam War, the film explores the corruption and abuse of power at the heart of war. Army captain Benjamin L. Willard has been given the task of assassinating Kurtz, a highly decorated American officer, who has gone rogue and is now commanding Montagnard forces in Cambodia. Willard travels to his last known location up the Nung River. Some of the crewmembers are killed, but Willard finally arrives at Kurtz's outpost, which is littered by decapitated heads and decomposing bodies. Willard leaves one crewmember – Chef – with instructions to call in an airstrike if he does not return by a certain time. Kurtz's men take Willard to their leader, imprisoning him in a tiger cage. During the night, Chef's head is thrown into Willard's lap and he screams frantically. During the following days, Willard is let out and Kurtz lectures him on war and philosophy. He asks Willard to tell his son about him if he should die. At night, Willard steals into Kurtz's quarters and kills him with a machete. Kurtz utters 'the horror ... the horror'. With Kurtz's words ringing in his ears, Willard travels back down the river, his mission accomplished.

Stars: Martin Sheen, Marlon Brando, Robert Duvall
Awards: Nominated for six Academy Awards, winning two (Best Cinematography and Best Sound)
Amazing fact: Both Steve McQueen and Al Pacino were offered the part of Willard, but McQueen did not want to leave the USA for the 17-week shoot and Pacino was concerned about falling ill in the jungle, as he had done in the Dominican Republic on the set of *The Godfather Part II*.

THE 10 PLAYWRIGHTS YOU SHOULD HAVE HEARD OF

Sophocles
'Hide nothing, for time, which sees all and hears all, exposes all'.

Sophocles (496–406 BC) was a Greek tragedian, one of the three greats whose plays have survived. Best known for his Theban plays, and the characters of Oedipus and Antigone, Sophocles is credited with a number of innovations, most notably for introducing a third actor, but also for pioneering scene paintings. He also developed the individuality of his characters to a greater extent than his predecessor, Aeschylus.

Influences: Aeschylus
Influenced: Sophocles' influence spans across a phenomenal range of thinkers and writers from ancient to modern times, including Aristotle, Sigmund Freud and Bertolt Brecht.
Plays written: 7 (intact)
Most famous plays: *Oedipus the King, Antigone*
Amazing fact: Aeschylus was the heavyweight tragedian when the drama festival of 468 BC took place and expected to win first place, but he was beaten by the 28-year-old upstart, Sophocles.

Christopher Marlowe

'Hell hath no limits, nor is circumscribed/In one self place; for where we are is hell/And where hell is, there must we ever be'.

A contemporary of Shakespeare's, Christopher Marlowe (1564–93) was a prominent Elizabethan playwright, poet and translator. His plays are known for their heightened drama, hubristic protagonists and the notable use of blank verse. Marlowe's plays were regarded as blasphemous by some of his contemporaries, and a warrant was issued for his arrest in 1593. Marlowe was killed in mysterious circumstances during a bar-room brawl later that year.

Influences: Ovid, Virgil, Niccolò Machiavelli
Influenced: William Shakespeare
Plays written: 7
Most famous plays: *Dr Faustus, The Jew of Malta, Tamburlaine*
Amazing fact: In 1587, Marlowe was completing his master's degree at Cambridge University, but the university decided to withhold his MA on account of his frequent absences. This decision was overturned after the Privy Council sent a letter explaining that Marlowe had been working 'on matters touching the benefit of his country', giving credence to the suspicion that he worked as a spy.

Henrik Ibsen

'The spectacles of experience; through them you will see clearly a second time'.

Henrik Ibsen (1828–1906) was a Norwegian playwright and a major influence on modern drama. He was considered a master of representing his characters in a psychologically truthful way, for his use of irony and his exploration of contentious issues in society. His plays demonstrated a heightened realism in theatre and were considered to be very controversial during his time.

Influences: Sallust, Cicero, William Shakespeare
Influenced: Anton Chekhov, James Joyce, Arthur Miller
Plays written: 26
Most famous plays: *A Doll's House, Hedda Gabler, Ghosts*
Amazing fact: It is believed that second to Shakespeare, Ibsen's plays are the most performed in the world.

Oscar Wilde

'There is no such thing as a moral or an immoral book. Books are well written, or badly written. That is all'.

Oscar Wilde (1854–1900) was an Irish novelist, dramatist and poet. His four society plays made him one of the most successful 19th-century playwrights. Wilde is also popularly known for his acerbic wit and outspoken aestheticism. After his private prosecution against the Marquess of Queensberry for criminal libel spectacularly backfired, Wilde was placed on trial for 'gross indecency' and sentenced to two years hard labour. He died penniless in Paris aged 46 and was buried in Père Lachaise Cemetery.

Influences: Plato, William Shakespeare, Walter Pater, John Ruskin
Influenced: James Joyce, Samuel Beckett, Tom Stoppard, André Gide
Plays written: 9
Most famous plays: *An Ideal Husband, The Importance of Being Earnest, Lady Windermere's Fan*
Amazing fact: *The Picture of Dorian Gray* was the only full-length novel Oscar Wilde wrote.

Anton Chekhov

'Don't tell me the moon is shining; show me the glint of light on broken glass'.

Anton Chekhov (1860–1904) was a Russian playwright and short-story writer. His plays are major landmarks of Russian realism, celebrated for the psychological depth of the characters and the evocative atmosphere orientated around everyday life. In 1889, Chekhov made the observation that 'One must not put a loaded rifle on the stage if no one is thinking of firing it.' This became known as Chekhov's gun, a literary device whereby a seemingly unimportant detail becomes significant later on.

Influences: Leo Tolstoy, Henrik Ibsen
Influenced: James Joyce, George Bernard Shaw, Ernest Hemingway
Plays written: 14
Most famous plays: *The Seagull, The Cherry Orchard, Uncle Vanya*
Amazing fact: The premiere of *The Seagull* was such an unmitigated disaster that Chekhov stated afterwards 'Not if I live to be 700 will I write another play!'

Bertolt Brecht

'Art is not a mirror held up to reality, but a hammer with which to shape it'.

Bertolt Brecht (1898–1956) was an influential dramatist and poet. He developed certain ideas relating to dramaturgy, among which was the 'defamiliarisation effect' (in which the stage action is presented in a more direct, shocking way so that from the audience can actively engage with the play). His plays often deal with the realities of poverty, corruption and censorship which threaten the characters' freedom of expression and the survival of virtue.

Influences: Karl Marx, William Shakespeare
Influenced: John Osborne, Tony Kushner, Caryl Churchill
Plays written: 53
Most famous plays: *Life of Galileo, Mother Courage and Her Children*

Amazing fact: W. H. Auden suggested that Brecht was one out of the three 'positively evil' men he had ever met and deserved the death sentence, stating 'In fact I can imagine doing it to him myself.'

Samuel Beckett

'In the landscape of extinction, precision is next to godliness'.

Samuel Beckett (1906–89) was an Irish avant-garde novelist, playwright, poet and theatre director. His plays are best known for their absurdist themes, their exploration of the human condition, fragmented writing style and black humour. Beckett settled in Paris in the late 1930s and wrote most of his plays in French before translating them into English. He was a major writer in the 'Theatre of the Absurd' and was awarded the Nobel Prize in Literature in 1969.

Influences: James Joyce, Marcel Proust, Dante
Influenced: Harold Pinter, Tom Stoppard, John Banville
Plays written: 21
Most famous plays: *Waiting for Godot, Happy Days, Endgame*
Amazing fact: Beckett joined the French Resistance in 1940, and was later awarded the Croix de guerre and Médaille de la Résistance for his valour.

Tennessee Williams

'Life is an unanswered question, but let's still believe in the dignity and importance of the question'.

Thomas 'Tennessee' Williams III (1911–83) was an important American playwright, as well as a poet and fiction writer. His plays are best known for their Southern United States setting, exploration of the American Dream and for their depiction of the gloomy realities of sex and violence which thwart characters' dreams and romantic aspirations. He won two Pulitzer Prizes for drama for *A Streetcar Named Desire* and *Cat on a Hot Tin Roof*. In 1980 he received the Presidential Medal of Freedom.

Influences: Hart Crane, Anton Chekhov, D.H. Lawrence
Influenced: Tony Kushner, Gore Vidal
Plays written: 38 plays (and over 70 one-act plays)
Most famous plays: *A Streetcar Named Desire, Cat on a Hot Tin Roof, The Glass Menagerie*
Amazing fact: While studying at the University of Iowa, Thomas was nicknamed 'Tennessee' on account of his southern roots. Williams decided to keep the name and joked, 'It's better than being called Mississippi'.

Arthur Miller

'A playwright lives in an occupied country. And if you can't live that way you don't stay'.

Arthur Miller (1915–2005) was an American playwright, widely considered to be one of the greatest playwrights of the 20th century. His best-known plays combine a critical awareness of the values of society and the flaws of the American Dream. He won both a Pulitzer Prize for Drama in 1949 and a Tony Award for Best Play for *Death of a Salesman*. He was also well known for his marriage to Marilyn Monroe.

Influences: Henrik Ibsen; Greek classical drama
Plays written: 50
Most famous plays: *Death of a Salesman, A View from the Bridge, All My Sons, The Crucible*
Amazing fact: Miller's account of his first meeting with Marilyn Monroe seemed like love at first sight on his part: 'When we shook hands, the shock of her body's motion sped through me.'

Tom Stoppard

'My whole life is waiting for the questions to which I have prepared answers'.

Tom Stoppard (*b*.1937) is an acclaimed British playwright and screenwriter. His plays incorporate philosophical, existential and political themes and are noted for their sharp wit and language play. One of the most performed playwrights of his generation, Stoppard was knighted in 1997 and has won four Tony Awards as well as the Academy Award for Best Original Screenplay for *Shakespeare in Love*.

Influences: George Bernard Shaw, Oscar Wilde, Samuel Beckett
Plays written: 62 (including TV and Radio)
Most famous plays: *Rosencrantz and Guildenstern are Dead, Arcadia, The Real Inspector Hound, The Real Thing*
Amazing fact: Stoppard decided against attending university because he was 'thoroughly bored by the idea of anything intellectual'.

THE 10 NOVELISTS YOU SHOULD HAVE HEARD OF

Jane Austen

'Let other pens dwell on guilt and misery'.

Jane Austen (1775–1817) completed six novels during her short lifetime and remains one of the most widely read authors in English literature. Her novels are set among the upper echelons of English society and explore how marriage was an alliance upon which women depended for financial and social security. Her books are notable for their insightful wit and incisive social commentary. All of her novels were published anonymously.

Movement: Romanticism
Influences: Lord Byron, Ann Radcliffe, Samuel Richardson
Novels written: 6
Most famous novels: *Pride and Prejudice, Sense and Sensibility, Emma*
Amazing fact: In 1802, Austen received her only proposal of marriage. The match offered many potential financial and practical advantages to her family so she accepted. The engagement was short-lived, however, as Austen changed her mind the following morning.

George Eliot

'The golden moments in the stream of life rush past us, and we see nothing but sand'.

George Eliot (Mary Anne Evans, 1819–80) was a novelist and translator of the Victorian era. She is famous for the realism with which she depicts rural England and the psychological depth of her characters. Her novel *Middlemarch* is considered a pinnacle of literary realism and was famously described by both Martin Amis and Julian Barnes as 'the greatest novel in the English language'.

Movement: Realism
Influences: Jane Austen, Charlotte Brontë, William Wordsworth
Influenced: Marcel Proust, Virginia Woolf, Martin Amis
Novels written: 7
Most famous novels: *Middlemarch, Daniel Deronda, The Mill on the Floss*
Amazing fact: After living with a married man for over 20 years, Eliot once more risked her reputation when in 1880, shortly before her death, she married a man 20 years younger than herself. The threat of scandal that both relationships posed may have contributed to her use of a pen name.

Leo Tolstoy

'Art is a microscope which the artist fixes on the secrets of his soul, and shows to people these secrets which are common to all'.

Leo Tolstoy (1828–1910) was a Russian novelist and short-story writer. His novels took literary realism to great heights exploring the faults and foibles of individuals and of society with remarkable profundity. In later life, Tolstoy became deeply pious and wrote moralistic and socially reforming tracts which went on to influence seminal figures such as Mohandas Gandhi and Martin Luther King, Jr.

Movement: Realism
Influences: Stendhal, Jean-Jacques Rousseau

Influenced: Maxim Gorky, James Joyce, Aleksandr Solzhenitsyn
Novels written: 12
Most famous novels: *War and Peace, Anna Karenina*
Amazing fact: Tolstoy was excommunicated by the Russian Orthodox Church in 1901 after criticising the church heavily in his 1899 novel *Resurrection*.

Henry James

'Experience is never limited . . . it is an immense sensibility, a kind of huge spider-web of the finest silken threads suspended in the chamber of consciousness, and catching every air-borne particle in its tissue'.

Henry James (1843–1916) was an American author who became a major player in the early modernism movement. He is renowned for his elaborate style and for his examination of philosophical themes including freedom and morality. He is also well-known for employing interior monologue and point-of-view techniques in his novels. James was a prolific writer, penning novels, short stories, travel books, biographies and literary criticism.

Movement: Modernism
Influences: Nathaniel Hawthorne, Henrik Ibsen, Honoré de Balzac
Influenced: Edith Wharton, Virginia Woolf
Novels written: 33
Most famous novels: *The Wings of a Dove, The Turn of the Screw, The Portrait of a Lady, Washington Square*
Amazing fact: The line 'Live all you can, it's a mistake not to' from *The Ambassadors* was used to promote Rolls Royce cars in the 1980s.

Virginia Woolf

'Fiction is like a spider's web, attached ever so slightly perhaps, but still attached to life at all four corners. Often the attachment is scarcely perceptible'.

Virginia Woolf (1882–1941) was an English novelist, essayist and short-story writer. She was central to the modernist movement of the 20th century. Famous for her exploration of the inner worlds and mental processes of her characters, Woolf experimented with novelistic form and made use of the stream-of-consciousness technique and interior monologue. Tragically, Woolf was plagued by depression for most of her life and she drowned herself in the River Ouse on 28 March 1941.

Movement: Modernism
Influences: James Joyce, George Eliot, Leo Tolstoy
Novel written: 9
Most famous novels: *Mrs Dalloway, To the Lighthouse, The Waves*

Amazing fact: Woolf was a member of the influential Bloomsbury Set, a group of writers, artists and intellectuals that included John Maynard Keynes and E. M. Forster.

James Joyce

'I go to encounter for the millionth time the reality of experience and to forge in the smithy of my soul the uncreated conscience of my race'. (From *A Portrait of the Artist as a Young Man*)

James Joyce (1882–1941) was a highly influential novelist, short-story writer and poet. Although Joyce spent most of his adult life in continental Europe, all of his novels are set in Dublin. His major works, *Ulysses* and *Finnegans Wake,* pioneered new novelistic techniques such as stream-of-consciousness and experimented with different literary styles. Serialisation of *Ulysses* was halted in the USA in 1921 after the publisher was convicted of printing obscenity and the book was banned in the UK until the 1930s.

Movement: Modernism
Influences: Henrik Ibsen, Dante, Homer
Influenced: Samuel Beckett, Katherine Mansfield, Virginia Woolf
Novels written: 4
Most famous novels: *Ulysses, Finnegans Wake*
Amazing fact: When he was a child, Joyce was attacked by a dog, an event that resulted in a canine phobia that persisted throughout his life.

Franz Kafka

'A book must be the axe for the frozen sea within us'.

Franz Kafka (1883–1924) was a Czech novelist and short-story writer. Goaded by his robust father, Kafka pursued a career in law, alongside his literary interests. The need to earn a living through law work and his troublesome relationships with his father and fiancée led to the themes of paranoia and punishment, isolation and judgement for which his works are best known.

Movement: Modernism
Influences: Benedict de Spinoza, Friedrich Nietzsche, Sigmund Freud
Influenced: Albert Camus, Jean-Paul Sartre
Novels written: 3
Most famous novels: *The Trial, America*
Amazing fact: Kafka fell for a German lady called Felice Bauer, but it was an attraction riddled with doubt and self-division. Kafka wanted to be with and without her at the same time, writing to her: 'my two requests are equally serious: "Go on loving me", and "Hate me!"'

William Faulkner

'An artist is a creature driven by demons. He doesn't know why they choose him and he's usually too busy to wonder why'.

William Faulkner (1897–1962) was, among other things a great American novelist, short-story writer, poet and essayist. Faulkner is well-known for the vividness with which he painted his fictional setting, Yoknapatawpha County, bringing together a high modernist aesthetic with local colour. He is also known for his elusive style and poly-vocal, stream-of-consciousness prose. He received the 1949 Nobel Prize in Literature and the Pulitzer Prize for Fiction in 1953 and 1963.

Movement: Modernism
Influences: James Joyce, T.S. Eliot, Herman Melville
Influenced: Cormac McCarthy, Gabriel García Márquez, Toni Morrison
Novels written: 19
Most famous novels: *The Sound and the Fury, As I Lay Dying, A Fable*
Amazing fact: Faulkner was in love with the local belle, Estelle Oldham, but someone else proposed to her first. Faulkner waited ten years for Estelle, and when they did finally marry (after her divorce) Faulkner had numerous affairs.

Ernest Hemingway

'My aim is to put down on paper what I see and what I feel in the best and simplest way'.

Ernest Hemingway (1899–1961) was an American novelist, journalist and short-story writer. Well-known for his terse, understated style and his ability to vividly capture scenes without gratuitous detail, Hemingway influenced many writers of the 20th century. He became a journalist after the First World War and was sent to Europe to cover news events such as the Greek Revolution and the Spanish Civil War; the latter provided much material for his most ambitious novel, *For Whom the Bell Tolls*. He was awarded the Nobel Prize in Literature in 1954.

Movement: Modernism
Influences: F. Scott Fitzgerald, Rudyard Kipling
Influenced: J. D. Salinger, Russell Banks
Novels written: 7
Most famous novels: *A Farewell to Arms, For Whom the Bell Tolls*
Amazing fact: Hemingway became a volunteer ambulance driver in Italy in 1918 after responding to a Red Cross recruitment drive in Kansas City. While in Italy, he was awarded the Italian Silver Medal for Bravery for carrying a wounded soldier to safety while gravely wounded himself. Hemingway's experiences in Italy inspired his novel *A Farewell to Arms*.

Gabriel García Márquez

'It is not true that people stop pursuing their dreams because they grow old, they grow old because they stop pursuing their dreams'.

Gabriel García Márquez (*b.*1928) is a Colombian writer who changed the direction of 20th-century prose. Breaking away from modernist modes of writing, he has his own, unique way of telling stories and remaking national myths. García Márquez is well known for his exploration of solitude, both of the individual and of the human race. In 1982, he was awarded the Nobel Prize in Literature.

Movement: Magical realism
Influences: Franz Kafka, William Faulkner, Jorge Luis Borges
Influenced: Salman Rushdie, Mario Vargas Llosa, Angela Carter
Novels written: 5
Most famous novels: *One Hundred Years of Solitude, Love in the Time of Cholera*
Amazing fact: When García Márquez started writing *One Hundred Years of Solitude,* he sold his car so that his family would have enough money while he wrote.

THE 10 ARTISTS YOU SHOULD HAVE HEARD OF

Caravaggio

'In painting not equal to a painter, but to Nature itself' (Caravaggio's epitaph).

Born in 1571, Michelangelo Merisi da Caravaggio was an Italian painter active during the Renaissance. A true pioneer, he was renowned for masterful lighting, his unidealised style and his skill at capturing the physical form and human emotion. His work was largely forgotten after his death, and it was only in the 20th century that his significance to Western Art was truly recognised.

Movement: Renaissance
Influences: Giuseppe Cesari
Influenced: Baroque school, Rubens, Rembrandt
Famous works: *The Taking of Christ* (National Gallery of Ireland), *The Calling of St Matthew* (San Luigi dei Francesi, Rome)
Amazing fact: Pope Paul V issued a death warrant for Caravaggio after he murdered a man over a gambling debt.

Velázquez

'I would rather be the first painter of common things than second in higher art'.

Born in 1599, Diego Rodríguez de Silva y Velázquez was a Spanish painter active during the Baroque period. He was the leading light of the Spanish Golden Age and was one of King Philip IV's court painters. Velázquez painted many portraits of members of the Spanish royal family as well as ordinary people. He is renowned for his naturalistic style, the fluency of his brushwork and his paintings' lifelike quality.

Movement: Baroque
Influences: Caravaggio, Rubens, Titian
Influenced: Manet, Picasso
Famous works: *Las Meninas* (Prado, Madrid) and the *Rokeby Venus* (National Gallery, London)
Amazing fact: Had it not been for his royal appointment, Velázquez's *Rokeby Venus* would not have escaped the censorship of the Spanish Inquisition.

Monet

'Colour is my day-long obsession, joy and torment'.

Born in 1840, Claude Monet was a French landscape painter. He was one of the founders of Impressionism and undoubtedly the movement's most famous exponent. Some of his most famous paintings were created in the garden of his house at Giverny, but he travelled extensively, painting famous scenes of London and Venice. He is renowned for his vibrant use of colour and his masterful handling of light.

Movement: Impressionism
Influences: Turner, Renoir, Manet
Influenced: Van Gogh, Cezanne, Degas, Seurat, Pissarro
Famous works: *Water-Lily Pond* (National Gallery, London), *Rouen Cathedral* (Musée d'Orsay, Paris), Water Lilies and the Houses of Parliament series
Amazing fact: It's possible that after cataract surgery, Monet was able to see certain ultraviolet wavelengths of light that are normally excluded by the lens of the eye, affecting the colours he perceived.

van Gogh

'I dream of painting and then I paint my dream'.

Born in 1853, Vincent Willem van Gogh was a Post-Impressionist Dutch painter. He was not well known during his time and died aged 37 from a gunshot wound to the chest, which is thought to have been self-inflicted. He struggled with mental health problems for most of his adult life, but it is not known how much these encroached on or inspired his work. He is renowned for his bold, vivid colours and heavily built-up layers of paint.

Movement: Post-Impressionism
Influences: Monet, Millet
Influenced: Picasso, Matisse, Klee
Famous works: *The Starry Night* (Museum of Modern Art, New York City), *Irises* (Getty Museum, Los Angeles), *Portrait of Dr Gachet* (privately owned); Sunflowers series and various self-portraits
Amazing fact: van Gogh only sold one painting – *The Red Vineyard* – during his lifetime. It fetched 400 francs.

Rodin

'To any artist, worthy of the name, all in nature is beautiful, because his eyes, fearlessly accepting all exterior truth, read there, as in an open book, all the inner truth'.

Born in 1840, François-Auguste-René Rodin was a French sculptor, widely acknowledged to be the father of modern sculpture. He eschewed the established dependence on classical themes and polished pure materials in favour of simple, modern themes, using rougher materials to convey transience and movement. Although many of his early works were criticized, he was a world-renowned artist by the turn of the 20th century.

Influences: Donatello
Influenced: Matisse
Famous works: *The Thinker*, *The Kiss*, *The Gates of Hell* (all in the Musée Rodin, Paris)
Amazing fact: Rodin bequeathed all of his work to the state of France with two conditions. Firstly, that they let him continue to live in the Hôtel Biron, a grand hotel scheduled for demolition, and secondly, that the government create a museum to hold and honour all of his works.

Michelangelo

'The true work of art is but a shadow of the divine perfection'.

Born in 1475, Michelangelo di Lodovico Buonarroti Simoni was an Italian sculptor, painter and architect. He was one of the pioneering influences of the Renaissance, producing some of the most well-known art in existence. Many of his works were religious in theme, commissioned by patrons including seven different popes and Lorenzo di Medici. His technical skill was truly extraordinary and his influence on Western Art was incomparable.

Movement: Renaissance
Influences: Ghiberti, Ghirlandaio
Influenced: Rubens, Velázquez, Tintoretto, Titian

Famous works: *David* (Galleria della Academia, Florence), Sistine Chapel ceiling (St Peter's Basilica, Vatican City)
Amazing fact: The sculpture *The Pieta* is the only work that Michelangelo signed, but he chastised himself for his vanity and vowed to never sign another one.

Leonardo da Vinci
'Art is never finished, only abandoned'.

Born in 1452, Leonardo di ser Piero da Vinci was a Renaissance polymath, widely regarded as the most diversely talented individual in history. He is primarily regarded as a painter, responsible for two of the most renowned works ever created. His detailed knowledge of anatomy and human expression in addition to his technical skill in applying paint and gradation are just some of the qualities that make Leonardo's work unique.

Movement: Renaissance
Influences: Verocchio
Influenced: Raphael, Lippi, Rubens
Famous works: *Mona Lisa* (Louvre, Paris), *The Last Supper* (Santa Maria delle Grazie, Milan)
Amazing fact: Leonardo was on the committee that decided where Michelangelo's statue of David should be positioned. His derisive contribution was that it should be placed where it wouldn't 'get in the way'.

Picasso
'Art is the lie that enables us to realize the truth'.

Born in 1881, Pablo Picasso was a Spanish painter and sculptor, considered one of the most influential artists of the 20th century and one of the greatest artists in history. Picasso's work falls into identifiable periods in which his style, subject and use of colour changed dramatically; these were the Blue period; Rose period; African period; Cubism, which he pioneered; and Classicism. Picasso was a prolific artist; it is estimated that he created 50,000 different works in his lifetime.

Movement: Cubism
Influences: Goya, Gauguin, Cézanne, Matisse
Influenced: Modigliani, Johns, De Kooning
Famous works: *Guernica* (Museo Reina Sofia, Madrid), *Girl Before a Mirror* (MOMA, New York), *Garcon à la Pipe* (privately owned), *Les Demoiselles d'Avignon* (MOMA, New York)
Amazing fact: Picasso's first word was '*piz*', short for *lapiz*, meaning 'pencil' in Spanish.

Rembrandt
'Without atmosphere a painting is nothing'.

Born in 1606, Rembrandt Harmenszoon van Rijn was a Dutch painter and etcher active during the Dutch Golden Age, a period of remarkable cultural achievement in the 17th century. Rembrandt is renowned for his atmospheric portraiture, the expressiveness of his subjects' faces and his dexterous use of chiaroscuro. Although his self-portraits are his most recognizable works, he also achieved renown for his religious scenes and landscapes.

Movement: Dutch Golden Age
Influences: Caravaggio
Influenced: Picasso
Famous works: *The Night Watch* (Rijksmuseum, Amsterdam), *The Return of the Prodigal Son* (Hermitage, St Petersburg), 27 self-portraits
Amazing fact: In 1656 Rembrandt was declared bankrupt and his paintings and house were auctioned to pay his debts.

Raphael
'Time is a vindicative bandit to steal the beauty of our former selves. We are left with sagging, rippled flesh and burning gums with empty sockets'.

Born in 1483, Raffaello Santi (or Sanzio) da Urbino is considered one of the great Renaissance masters along with Leonardo and Michelangelo. He is most famous for his paintings of Madonnas and the stunning biblical frescoes in the four Stanze di Raffaello in the Vatican. He produced significant altarpieces and a series of 10 cartoons for tapestries, the latter of which were bought by Charles I for £300.

Movement: Renaissance
Influences: Michelangelo
Influenced: Rembrandt, El Greco, Rubens
Famous works: *The School of Athens* (Apostolic Palace, Vatican City), *Bridgewater Madonna* (National Gallery of Scotland), *Aldobrandini Madonna* (National Gallery, London)
Amazing fact: According to the Renaissance artist Giorgio Vasari, Raphael died after a night of excessive sex with his mistress.

THE 10 ART MOVEMENTS YOU SHOULD HAVE HEARD OF

Pop Art

'*Popular, transient, expendable, low-cost, mass-produced, young, witty, sexy, gimmicky, glamorous, Big Business . . .*' British painter Richard Hamilton's description of Pop Art in 1957.

Pop Art in the 1960s challenged traditional fine art by taking its imagery from popular culture such as advertising and comic books. It was a direct response to the new consumer society, and reflected the vibrancy of music and youth culture. At the same time, Pop Art was a reaction both to the austerity years of World War II and to the intensity of the Abstract Expressionist works of the 1940s and 50s.

Influenced: Ed Ruscha, David Hockney
Key artists: Richard Hamilton, Roy Lichtenstein, James Rosenquist, Andy Warhol
Famous works: *Just What Is It That Makes Today's Homes So Different, So Appealing?* by Richard Hamilton (Kunsthalle, Tubingen), *200 Campbell's Soup Cans* by Andy Warhol (Leo Castelli Gallery, New York), *Drowning Girl* by Roy Lichtenstein (The Museum of Modern Art, New York)
Amazing Fact: Pop Art was detested by many art critics. Harold Rosenberg described it as being 'like a joke without humour, told over and over again. . . advertising which advertises itself as art that hates advertising.'

Futurism

'*Courage, audacity and revolt will be essential ingredients of our poetry. We affirm that the world's magnificence has been enriched by a new beauty: the beauty of speed*' First Futurist Manifesto 1909.

Futurism was the invention of Filippo Tommaso Marinetti, who called himself 'The Caffeine of Europe'. He attacked both memory and history for being backward-looking, and instead glorified speed, technology, and war. The machine (notably the car and the plane), and the industrial city were worshipped. The *Technical Manifesto of Futurist Painting* committed the Futurists to 'a universal dynamism' but the problem was how to translate this into paint. As a solution, the Futurists used the technique of Divisionism by breaking light and colour into stippled dots.

Influenced: Natalia Goncharova, Vladimir Mayakovsky, Kazimir Malevich, Antonio Sant'Elia
Key artists: Filippo Tommaso Marinetti, Umberto Boccioni, Carlo Carra, and Gino Severini

Famous works: *The City Rises* by Umberto Boccioni (MOMA, New York), *Dynamism of a Dog on a Leash* by Giacomo Balla (Albright-Knox Gallery, Buffalo), *Dynamic Hieroglyphic of the Bal Tabarin* by Gino Severini (MOMA, New York)

Amazing fact: Marinetti, in his enthusiasm to break with the customs of the past, even critised the eating of pasta, stating that 'it is heavy, brutalising and gross … it induces scepticism and pessimism. Spaghetti is no food for fighters.'

Impressionism

'Impressionism means taking inspiration directly from nature, trusting your senses rather than what you think you know' Michael McClure.

Impressionism was a revolutionary movement in painting in the late 19th century that rejected studio work and classical scenes in favour of landscapes and scenes from contemporary life. It was essentially an art of immediacy and movement, light and colour. The Impressionists preferred to work *en plein air* using vibrant colour, and light, short brushstrokes to capture the essence of a subject, rather than its details. When, alongside others, Manet's *Le déjeuner sur l'herbe* was rejected by the jury for the annual Salon de Paris show in 1863 because it portrayed a nude woman with two clothed men, Napoleon III set up the Salon des Refusés so that the public could view the rejected paintings. This show attracted far more attention that the regular Salon. In 1873 Monet, Renoir, Sisley and Pissarro organised a separate society to show their works, and they were soon joined by others.

Influenced: Vincent van Gogh, Paul Gauguin, Henri de Toulouse-Lautrec, Edgar Degas

Key artists: Claude Monet, Pierre-Auguste Renoir, Edouard Manet, Alfred Sisley, Camille Pissarro

Famous paintings: *Impression, Sunrise* by Claude Monet (Musée Marmottan, Paris), *Le déjeuner sur l'herbe* by Edouard Manet (Musée D'Orsay, Paris), *Bal du Moulin de la Galette* by Pierre-Auguste Renoir (Musée D'Orsay, Paris), *L'Absinthe* by Edgar Degas (Musée D'Orsay, Paris)

Amazing fact: The name Impressionism was coined from the title of Monet's painting *Impression, Sunrise*, which provoked derisory reviews when it was first exhibited in 1872 because it was considered to be little more than a sketch.

The Pre-Raphaelites

'Every Pre-Raphaelite landscape background is painted to the last touch, in the open air, from the thing itself. Every Pre-Raphaelite figure, however studied in expression, is a true portrait of some living person' John Ruskin.

Founded in 1848 by William Holman Hunt, John Everett Millais, and Dante Gabriel Rossetti, the Pre-Raphaelite Brotherhood set out to reform art radically. They vowed to restore art to the clearer depictions of nature as seen in Quattrocento Italian and Flemish painting before the classical compositions of Raphael had their deleterious effect. The brotherhood made detailed studies of the natural world using brilliant colours and a sharp-focus technique. Despite their emphasis on naturalism, the majority of their subjects came from literature: the Bible, Tennyson, Shakespeare, Dante, and Keats in particular.

Influenced: Edward Burne-Jones, William Morris, Arthur Hughes
Key artists: William Holman Hunt, John Everett Millais, Dante Gabriel Rossetti
Famous works: *The Awakening Conscience* by William Holman Hunt (Tate Britain), *Christ in the House of His Parents* by John Everett Millais (Tate Britain), *Beata Beatrix* by Dante Gabriel Rossetti (Tate Britain)
Amazing fact: When Millais' *Christ in the House of His Parents* was first exhibited in 1850 it caused such a public outcry for its bluntly realistic portrayal of the Holy Family that Queen Victoria asked for the painting to be taken to Buckingham Palace for a private viewing.

Cubism

'Fragmentation helped me to establish space, and movement in space' Georges Braque.

A revolutionary way of depicting images, Cubism was pioneered by Pablo Picasso and Georges Braque in the early years of the 20th century. It was Picasso's *Les Demoiselles d'Avignon* of 1906–7 that sowed the seeds of the Cubist movement, together with Georges Braque's *Houses at L'Estaque* of 1908 which prompted the description of 'cubes'. In cubist art, objects are broken up, analysed and reassembled, and artists often view their subjects from different viewpoints. It was a re-interpretation of the visual world, but stopped short of abstraction, at least in the works of Picasso and Braque.

Influenced: Jean Metsinger, Robert Delaunay, Albert Gleizes and Marcel Duchamp.
Key artists: Pablo Picasso, Georges Braque, Juan Gris, Fernand Léger
Famous works: *Violin and Palette* by Georges Braque (Solomon R. Guggenheim Museum, New York), *Portrait of Picasso* by Juan Gris (Art Institute of Chicago), *Man with a Pipe* by Pablo Picasso (Art Institute of Chicago)
Amazing fact: The real roots of Cubism can be found in Paul Cézanne's work as early as the 1880s and 90s. Called 'the father of us all' by both Picasso and Matisse, Cézanne was the first to break up the painting's surface into different facets and declared 'treat nature by the cylinder, the sphere and the cone'.

Surrealism

'Beautiful as the chance encounter, on an operating table, of a sewing machine and an umbrella' from 'Songs of Maldoror' by Isidore Ducasse.

Surrealism was essentially a literary movement that began in 1920s Paris and was, above all, for the liberation of the imagination from all rational or bourgeois thought. André Breton, Surrealism's inspirational leader, was influenced by Sigmund Freud's work on dreams and the unconscious mind, and soon gathered around him a group of like-minded writers and artists. Breton defined Surrealism as 'pure psychic automatism ... dictation of thought in the absence of all control exercised by reason ...'. The Surrealists were hugely influenced by the early dreamlike paintings of Giorgio de Chirico which they felt had the right ingredients of chance, memory, desire and coincidence meeting in a new reality: a 'sur-reality' (a term borrowed from Guillaume Apollinaire).

Influenced: The films of Luis Buñuel, Jean Cocteau, and René Clair, and the plays of Federico García Lorca
Key artists: Max Ernst, Salvador Dalí, René Magritte, Joan Miró, Man Ray
Famous works: *The Elephant Celebes* by Max Ernst (Tate Modern), *The Persistence of Memory* by Salvador Dalí (MOMA, New York), *The Treachery of Images* by René Magritte (Los Angeles County Museum of Art)
Amazing fact: The Surrealist group even held a serious enquiry as to whether excrement could be classified as an acceptable dream image after André Breton was offended by a depiction of it in Salvador Dalí's painting *Lugubrious Game* of 1929.

The Renaissance

'*This century, like a golden age, has restored to light the liberal arts which were almost extinct: grammar, poetry, rhetoric, painting, sculpture, architecture, music ... and all this in Florence*' philosopher Marsilio Ficino.

The Renaissance in art began in Florence in the 14th century, arguably with the paintings of Giotto di Bondone and ended after the death of Raphael in 1520. This transformation in the arts was part of a far wider cultural change in the whole of European intellectual life. In Florence, the generous patronage of the Medici family did much to encourage the works of Leonardo da Vinci, Sandro Botticelli, and Michelangelo Buonarotti, among others. Florentine painters, led by the example of Giotto and Masaccio, strove to portray the human form realistically, utilising the realistic linear perspective technique developed by the architect Filippo Brunelleschi.

Influenced: Albrecht Dürer, Hieronymus Bosch, Pieter Brueghel, Jean Clouet
Key artists: Giotto di Bondone, Sandro Botticelli, Leonardo da Vinci, Michelangelo Buonarotti
Famous works: *Primavera* by Sandro Botticelli (Uffizi, Florence), *Baptism of Christ* by Piero della Francesca (National Gallery, London), *Mona Lisa* by Leonardo da Vinci (Louvre, Paris), *The Arnolfini Portrait* by Jan van Eyck (National Gallery, London)

Amazing fact: It was not until the mid 19th century that the word 'Renaissance', literally meaning 'rebirth', was coined by the French historian, Jules Michelet, in his 1855 work *Histoire de France*.

Conceptual Art

'It's *amazing what you can do with an 'E' in Art A-Level, a twisted imagination, and a chainsaw*' Damien Hirst on winning the Turner Prize in 1999.

In Conceptual Art the idea, or concept, is the most important part of the work. It was actually the brainchild of the French artist, Marcel Duchamp who, as early as 1917, broke all the barriers of tradition and displayed his *Fountain*, a common urinal at the exhibition of the Society of Independent Artists in New York. Duchamp was way ahead of his time, and it was not until the 1960s that Conceptual Art as a movement really got under way. At its most radical it can be reduced to no more than a set of instructions for making a work of art, such as in the work of Yoko Ono.

Influenced: Tracey Emin, Damien Hirst, Simon Starling
Key artists: Joseph Kosuth, Yves Klein, Walter de Maria
Famous works: *Vertical Earth Kilometer* by Walter de Maria, *Immaterial Pictorial Sensitivity* by Yves Klein, *The Physical Impossibility of Death in the Mind of Someone Living* by Damien Hirst
Amazing fact: In 2002, the Chairman of the London Institute of Contemporary Arts, Ivan Massow, was forced to resign for denouncing Conceptual Art as '*pretentious, self-indulgent, craftless tat . . . in danger of disappearing up its own arse . . .*'

Abstract Expressionism

'*Today painters do not have to go to a subject matter outside of themselves. Most modern painters work from a different source. They work from within*' Jackson Pollock.

Wassily Kandinsky was probably the first artist to entirely dispel the representation of objects from his work in order to reach a higher intensity of feeling and, in this, he was the pioneer of abstract art. The retrospective exhibition of his work in 1945, a year after his death, at the Museum of Non-Objective Art in New York City (now known as the Guggenheim Museum) was a catalyst for American Abstract Expressionism. This movement flourished until the 1960s, and was championed by the influential critic, Clement Greenberg, who identified two different styles: 'action painting' and 'colour field painting'. In the late 1940s Jackson Pollock began to drip paint onto a canvas laid flat on the floor, which marked the beginning of his 'action paintings'. The contrast between these, and Rothko's sublime, contemplative, soft-edged 'colour field paintings' could not be greater.

Influenced: Hans Hofman, Philip Guston, Stuart Davis, Cy Twombly, Jasper Johns
Key artists: Jackson Pollock, Arshile Gorky, Barnett Newman, Clyfford Still, Mark Rothko
Famous works: *Lavender Mist Number I* by Jackson Pollock (National Gallery of Art, Washington D.C.), *Ochre and Red on Red* by Mark Rothko (Phillips Collection, Washington D.C.)
Amazing fact: The CIA financed and organised the promotion of American Abstract Expressionists from 1950–67. They saw the movement as representative of both the independent thought and free market of the USA in contrast to the Socialist Realist styles of art prevalent in Communist nations at the time.

Romanticism
'The artist's feeling is his law' Caspar David Friedrich.

The Romantic movement in art originated in Europe at the end of the 18th century. It was a reaction to the Industrial Revolution, the rationalism of the Enlightenment, and to the confines of the Neoclassical movement, particularly in France. The Romantics believed in spiritual freedom and individual creativity and a close connection between man and nature. Originality was felt to be essential, as the Romantics scorned the derivative. Indeed, such was the belief in the primacy of the imagination that some artists abandoned classical drawing and ideas of correct proportions or perspective altogether.

Influenced: Albert Bierstadt, Frederic Edwin Church, Edvard Munch, Paul Nash, Mark Rothko
Key artists: Caspar David Friedrich, Philipp Otto Runge, Eugene Delacroix, J. M. W. Turner
Famous works: *The Death of Sardanapulus* (Louvre, Paris), *The Raft of the Medusa* by Theodor Gericault (Louvre, Paris), *Moonrise over the Sea* by Caspar David Friedrich (Alte Nationalgalerie, Berlin), *The Fighting Temeraire* by J.M.W. Turner (Tate Britain, London)
Amazing fact: Samuel Beckett, standing before Caspar David Friedrich's painting *Man and Woman Contemplating the Moon*, said that it was the inspiration for his play, *Waiting for Godot*.

THE 10 PHILOSOPHERS YOU SHOULD HAVE HEARD OF

Socrates
'I only know that I know nothing'.

Born in 469BC, Socrates is widely regarded as one of the founders of philosophy. His life is shrouded in mystery as he left no philosophical writings; the details we know of his life are through the writings of his pupils: Plato, Xenophon and the playwright Aristophanes. He is renowned for what became known as the Socratic Method – his mode of inquiry involving reasoned argument as a means of establishing truth. He lived a frugal life, caring little for material wealth. After making countless enemies in Athenian society, Socrates was arrested and was found guilty of corrupting the youth of Athens and heresy. He was condemned to die by being made to drink hemlock.

Amazing fact: Socrates could have escaped from prison but actually chose to die, on the grounds that (i) escaping would have admitted a fear of death (ii) he would suffer the same fate wherever he fled to, and (iii) he had agreed to live under Athenian law and would honour it.

Descartes
'I think, therefore I am'.

Born in 1596, René Descartes is one of history's most influential philosophers. He was also a pre-eminent mathematician, and is renowned for his legacy in the field of analytic geometry. Descartes is well known for his theory on dualism – that the body is physical matter, while the mind is an immaterial substance. He is also known for pioneering a system to establish unequivocal truth, by rejecting everything that could be doubted and isolating the things he knew could not be doubted. This gave rise to his assertion 'cogito ergo sum', or 'I think, therefore I am'.

Amazing fact: Descartes suggested that the seat of interaction between the physical brain and immaterial mind was the pineal gland; we now know this gland produces the hormone melatonin.

Hume
'Reason is, and ought only to be the slave of the passions'.

Born in 1711, Hume was a Scottish philosopher, who believed that we are not born with pre-existing ideas, but rather that we acquire knowledge through sensory experiences. He refuted the popular notion that reason governed human behaviour, asserting that desire motivates us instead. He is well known for rejecting the design argument (that we can infer a divine origin from order, design and purpose in the universe) on several grounds, including (i) that we have not seen other parts of the universe, so don't know whether or not chaos may be present (ii) that nature could have a system of order intrinsic to it and that (iii) even if the universe was designed, why should we infer that an omniscient God created it?

Amazing fact: Hume asked that he be interred in a 'simple Roman tomb', inscribed only with his name and the year of his birth and death, 'leaving it to posterity to add the rest'.

Aristotle

'Man is by nature a political animal'.

Born in 384BC, Aristotle was a student of the philosopher Plato and is considered one of the founders of Western philosophy. Aristotle's legacy covers a diverse range of philosophical doctrines, but he is perhaps best known for his pioneering work in the field of formal logic. In contrast to his master Plato, who believed that ultimate reality existed in ideas, Aristotle held that it existed in physical objects, which he asserted possessed matter (their potential) and form (their reality). Aristotle's influence was not solely limited to philosophy. He was a keen student of natural history and elements of his classification of living organisms were still studied in the 19th century. His writings also include the first known instance of the camera obscura, which he used to observe the Sun.

Amazing fact: Aristotle was Alexander the Great's teacher and also taught two future Macedonian kings, Ptolemy and Cassander.

Kant

'There can be no doubt that all our knowledge begins with experience'.

Born in 1724 in Prussia, Immanuel Kant was one of the key thinkers of the Enlightenment and exerted a profound influence on subsequent Western philosophy. His *Critique of Pure Reason* in 1781 revolutionised 18th-century philosophy, offering a new approach that advanced debate beyond the prevailing rationalist and empiricist schools of thought. In this *magnum opus*, Kant suggested that rather than employing reason and sensory experience to force concepts to match the nature of objects, we should allow the structure of our concepts to govern our experience of objects. Kant's writings in the field of moral philosophy are well known, particularly his assertion that there is a sole moral responsibility determining whether an action or inaction is necessary, which he called the 'categorical imperative'.

Amazing fact: Kant's tomb, which was erected in Konigsberg (now known as Kaliningrad), is one of the few buildings and monuments to survive the conquest and annexation by Soviet forces in 1945.

Mill

'Over himself, over his own body and mind, the individual is sovereign'.

Born in 1806, John Stuart Mill was a significant figure in political philosophy. In his extremely influential work *On Liberty,* Mill asserted that people's freedom from the state should only be curtailed if they cause injury to others, a belief known as the 'Harm Principle'. He believed that without three crucial freedoms: freedom of speech, freedom of assembly, and the freedom to enjoy tastes and pursuits, a person could not be considered free. Mill was also anti-censorship, anti-slavery and in favour of greater rights for women. He is well known for being a strong proponent of utilitarianism, the idea that actions should be performed with the intention of causing the greatest cumulative happiness. However, unlike Jeremy Bentham, another advocate of utilitarianism, Mill held that intellectual pleasures should be considered more important than physical pleasures.

Amazing fact: In 1866, while MP for City and Westminster, Mill became the first person in the history of the Houses of Parliament to argue that women should be allowed to vote.

Wittgenstein

'the most perfect example I have ever known of genius as traditionally conceived, passionate, profound, intense, and dominating' Bertrand Russell.

Born in 1889, Ludwig Josef Johann Wittgenstein was an Austrian-British philosopher considered by some to be the greatest philosopher of the 20th century. He worked in the fields of mathematics, logic, philosophy of mind and philosophy of language. His first published work, the *Tractatus Logico-Philosophicus* attempted to explore the relationship and establish the limits of language, thought and reality. In his posthumously published *Philosophical Investigations*, Wittgenstein suggested that the cause of many philosophical problems was conceptual ambiguity associated with language, which effectively rejected his earlier conclusions in the *Tractatus Logico-Philosophicus*. The philosopher Douglas Lackey described the book as 'the one crossover masterpiece in 20th-century philosophy, appealing across diverse specializations and philosophical orientations'.

Amazing fact: Wittgenstein finished the *Tractatus* in a prisoner-of-war camp in Italy in 1918.

Confucius

'What you do not want done to yourself, do not do to others'.

Thought to have been born in 551BC, Confucius was a Chinese philosopher and politician who profoundly influenced Chinese history. His teachings were developed into a philosophical system known as Confucianism, which was the official state ideology of China for over 2,000 years. Confucianism is a humanistic and non-theistic ideology, which focuses on social harmony through virtuous living and the honouring of the five constants: Ren (humaneness), Yi (righteousness), Li (propriety), Zhi (knowledge) and Xin (integrity). Among the other crucial components is a reverence for one's parents, the cultivation of knowledge and sincerity and the belief that people should treat each other the way they would like to be treated. He is also credited with introducing the idea of meritocracy, the concept that people should be assigned to occupations on the basis of their intelligence and competency.

Amazing fact: Confucius became Justice Minister in the State of Lu, but disliked the behaviour of his master the Duke, so waited for him to make a mistake so that he could legitimately leave his service. This mistake? Forgetting to honour Confucius with sacrificial meat.

Marx

'The philosophers have only interpreted the world, in various ways. The point, however, is to change it'.

Born in 1818, Karl Marx was a German philosopher who played a crucial role in the socialist political movement. The first of his two most famous works, *The Communist Manifesto* (1848), which Marx wrote with his friend Friedrich Engels, explores the struggle between the different classes and the pitfalls of capitalism. It is regarded as one of history's most influential political documents. The second of Marx's most significant works, *Das Kapital*, was completed in 1894 by Engels after Marx's death. It is a critique of capitalism, focusing heavily on the exploitation of workers and its economic instability. Marx believed that capitalism would implode and be replaced by socialism, a system in which society would be governed by the working classes. However, this system would inevitably self-destruct and be replaced by communism, a society without classes or states.

Amazing fact: Marx's tomb, in Highgate Cemetery in London, features the epitaph 'Workers of all lands unite', the last line of *The Communist Manifesto*.

Nietzsche

'God is dead'.

Born in 1844, Friedrich Nietzsche was an influential German philosopher, although neither widely read nor regarded during his lifetime. Nietzsche did not develop a unifying philosophical system, but he is well known for questioning the objectivity of truth, his proclamation that 'God is dead' and his idea of the *Übermensch* (Over-man), which he regarded as a goal for humanity: 'Man is a rope, tied between beast and Übermensch'. Another central element to his philosophy is the belief in two types of morality: master morality, which he believed emanated from the strong-willed, and slave morality, which he believed emerged reactively from the weak. Hitler famously employed elements of Nietzschean philosophy, although there are doubts as to how extensively he read or understood Nietzsche's work.

Amazing fact: In 1889, while in Turin, Nietzsche suffered a mental breakdown. A few days afterwards, he wrote to his erstwhile colleague Burckhardt explaining that 'last year I was crucified by the German doctors in a very drawn-out manner.'

THE 10 SCIENTISTS YOU SHOULD HAVE HEARD OF

Albert Einstein

'Imagination is more important than knowledge'.

Born in 1879, Albert Einstein was a German-born physicist who revolutionised science in 1916 with his publication of the general theory of relativity, which identified the relationship between gravity, space and time. Another of Einstein's astonishing contributions to science was his mass-energy equivalence formula, $E = mc^2$, which he proposed in 1905. His formula basically says that energy (E) and mass (m) are two forms of the same thing and that conversion between the two is possible through the constant c^2, a number equivalent to two times the speed of light in a vacuum. Einstein won the 1921 Nobel Prize in Physics for his work on the photoelectric effect, which proved critical in the study of quantum mechanics.

Amazing fact: In 1895, the 17-year-old Einstein failed the examination to the Swiss Federal Polytechnical School.

Michael Faraday

'Nothing is too wonderful to be true if it be consistent with the laws of nature'.

Born in 1791, Michael Faraday was a renowned chemist and physicist credited with pioneering work in the fields of electromagnetism and electrochemistry. In 1821 he performed experiments that led to the publication of a paper on electromagnetic rotation (the means to drive an electric motor). In 1831, he discovered electromagnetic induction (the principle behind the transformer and generator), which proved critical in the development of electricity as a viable technology. In 1845, he discovered that some objects display a weak repulsion from a magnetic field, a condition that he named diamagnetism. His achievements in chemistry include the discovery of the element benzene and the system of oxidation numbers. The SI unit of electrical capacitance, the 'farad' is named in Faraday's honour.

Amazing fact: In 1812, Faraday had just finished an apprenticeship to a bookbinder when he attended the famous chemist Humphry Davy's lectures at the Royal Institution. He was so inspired that he sent Davy a 300-page book of notes he had taken at the lectures and Faraday soon became Davy's secretary.

Issac Newton

'If I have seen further it is by standing on the shoulders of giants'.

Born in 1643, Issac Newton is considered one of the greatest scientists in history. He won acclaim from the scientific community after he created the first reflecting telescope in 1668, and he was subsequently made a fellow of the Royal Society. Newton began to investigate light refraction in the 1670s and discovered that a prism separates white light into a spectrum of colours and that the separate colours reform when met with a lens and a second prism. In 1687, he produced his greatest work, the *Philosophiae Naturalis Principia Mathematica* in which he explained universal gravitation and the three universal laws of motion. Among his many achievements in mathematics was the development of infinitesimal calculus and approximating, which thereafter became known as Newton's Method.

Amazing fact: Newton became warden of the Royal Mint in 1696 and took charge of moving Britain from the Silver Standard to the Gold Standard.

Galileo

'All truths are easy to understand once they are discovered; the point is to discover them'.

Born in 1564, Galileo Galilei was an Italian scientist, mathematician and philosopher, renowned for his extraordinary contributions to astronomy. In 1610, he discovered the four largest satellites of Jupiter, now known as the Galilean satellites. The same year, he observed that the Milky Way comprised countless individual stars. The following year, he identified the phases of Venus. His assertion that the Sun was the centre of the Solar System ultimately led to his trial in Rome, after which he was found 'vehemently suspect of heresy' and forced to 'abjure, curse and detest' his opinions. He was placed under house arrest for the rest of his life. In addition to his astronomical observances, Galileo also invented an early thermometer and a military compass.

Amazing fact: In 1992, Pope John Paul II expressed regret and made a declaration announcing that mistakes had been made by the members of the Inquisition in the case against Galileo. This admission came 377 years after the original trial.

Charles Darwin

'A man who dares waste one hour of time has not discovered the value of life'.

Charles Darwin was an English naturalist who revolutionised the scientific world with his 1859 book *On the Origin of the Species*. He was already well-known to the public after publishing the journal of his five-year voyage around the world on HMS *Beagle* from 1831–6, during which he took detailed observations of plants and animals. These experiences proved invaluable to his *magnum opus*, which took him over 20 years to complete. *On the Origin of the Species* established that every living species was descended from common ancestors through a process known as natural selection. This effectively explained the diversity of life on earth and provides the foundation of biology. In 1871, he published his second book on evolutionary theory, *The Descent of Man and Selection in Relation to Sex*, a wide-ranging examination of human evolution.

Amazing fact: More than 120 species and nine genera have been named after Darwin.

Marie Curie

'I have frequently been questioned, especially by women, of how I could reconcile family life with a scientific career. Well it has not been easy'.

Born in 1867, Marie Skłodowska was a Polish scientist renowned for her pioneering work in the field of radioactivity. She met the scientist Pierre Curie in 1894 in Paris and they married a year later. They worked together and made major breakthroughs, including the discovery of the rare and highly radioactive element Polonium, and the highly radioactive earth-metal Radium. They were awarded the Nobel Prize in Physics in 1903 for their work on radiation (jointly with Henri Becquerel, the man who discovered radiation). After Pierre's tragic death in 1906, she succeeded him as Head of Physics at the Sorbonne. Five years later, she was awarded the Nobel Prize in Chemistry in 1911, becoming the first person to win in two disciplines. Her later achievements included instigating the first studies to treat neoplasms with radioactive isotopes.

Amazing fact: Curie's research papers from the 1890s and even her cookbook are considered too radioactive to be handled safely so are kept in a lead-lined box.

Louis Pasteur

'Chance favours the prepared mind'.

Born in 1822, Louis Pasteur was a French chemist and biologist well-known for his work in the origin and prevention of diseases. Although he did not discover germ theory (the idea that micro-organisms are responsible for significant numbers of diseases), his experiments demonstrated that micro-organisms responsible for spoiling liquids did not generate spontaneously from the liquid, but rather came from outside. His solution of heating the liquid and then cooling it dramatically reduced the bacteria count. This process is named pasteurisation in Pasteur's honour. Pasteur's subsequent work included major breakthroughs in vaccine development, including the synthesis of an anthrax vaccine by exposing the bacteria to oxygen. He also developed vaccines for rabies and cholera.

Amazing fact: The Swedish psychiatrist Axel Munthe was involved in Pasteur's rabies vaccine trials and recalled Pasteur with a test-tube between his teeth trying to extract saliva from the jaws of a rabid pit bull that was held down by Pasteur's two assistants.

Alan Turing

'Machines take me by surprise with great frequency'.

Born in 1912, Alan Turing was an English mathematician many consider to be the founder of computer science and artificial intelligence. In 1936, he formulated a proof that automatic computation cannot solve every mathematical problem. Now known as the Turing machine, this proof played a pivotal role in the development of the modern computer. During the Second World War, Turing worked at Bletchley Park, Britain's codebreaking hub. His work there was critical in deciphering German messages encrypted by the Enigma machine. After the war, Turing worked for the National Physical Laboratory on the design of the Automatic Computing Engine. He succeeded in producing the first extensive design of a stored-program computer. Turing was convicted of homosexuality in 1952 and was subjected to chemical castration. His security clearance was revoked and he committed suicide two years later.

Amazing fact: Turing died from arsenic poisoning and it is speculated that the half-eaten apple found next to him was used to administer the poison. It has often been suggested that the company Apple designed their half-eaten apple logo in honour of Turing, but this is not true.

Niels Bohr

'An expert is a person who has found out by his own painful experience all the mistakes one can make in a very narrow field'.

Born in 1885, Niels Bohr was a Danish physicist who made pioneering contributions to the study of atomic structure and quantum mechanics. Bohr introduced the revolutionary theory that electrons travel in orbit around the nuclei of atoms and that the properties of the elements are determined by the number of electrons in the outer orbits around a nucleus. He was rewarded for his investigations with the Nobel Prize in Physics in 1922. Bohr was due to be arrested by German police during the occupation of Denmark, but escaped to London, where he was soon recruited for the Manhattan Project, the programme to build an atomic bomb. He strongly believed that nuclear technology should be shared with the international scientific community, but was faced with stiff opposition from Winston Churchill among others.

Amazing fact: During his youth, Niels played as goalkeeper for professional Danish football club Akademisk Boldklub

Archimedes

'Give me a place to stand on, and I will move the Earth'.

Born around 287 BC, Archimedes was a Greek mathematician, philosopher, engineer and inventor. One of the most notable scientists of the classical world, Archimedes discovered the law of hydrostatics. Also known as 'Archimedes' Principle', the law states that an object floating in liquid is carried by a force equal to the weight of the displaced liquid. Archimedes was so excited upon discovering this principle that he famously cried 'Eureka!' upon stepping into his bath. Archimedes served Syracuse during the Second Punic War in 214 BC by inventing weapons which could be used to defend the city against Roman attack. Such weapons included the Claw of Archimedes, which was a type of crane able to lift or capsize invading ships, the catapult and the 'Archimedes heat ray' (in which a mirror is used to reflect the sun's rays onto invading ships, setting them alight).

Amazing fact: When Syracuse was seized by the Romans, Archimedes was so preoccupied in his work that he is believed to have said 'do not disturb my circles' to the Roman soldier who was about to kill him.

NOSTALGIA

TV SHOWS
Original series' run dates given in parentheses.

The Flintstones (1960-6)
The Flintstones was a prime-time television cartoon about the life and pre-historic times of Fred Flintstone, a working-class quarry worker living in the town of Bedrock. Set in a fantasy version of a stone-age era with modern-day technology, the show was first broadcast on the ABC network in the USA on 30 September 1960 and went on to spawn some six series and over 160 episodes, becoming the first cartoon to broadcast for more than two series – a record held for nearly 30 years before finally being broken by *The Simpsons*.

No. of series: 7 (166 episodes)

Classic quote: 'WILMA!!'

Did you know? Alan Reed, the original Fred Flintstone voice artist, appeared in numerous film roles including *Breakfast at Tiffany's* and *The Lady and the Tramp*.

Thunderbirds (1965-6)
Devised by British children's television producers Gerry and Sylvia Anderson, *Thunderbirds* was a British sci-fi 'Supermarionation' show based on the adventures of millionaire Jeff Tracy and International Rescue – a covert organisation operating from a secret island located in the South Pacific. Tracy and his five sons – Scott, John, Virgil, Gordon and Alan – pilot the *Thunderbird* rescue vehicles, which range from a hypersonic variable-sweep wing rocket plane (*Thunderbird 1*, piloted by Scott) to a reusable, vertically launched spaceship (*Thunderbird 3*, piloted by Alan). With help from Brains, a scientific genius, and agent Lady Penelope, the Tracy team does battle with 'The Hood' and his villainous agents.

No. of series: 2 (34 episodes)

Classic quote: '5, 4, 3, 2, 1, Thunderbirds are go!'

Did you know? Two feature-length films, *Thunderbirds Are Go* and *Thunderbird 6*, brought the world-famous International Rescue team to the big screen in the late 1960s and paved the way for the likes of *Team America: World Police* to continue the 'Supermarionation' legacy.

The Magic Roundabout (1965-77)
The Magic Roundabout was originally created by French animator Serge Danot before being snapped up by the BBC for its early afternoon children's slot. The first episode was aired in 1965 and the hugely popular show went on to span nearly 450

episodes over the course of seven years. Using stop motion animation, *The Magic Roundabout's* appeal stemmed from the much-loved characters (such as Dougal and Zebedee) and the show's hugely entertaining scripts, written and performed by actor Eric Thompson.

No. of episodes: 441

Classic quote: 'Boing' and 'Time for bed'

Did you know? Thompson's stories were published as a series of four paperbacks in 1998 with forewords by actor Emma Thompson, Eric's daughter.

Danger Mouse (1981–92)

What do you get when you cross James Bond with Mighty Mouse? Danger Mouse. A loose parody of the spy fiction which partly inspired it, *Danger Mouse* was first shown on British television in 1981 and went on to span 161 episodes over the course of ten series. Developed by the Manchester-based graphics partnership Cosgrove Hall Films, it was snapped up by Thames Television, and later by the Nickelodeon channel for the US market. Danger Mouse, a quintessentially British character – replete with eye-patch and quick-witted refrains – and his bumbling sidekick, Penfold (a hamster) are given assignments by Colonel K. (a chinchilla) to save the world from various villains, the most prolific being their arch-enemy, Baron Silas Greenback (a toad), and his henchman Stiletto (a crow).

No. of series: 10 (161 episodes)

Classic quote: 'Oh crumbs!'

Did you know? Danger Mouse was voiced by actor David Jason, who was also the voice behind a number of other characters on the show.

Knight Rider (1982–6)

An American television series which starred David Hasselhoff as Michael Knight, a former Los Angeles Police Department detective rescued by billionaire Wilton Knight after being shot in the face. Wilton pays for facial reconstructive surgery and employs Michael as a field agent at his Foundation for Law and Government (FLAG). With the help of Knight Industries Two Thousand (KITT), an artificially intelligent, near-indestructible car (a heavily modified Pontiac Trans Am), Michael Knight travels the back-streets of America as a modern-day knight 'to champion the cause of the innocent, the helpless, the powerless in a world of criminals who operate above the law.'

No. of series: 4 (90 episodes)

Classic quote: 'Michael Knight, a lone crusader in a dangerous world. The world ... of the Knight Rider.'

Did you know? The Knight Rider theme tune has been sampled by six different recording artists include Busta Rhymes and Punjabi MC.

SuperTed (1982–94)

SuperTed is a Welsh teddy bear found to be defective in the toy factory where he was made and thrown away '...like a piece of rubbish into an old dark storeroom'. Here he was found by Spotty (a yellow alien covered in green spots) and brought back to life with Spotty's 'cosmic dust'. SuperTed is then given superpowers by Mother Nature which, once activated by a secret magic word, transforms him into a superhero able to fight evil, including his arch-enemy Texas Pete and his sidekicks: hapless Bulk and cowardly Skeleton.

No. of series: 3 (36 episodes)

Did you know? *SuperTed*'s creator Mike Young originally told the *SuperTed* stories to his young son to help him overcome his fear of the dark. After publishing a few of the tales as books, Mike set-up Siriol Productions, creating the fully fledged animated character we know today.

The A-Team (1983–7)

Originally broadcast in 1983, *The A-Team* was put together by American television supremos Frank Lupo and Stephen J. Cannell following the direct request from NBC television president Brandon Tartikoff for a fresh, prime-time action-adventure television series. The resulting show – about a group of ex-US Army Special Forces personnel who work as 'good-guy' mercenaries – featured some of the most memorable characters of the 1980s, including the group's leader John 'Hannibal' Smith, con-man Templeton 'Faceman' Peck, and, of course, the legendary B. A. Baracus (played by the inimitable Mr T).

No. of series: 5 (98 episodes)

Classic quote: 'I love it when a plan comes together' (Hannibal) and 'I ain't gettin' on no plane!' (B. A. Baracus)

Did you know? Dwight Schultz, who played Murdock in the show, also appeared in a number of *Star Trek* episodes as Lieutenant Reginald Barclay. Schultz was also the voice of Dr Animo in *Benlo*. Mr T, meanwhile, has had a colourful career and has made numerous television appearances as himself.

Fraggle Rock (1983–7)

Fraggle Rock was essentially a spin-off of *The Muppets*, both of which were created by American puppeteer Jim Henson. The show revolved around the adventures of a group of colourful, furry, humanoid creatures called Fraggles who live in a place called Fraggle Rock. The Rock is also home to the all-knowing trash heap, Marjorie, as well as the Doozers and the Gorgs. According to Henson *Fraggle Rock* was 'a high-energy, raucous musical romp' although the show did deal with issues such as prejudice, spirituality and the environment.

No. of series: 5 (96 episodes)

Classic quote: 'Down at Fraggle Rock!'

Did you know? The Gorgs required two performers each: an actor to perform in the costume, and a puppeteer to do the voice and operate the radio-controlled face.

Airwolf (1984–7)

Distinctively 'cold war' in theme, the show followed the various 'missions' of a high-tech supersonic helicopter code-named 'Airwolf' and its crew. Originally built by the 'FIRM', a covert division of the CIA, Airwolf was stolen and the FIRM asks Stringfellow Hawke (played by Jan-Michael Vincent), a reclusive former test pilot for Airwolf, to retrieve the helicopter. The FIRM, during the first three seasons, served as both ally and enemy for Hawke and his older mentor Dominic Santini (played by Ernst Borgnine) with FIRM operatives often seizing *Airwolf* when the opportunity arose. Dubbed the '*Knight Rider* for the sky' when it was first released in 1984, the show was a big success in both the USA and Europe.

No. of episodes: 79 (4 series)

Classic quote: 'Why can't we hover like regular helicopter people?'

Did you know? The Bell 222 helicopter used in the series was sold to a German company and became an air ambulance. Tragically, it crashed in 1992, killing all three passengers.

ThunderCats (1984–9)

A hugely popular animated TV series, *ThunderCats* follows the adventures of the eponymous team of heroes as they battle the evil Mutants of Plun-Darr. With their own planet of Thundera dying, Lion-O and his band of cat-like humanoid aliens are forced to relocate to Third Earth, where they must protect the Sword of Omens from the evil mummified sorcerer, Mumm-Ra. Originally debuting on children's television in 1984, the show went on to spawn numerous series and some very successful action figure merchandise.

No. of Series: 4 (130 episodes)

Classic quote: 'Sword of Omens, give me sight BEYOND sight.'

Did you know? A new *ThunderCats* animated series began airing on the Cartoon Network in July 2011.

DuckTales (1987–90)

DuckTales was an American animated television series revolving around the adventures of Scrooge McDuck and his great-nephews, Huey, Dewey and Louie. As the richest duck in the world, Scrooge McDuck is constantly looking for ways of both making more money but also protecting his vast fortune from the likes of the Beagle Boys and Flintheart Glomgold – his arch-nemesis. Supported by his great-nephews, Webbigail 'Webby' Vanderquack and hapless pilot Launchpad McQuack, Scrooge McDuck did whatever it took to protect both his family and his over-sized money vault.

No. of series: 4 (100 episodes)

Classic quote: 'Since I'm the richest duck in the world, I am going to celebrate by taking everyone out the world's biggest hamburger stand!' (Scrooge McDuck)

Did you know? The great-nephews originally lived with their uncle, Donald Duck, but were left in Scrooge's care when Donald joined the navy.

Teenage Mutant Ninja Turtles (1987–96)

Based on a series of comic books originally released in the early 1980s, the internationally successful animation series – commonly abbreviated to *TMNT* – follows the adventures of a team of anthropomorphic, pizza-loving, teenage turtles. Under the guidance of former jujitsu master (and now humanoid rat) Splinter, Donatello, Michelangelo, Raphael and Leonardo do battle with arch-enemy Shredder while maintaining a low-profile in the sewers of a criminal-ridden Manhattan island. Spanning three animated series, four feature films, concert tours and countless food tie-ins, *TMNT* was one of the biggest-selling animated series of the late 1980s.

No. of series: 10 (193 episodes)

Classic quote: 'Heroes in a half-shell – TURTLE POWER!'

Did you know? Robbie Rist, who voiced Michelangelo in the 1987 feature-length film *Teenage Mutant Ninja Turtles*, publicly criticised film-director Michael Bay after it was reported that Bay was looking into significantly changing the turtles' back-story for a re-launch of the original film.

Baywatch (1989–99)

Baywatch premiered on NBC in the USA in 1989 and went on to become one of the most successful prime-time television shows of all time. The show revolved around the work of a team of lifeguards patrolling a stretch of beach in sunny California, with each episode focusing on both a significant event for the team to resolve and their 'off-beach' interpersonal relationships. David Hasselhoff's Mitch Buchannon was the show's mainstay protagonist and, along with support from the likes of Pamela Anderson, Yasmine Bleeth, and Carmen Electra, went on to star in over 240 episodes of the sun-kissed drama.

No of series: 11 (242 episodes)

Classic Quote: 'Uh . . . we just had a serious ordinance violation committed' (Mitch Buchannon)

Did you know? Hobie Buchannon, Mitch Buchannon's tearaway son, was played by two different actors during the show's run between 1989 and 1999. Brandon Call played him in the show's first season before the role was taken over by Jeremy Jackson for the remaining ten series and the spin-off feature-length film, *Baywatch: Hawaiian Wedding.*

Round the Twist (1989–2001)

Round the Twist was an Australian children's television programme, based on fantasy stories written by children's author Paul Jennings. The show centres around the magical adventures of three children – Pete, Linda and Bronson – who live with their widowed father Tony Twist in a mysterious and ghostly old lighthouse. In episodes ranging from 'Skeleton on the Dunny' – in which Bronson discovers a ghost in the lighthouse's outdoor toilet – to 'Without my Pants' – in which a ghost casts a spell on Pete causing him to blurt out 'without my pants' at the end of every sentence, *Round the Twist* remains one of the most entertaining and original children's television shows of all time.

No. of series: 4 series (52 episodes)

Classic quote: 'Have you ever, ever felt like this? How strange things happen, or are you going round the twist?'

Did you know? Tamsin West, who played the original Linda Twist in the first series, provided the vocals for the show's opening song. After a brief stint playing Emma Gordon in the long-running hit Australian television soap *Neighbours*, West returned to Queensland to concentrate on her singing career.

Captain Planet and the Planeteers (1990–6)

Seeing the Earth is in profound environmental peril, Gaia, goddess of the Earth, chooses five teenagers – Kwame, Wheeler, Linka, Gi and Ma-Ti (each originating from a different region of the world) – to become the 'Planeteers', a force to protect the planet. To accomplish that task, each member of the quintet is given a magic ring which allows them to temporarily control one of five elements: earth, wind, water, fire and 'heart'. When the threat is too big for them to face alone, they can summon Captain Planet by combining their powers. Captain Planet can shape-shift and take on the properties of any element, however he is weakened when he comes into contact with pollutants. Captain Planet and the Planeteers are tasked with stopping the Eco-Villains, a small group of antagonists (such as Hoggish Greedily and Duke Nukem), who endanger the Earth through polluting, poaching and deforestation.

No. of series: 6 (113 episodes)

Classic quote: 'With the five powers combined they summon earth's greatest champion – CAPTAIN PLANET!'

Did you know? Actor Whoopi Goldberg voiced Gaia in the episodes produced between 1990 and 1993.

VIDEO GAMES
Original release date given in parentheses

Space Invaders (1978)

Along with Asteroids and Pac-Man, Space Invaders set a precedent for computer gaming and went on to become one of the most popular and memorable games ever created in the medium. The aim of the game was to destroy all of the aliens as they descended from the sky and attempted to invade Earth. Originally released to a sceptical Japanese public in 1978, by 1982 the game had become one of the highest-grossing entertainment products of all time, amassing a healthy $450m net profit for the game's publisher Taito and in turn heralding the start of the golden generation of video gaming.

Asteroids (1979)

Atari's Asteroids was originally released in 1979; the aim of the game was to guide your space ship through a hostile asteroid field by shooting flying-saucers and avoiding the alien ship's counter fire. Asteroids had its fair share of devotees and champion players, including the late Scott Safran, who held the longevity record for a video game high score; in November 1982, Safran's mother drove her 15-year-old son to participate in an Asteroid charity event, where he scored 41,336,440 points over the course of three days. Twenty-seven years later, John McAllister finally cracked Safran's high score, scoring 41,338,740 in just under 58 hours!

Pac-Man (1980)

The game that defined the arcade-generation, Pac-Man was developed by Japanese video-game giant Namco and first released in 1980. It hit the arcades amid a flurry of hype but failed to compete against the more established space invader games, and was at one point completely overlooked by marketing executives at a trade show in the first 12 months of its release. Nearly 20 years later, the video game – which consisted of guiding Pac-Man through a maze of pellets, power pellets and, of course, ghosts – had grossed over $2.5bn, and had become the most popular arcade game of all time!

Tetris (1984)

Possibly one of the simplest video games, Tetris, was first developed in 1984 by computer engineer Alexey Pajitnov, while working at the Soviet Academy of Sciences in the USSR, and went on to become a worldwide phenomenon. Pirated versions spread like wildfire across Europe, before the game was finally (and somewhat controversially) picked-up by UK-based developers Andromeda. Some five years later, Tetris – in which the aim is to manipulate a series of 'Tetriminos' into a line of ten blocks without gaps – was one of the biggest-selling games in the world and, thanks to a licensing agreement with gaming giants Nintendo, has become an international household name.

The Legend of Zelda (1986)

A mixture of puzzle-solving and general action adventure – and one of Nintendo's most important franchises – The Legend of Zelda has been released, in various formats, 16 times over the course of 25 years. In each of the game's 16 guises and various spin-offs, Link, an elf-like 'Hylian' and reluctant hero, travels through the kingdom of Hyrule, defeating evil forces and collecting parts of the magical 'Triforce' in order to find and rescue Princess Zelda, who has been kidnapped by the evil Ganon. The game has sold approximately 67.9 million copies since the first release on the Nintendo Entertainment System in 1986.

Street Fighter (1987)

The first Street Fighter game was released in 1987 and allowed the player to take control of martial arts expert Ryu as he travelled the globe to take part in an international martial arts tournament. Four years and a few major developments later, Capcom released Street Fighter 2, a vastly improved version of the original release, which offered players a selection of playable characters, each with their own unique style. The sequel became an instant classic and went on to spawn numerous spin-offs and updated versions (the latest, Super Street Fighter 4, was released in 2010), and even a feature-length film!

Golden Axe (1989)

Sega's Golden Axe was released on the Sega Mega Drive system in 1989 and has since been heralded as one of the first successful 'hack 'n' slash' platform games. Set in the medieval town of 'Yuria', the game revolved around several heroes (including the excellently named green dwarf Gilius Thunderhead) who take on the task of recovering the legendary Golden Axe. The game was one of the first successful games for Sega's flagship Mega Drive console and went on to produce five sequels and numerous, albeit less successful, spin-offs.

Super Mario Kart (1992)

Developed by video game designer Shigero Miyamoto with a view to produce a game which featured a two-player split-screen mode, Super Mario Kart allowed players to choose from eight characters in the Super Mario series – Mario, Luigi, Toad, Donkey Kong Jr, Bowser, Princess Peach, Koopa Troopa and Yoshi – and race them against another player simultaneously. Extremely popular on the Super Nintendo games console when it was originally released in 1992, Super Mario Kart was revived for Nintendo Wii for the 'three-dimension' games market, going on to sell approximately 31 million copies on the Wii console alone.

Doom (1993)

In a press release dated 1 January 1993, id Software, an American video game development company, wrote that they expected their brand-new first-person shooter to be 'the number one cause of decreased productivity in businesses around the world'. Some three years later, Doom – a game in which a player has to literally shoot his way out of hell – was thought to have been installed in more computers than Microsoft's Windows '95. Three sequels and numerous expansion packs were added and it was even made into a feature-length film in 2005.

GoldenEye 007 (1997)

When British-based video-game developer Rare was approached by Nintendo to produce a game based on the 1995 James Bond film *GoldenEye*, the inexperienced team of designers would never have guessed that they would end up developing one of the most influential video games of all time. Originally released for the Nintendo 64 games console in 1997, GoldenEye 007 was one of the 'first-person-shooter' games for a home console and could be played in single player mode or in a split-screen multiplayer mode for up to four players. Players assume the role of British secret agent James Bond in his mission to prevent a criminal syndicate from using a satellite weapon to trigger global financial meltdown.

MUSIC

Rick Astley

Richard Paul Astley was born on 6 February 1966 in Lancashire and began his music career by singing in his local church choir. Nearly 20 years later he was approached by music impresario Pete Waterman after the producer had seen him sing with the short-lived band, FBI. Under the tutelage of Waterman's song co-writers, Mike Stock and Matt Aitken, Rick Astley was transformed into a pop sensation and a heartthrob for young pop fans the country over. Known for his boy-next-door looks and for his mega-selling hit single, 'Never Gonna Give You Up' (which became 1987's highest-selling single), Rick retired aged 27, but made a comeback in 2007 after becoming a surprise Internet phenomenon.

Billy Ray Cyrus

Despite only having one hit of any substance in the UK, Billy Ray Cyrus is hailed as the 'saviour' of modern country music in his home state of Kentucky, USA. Born in 1961, the young Cyrus rose to stardom after playing various venues in and around the south of the USA before finally releasing his debut album *Some Gave All*. The first single from the album – 'Achy Breaky Heart' – reached number one in the American Hot Country Singles and Tracks chart and also reached number four in the USA pop charts; what's more, the single was a massive success around the world charting at number three in the UK and even achieving triple-platinum in Australia. His subsequent releases were less successful and Cyrus has since gone on to have a relatively successful acting career alongside his pop-star daughter Miley Cyrus in the television series *Hannah Montana*.

Hanson

Rolling out of Tulsa, Oklahoma, with photogenic looks and an irresistibly fresh sound, Hanson became the 'Jackson 5 of the 1990s' after they released their first single 'MMMBop' in 1997. Topping more or less every chart across the world, Isaac (guitar, piano, vocals), Taylor (keyboards, piano, guitar, drums, vocals) and Zac Hanson (drums, piano, guitar, vocals) set off on a tour of the world, cementing a dedicated fan-base. Twenty years later the three brothers are still performing as a band, and in 2010 released their eighth album, *Shout it Out*.

Chesney Hawkes

'I am the one and only!' boomed a 19-year-old Chesney Hawkes as he took to the stage to perform his first single in the spring of 1991. The young man from Berkshire, England, had just appeared in the film *Buddy's Song* in which he played Buddy Clark, a kid determined to make it as a pop star. Over a year later he was the darling of the British pop scene and his song – written by singer-songwriter Nick

Kershaw – was at the top of the UK charts. Success didn't last for young Chesney, however, as his subsequent releases failed to live up to his first hit. He now tours universities with his band and was due to appear on ITV's *Dancing with the Stars* in 2011, but pulled out after breaking his ankle.

Jazzy Jeff and the Fresh Prince

'In West Philadelphia born and raised, on the playground is where I spent most of my days...' chimed the devious Fresh Prince in the opening rap to the hit TV show *The Fresh Prince of Bel-Air*. The Fresh Prince and Jazzy Jeff – aka Will Smith and DJ Jeff Townes – had met some five years earlier at a house party in their hometown and decided to start a rap group with fellow beat-boxer Ready Rock C. They released 'Girls Ain't Nothing But Trouble' in 1985 and, after ditching Rock C and releasing a string of under-the-radar singles, the Fresh Prince was approached by legendary music producer Quincy Jones with an idea for a sitcom. NBC's *The Fresh Prince of Bel-Air* was first broadcast in September 1990 and featured Jazzy Jeff as a recurring (and somewhat tragic) character in the show. Spanning six years and some 146 episodes, the show was a massive hit and catapulted Jazz and the Fresh Prince on to worldwide acclaim. Will Smith subsequently made it as an internationally renowned actor while Jazzy Jeff stayed in the music business; they remain good friends to this day and are still making music together.

Timmy Mallett

Timmy Mallett began his entertainment career on the radio, most notably on Manchester's Piccadilly Radio where his energetic style won him fans and awards alike. However, it was on television where Mallett found his largest audience, and his stint as presenter of the *Wide Awake Cub* turned him into a household name. His trademark show *Wacaday* – a school-holidays children's series in which kids were invited on to the show to compete in tasks such as 'Mallett's Mallet' and other crazy tasks – was the perfect platform for the star's unique art of entertaining. In 1990, Mallett formed the band Bombalurina and released the single 'Itsy Bitsy Teeny Weeny Yellow Polka Dot Bikini'. The song sold more than a million copies and reached the top of the charts in over a dozen countries.

New Kids on the Block

Between 1985 and the early 1990s, New Kids on the Block (or NKOTB) were the biggest boy band in the world. Put together by American pop producer Maurice Starr, NKOTB consisted of brothers Jonathan and Jordan Knight, Joey McIntyre, Donnie Wahlberg and Danny Wood. Despite failing with their first album, the boys toured the United States extensively throughout the late 1980s and the first single from their second album, 'Please Don't Stop it Girl', finally captured the American public's imagination, pushing NKOTB to the top of the singles chart in 1988.

Hangin' Tough, NKOTB's second album, was released in 1988 and the single of the same name catapulted the boy band to worldwide fame and success. NKOTB disbanded in 1994 before reuniting in 2011 for a super-tour with the Backstreet Boys.

Van Halen

With 56 million album sales in the USA alone and some 75 million albums sold worldwide, Van Halen earned a well-deserved induction into the Rock and Roll Hall of Fame in 2007 after surviving some 35 years in the business. Formed in Pasadena, California, in 1972, the band originally revolved around the frenetic guitar workings of Eddie Van Halen and the vocal growl of David Lee Roth, before personal problems lead the latter to leave at the height of the band's success. A succession of lead singers came in to fill the void left by Roth – including Sammy Hagar and Gary Cherone, both of whom left the group shrouded in controversy – but it wasn't until the beginning of the 21st century that Roth decided to bury the hatchet and return to the group which originally made his name. By then Van Halen were world-beaters and tracks such as 'Why Can't This be Love?', 'Panama' and the timeless 'Jump' had entered into rock and roll folklore.

Vanilla Ice

Robert Van Winkle – aka Vanilla Ice – was born in South Dallas in 1976 and quickly established himself as a keen break-dancer and singer. His breakthrough single 'Ice Ice Baby' was originally B-side for the more mainstream 'Play That Funky Music', and became an overnight hit after a DJ opted to play the B-side instead of the original single. 'Ice Ice Baby' became the first hip-hop single to top the Billboard charts in the USA, making Vanilla Ice an instant star and the envy of the hip-hop scene the world over. His success didn't last long, however, and his second album (entitled *Mind Blowin'*) didn't manage to chart. He has since opened his own extreme sports shop in the USA.

Wham!

Wham! started life as a ska band before founders George Michael and Andrew Ridgeley formed a new band and signed to Innervision Records in 1982. Their first release, 'Wham Rap! (Enjoy What You Do)' failed to chart, but their subsequent single, 'Young Guns (Go For It!)' received widespread airplay on UK radio stations and kick-started Wham!'s rise to the top of the British pops. With the Wham! phenomenon well and truly in the ascendancy during the mid to late 1980s, Ridgeley and Michael enjoyed worldwide superstardom and a succession of number one albums in both the UK and the USA. After three platinum-selling albums, however, George and Andrew went their separate ways, the former achieving even greater superstardom.

TOYS

View-Master (1939)

Now a piece of photographic history as well as a classic children's toy, the View-Master is a hand-held device which shows 3-D images on paper-mounted disks. The original View-Masters, introduced in the mid-20th century, were intended mainly for adult use and included both tourism and educational content; given the development of the technology – which never really got beyond the paper-disk stage – the View-Master came to be cherished by the children's toy market, with various television and film series appearing on the stereoscopic toy. Today the View-Master is seen as 'classic' toy and, in 2002 it was mooted that Steven Spielberg's DreamWorks production company would base a feature film on it!

Subbuteo (1947)

There is little more iconic in the world of football (soccer) than a small plastic man standing atop a round plastic base. Subbuteo was invented by Peter Adolph just after the end of the Second World War and involves flicking model players across a tabletop pitch to make contact with the ball. After the name 'Hobby' was refused an official trademark, Adolph opted for the name Subbuteo (the Latin name for a bird of prey commonly known as the Eurasian Hobby or, just simply, 'Hobby'). By the early 1980s the table football game had taken much of Europe by storm. Indeed, by 1992, Subbuteo had become so big that the Federation of International Sports Table Football lobbied for the game to become an Olympic sport!

Play-Doh (1956)

What do you get when you combine flour, water, salt, boric acid and mineral oil? Wallpaper cleaner according to the 'grown-ups' of 1930s America. When Joe McVicker, the nephew of the compound's manufacturer, discovered kids at the local school were began using the cleaner as a modeling compound, he decided to pitch 'Play-Doh' to his local manufacturer of school supplies. By 1956, the McVickers had formed a company to make and sell the popular modeling putty, and by 1958 Play-Doh had made nearly $3m. Play-Doh was bought by Hasbro in 1991 and is still widely sold.

Troll Doll (1959)

A truly unique addition to the toy universe, the Troll Doll was invented by Danish fisherman and woodcutter Thomas Dam in 1959 after he couldn't afford to buy his young daughter a Christmas present. The doll was a hit in Dam's hometown, and by the beginning of the 1960s the Dane was producing Troll Dolls for the majority of the kids in his area. A mistake in his copyright notice, however, allowed a wave of cheaper imitations to find their way across Europe and by the beginning of the 1960s, the Troll Dolls were being stocked on the lucrative shelves of North America. The troll craze didn't survive into the new millennium and by 2007 manufacturing was significantly reduced; it was announced in 2010, however, that Steven Spielberg's DreamWorks is to create a film based on Thomas Dam's idiosyncratic playthings.

G.I. Joe (1964)

Although first developed in the mid-1960s under the tagline 'America's moving fighting man', the cult of G.I. Joe didn't really take off until the early 1980s, when the toy was relaunched as an out-and-out action hero – replete with play sets, vehicles and a compelling (and indeed rather complicated) back-story. The everyman hero – available in various different action guises, ranging from the classic aquanaut, marine soldier and pilot figures to the more recent 'Mortal Kombat' series – was developed by Hasbro as a way to tap into the male 'doll' market following the success of the 'Barbie' series. Nearly half a century later, the G.I. Joe collection is still going strong, and in 2010 a brand new collection – entitled 'Rise of the Cobra' – was released to whole new generation of fans.

Space Hopper (1968)

Space Hopper, Moon Hopper, Skippyball, Kangaroo Ball, Bouncer, Hoppity Hop or Hop Ball – whatever the name – the rubber ball with handles became one of the most popular toys in the world after it was invented by Italian Aquilino Coasani in the late 1960s. Serving practically no use whatsoever, the bouncing rubber ball has maintained a cult following throughout the past 40 years – particularly in the Netherlands, where in 2007 a record 2,518 people hopped simultaneously for one minute on their precious Space Hoppers.

Pogs (1971)

Pogs was the unlikely toy success story of the late-20th century; a story which began with a drink invented by a food product consultant in Hawaii in 1971. POG – a tropical fruit drink made up of passion fruit, orange and guava – was bottled and sold with a promotional lid, imprinted with the unique and collectable POG symbol. The lids, in turn, were then collected and used in a game which consisted of slamming a 'pog' on to a pile of other 'pogs'. They soared in popularity in the mid-1990s when the World Pog Federation reintroduced the game to the public – even bringing out a pog-making kit for home manufacturing!

Teddy Ruxpin (1985)

Who better to gently lull your three-year old to sleep than the legendary Teddy Ruxpin? Originally created by inventor and former Walt Disney employee Ken Forsse, Teddy Ruxpin was introduced in 1985 and immediately became a best-seller in both the USA and the UK. In its original guise, Teddy Ruxpin was released with approximately 40 'World of Wonder' audio cassette tapes, each including a separate adventure, which could be played on a cassette deck built into his back. Despite Teddy Ruxpin being granted his own television series in 1988, the original manufacturer went out of business in 1990.

Micro Machines (1986)

Micro Machines are tiny scale-model versions of various automobiles, normally no bigger than the average pencil sharpener. Originally invented by toy enthusiast Clem Heeden – who in turn licensed the idea to California toy manufacturer Galoob – the tiny toys were a success in the early 1980s, before Hasbro (who bought Galoob in 1999) marketed the 'Micros' into real world-beaters in the late 1990s. From cars, trucks, trains and emergency vehicles, to airplanes, helicopters and even G.I. Joe-themed merchandise, the Micro Machines franchise is arguably one of the most original and successful toys of the past 25 years.

Tamagotchi (1996)

When Akihiro Yokoi and Aki Maita presented a tiny, palm-sized computer with an interface consisting of just three buttons to their fellow developers at Bandai, little did they know that they were sitting on a truly golden egg. As of 2010, over 76 million Tamagotchis have been sold worldwide. Tamagotchi (or 'egg watch') has also undergone nearly 45 various rebirths (including the 2010 release, 'TamaTown'). A tiny, keychain-sized virtual pet simulation game, Tamagotchis allow the player (or, indeed, 'parent') to raise an alien species into an adult creature, nursing it through several stages of growth which include 'child', 'teen', 'adult' and 'senior'. From bedtimes, feedings, marriages and death, to sickness, happiness and toilet training, the Tamagotchi franchise is one of the most original and simple computer games ever developed.

CARS

Ford Capri

The Ford Capri was first produced by Ford of Britain in 1961 as a two-door coupé version of the Ford Classic saloon car. Relaunched in 1969 as the Ford Capri coupé, the new version was a big hit across Europe, with the success of the classic Ford Mustang at the forefront of the manufacturers' and marketers' minds. Banking on the success of the first two models (and its various, performance-enhancing facelifts), Ford once again redesigned the Capri towards the end of the 1980s, this time as a convertible roadster and, by the beginning of the 1990s, it was one of the most popular Ford models of all time.

Top speed: 135mph

Production: 1961–94

Appearances on the big screen: The Ford Capri features in *Willy Wonka and the Chocolate Factory* (1971), *Muriel's Wedding* (1994) and *The Professionals* (1977)

DeLorean DMC-12

'Wait a minute, Doc. Are you telling me that you built a time machine... out of a DeLorean?' So said Marty McFly in the classic film *Back to the Future* – only a decade or so after John DeLorean had originally drawn up the design for the most iconic car of the 1980s. With backing from various patrons and a few Hollywood celebrities, DeLorean – who was best known for working as an engineer on the Pontiac car at General Motors – managed to put out approximately 9,000 DeLorean DMC-12s before a slump in the car market consigned the outlandish design to the vaults of history. With its Italian sensibilities and idiosyncratic 'gull-wing' doors, the DeLorean is still considered a true design classic.

Top speed: 140mph (but 88mph to travel through time!)

Production: 1981–2

Appearances on the big screen: the DeLorean was used in all three *Back to the Future* films (1985–90) and made an appearance in Adam Sandler's *The Wedding Singer* in 1998.

Ferrari F40

Everyone has their favourite Ferrari model, but the F40 is considered by car enthusiasts the world over as being one of the greatest models of all time. A rear-wheel drive, two-door coupé, the F40 was, at the time of its release, the fastest, most powerful and most expensive car Ferrari sold to the public. Originally devised by Ferrari as a counterpoint to the flashier Lamborghini Countach and Porsche 959, the F40 went into development just as Enzo Ferrari was heading into his 90s, and the entrepreneur wanted the final design of his dynasty to be a true statement of intent. Released in 1987 – only a year before Enzo's death – the car has been hailed by none other than Jeremy Clarkson as the 'greatest supercar the world has ever seen'.

Top speed: 201mph

Production: 1987–92

Appearances on the big screen: *Gone in 60 Seconds* (2000), *Scent of a Woman* (1992), and *Mike Bassett: England Manager* (2001)

Ford Thunderbird ('T-Bird')

The story of the Ford Thunderbird spans over 50 years and nearly 11 different model generations. The T-Bird began life as a rival to Chevrolet's Corvette, a flashy convertible originally designed as a show car before being unleashed on the car-buying public in the early 1950s. Released a year after its rival in 1955, a sleeker T-Bird had a two-seat coupé layout with convertible hood and also included circular headlamps, tail lamps and hood scoop. Sold as a 'personal luxury car', the Thunderbird stole the show from the Corvette in the first year of its release, selling 16,155 against 700 Corvettes. Despite numerous redesigns and modifications – including a Jaguar-designed engine in the 11th generation T-Bird in 2005 – the Thunderbird remains one of the classiest cars of all time and a true game-changer in the world of car design and, of course, marketing.

Top Speed: 117mph (Ford Thunderbird 1961)

Production: 1955–97; 2002–5

Appearances on the big screen: *Thelma and Louise* (1991), *Summer Holiday* (1963), *Flubber* (1997)

McLaren F1

Whatever Ferrari did, McLaren could do better. Following the release of Enzo Ferrari's swansong of a car, the Ferrari F40, in the late 1980s, Formula One car designer Gordon Murray convinced the executive chair of McLaren, Ron Dennis, to back a brand-new supercar project which would compete with Ferrari. The result – the McLaren F1 – blew away the rest of the field when it was released in 1992 and even went on to win several races, including the 24 Hours of Le Mans in 1995. Featuring a more streamlined structure and an incredibly powerful engine, the McLaren F1 set a record for the fastest road car in the world upon its release and, in turn, became one of the most sought-after cars in the world.

Top speed: 231mph

Production: 1996–8 (106 produced)

Appearances on the big screen: None

E-Type Jaguar

The E-Type Jaguar was originally designed as a rear-wheel drive grand tourer (luxury automobile designed for long-distance driving) before it was relaunched as a competitively priced, high-performance car for the top-range market. Acclaimed by Enzo Ferrari as 'the most beautiful car ever made', the E-Type underwent three different series between 1961 and 1975. The first 300 or so versions of the first series had flat floors, although this was modified for more leg-room by the time the second series rolled off the production line (as was the engine size). Sleek, fashionable and timeless, the Jaguar E-Type was ranked first in the *Daily Telegraph*'s list of '100 most beautiful cars' of all time.

Top speed: 154mph

Production: 1961–75

Appearances on the big screen: *Austin Powers: International Man of Mystery* (1997), *Emmanuelle* (1974), *The Italian Job* (1964)

Ford Mustang

The oldest product on Ford's production line, the Ford Mustang began life as a second-generation compact car, based originally on the design of the Ford Falcon. The executive designer who worked on the car was such an admirer of the World War II P-51 Mustang fighter plane that he unveiled the prototype to the Ford board with the Mustang moniker already attached. Released in 1965, the Mustang took America, and to a lesser extent Europe, by storm, selling some 100,000 units in its first year alone. Subsequent models underwent various facelifts and size reconfigurations – indeed, Mustangs grew larger and larger every year until Ford finally returned to its original design in 1974 – but the Ford Mustang remains one of the most sought-after mass-market cars ever produced.

Top speed: 113mph

Production: 1964–present

Appearances on the big screen: *Gone in 60 Seconds* (1974 and 2000), *K-9* (1989), *Innerspace* (1987)

Lotus Esprit

Designed by Giorgetto Giugiaro, an Italian car designer voted 'car designer of the century', the Lotus Esprit was launched at the Paris Motor Show in 1975 before going into production in 1976. Lauded for its handling and powerful engine – along with Giurgiaro's patented 'folded paper' design – the Lotus Esprit went in to re-development five times, before a new generation Esprit was launched at the Paris Motor Show in 2010, featuring futuristic daytime running lights and an impressive dual-exhaust system at the rear. With a timeless design and new developments constantly in the pipeline, the future's bright for the Esprit and those who adore it.

Top speed: 137mph

Production: 1993–2004

Appearances on the big screen: *The Spy Who Loved Me* (1977), *Pretty Woman* (1990), *Basic Instinct* (1992)

Cadillac Miller-Meteor

It needed 'suspension work and shocks, brakes, brake pads, lining, steering box, transmission, rear-end, new rings, mufflers and a little wiring', but once Ghostbuster Ray Stantz had transformed his Cadillac Miller-Meteor into the Ecto-1, there was no looking back. The car's origins lie in the merger of car manufactures Miller and Meteor, who were bought out by Divco-Wayne Corporation after the latter entered the car market. The original car was used as an ambulance due to its ample space and low centre of gravity, but the Cadillac Miller-Meteor rose to fame after Stantz purchased it for the relatively high price of $4,800 in the quest to bust ghosts.

Top speed: Unknown

Production: Unknown

Appearances on the big screen: *Ghostbusters I* and *II* (1984 and 1989)

Aston Martin DB5

The quintessential James Bond car, the Aston Martin DB5 was originally introduced in 1963, following on from the final DB4 series (named after the David Brown, the head of Aston Martin between 1947 and 1972). It included an enlarged, all-aluminium engine, a brand-new speed transmission and, most impressive of all, three Skinners Union carburetors. Always pleasing on the eye, the DB5 underwent a few redesigns over the years, including a convertible model and a custom-made model for David Brown himself. The car has featured in numerous James Bond films, including the latest Bond instalment, *Skyfall*.

Top speed: 143mph

Production: 1963–1965 (1,023 produced)

Appearances on the big screen: *Goldfinger* (1964), *Thunderball* (1965), *GoldenEye* (1995), *Tomorrow Never Dies* (1997), *Casino Royale* (2006), *Skyfall* (2012)

WHITAKER'S TREASURE TROVE

INTRODUCTION

Whitaker's Almanack has been published annually since 1868 and as such provides a valuable historical record. What follows is a selection of notable events, remarkable occurrences, quirky information and facts and figures from the *Whitaker's* archive. The information has been reproduced exactly as it was recorded at the time incorporating grammatical idiosyncrasies and archaic phrasing present in the original editions.

REMARKABLE OCCURRENCES

A selection of 'Remarkable Occurrences', later re-named 'Events of the Year', as recorded in editions of *Whitaker's Almanack* dating from the first edition in 1869.

Each month below details 'occurrences' or 'events' one decade on from the previous month.

JANUARY (1868)
From the 1869 edition

4. Slight shock of earthquake felt in the Vale of Parret and other parts of Somerset. **4–11.** General swearing-in of special constables throughout England, in consequence of the Fenian outrage at Clerkenwell. – Great eruption of Mount Vesuvius, with earthquakes, descent of lava, etc. **8.** Sudden and mysterious disappearance of the Rev. B. Speke, causing great sensation throughout the country. He was discovered alive and well in Cornwall shortly afterwards. **9.** Committal of Burke, Casey, and Shaw, to Warwick gaol for Fenianism, from the Bow Street police-office, London. **11.** Wreck of the screw steamer, "Chicago," on a reef of rocks near Cork harbour; all lives saved. **17,18.** Severe gales on all coasts of the United Kingdom, with many wrecks and great loss of life. **18.** Explosion of gunpowder at Newcastle-on-Tyne, with death of two men and injury to others – Attempted murder by Clancy, a Fenian, of two policemen, in Bedford Square. **18–25.** Heavy gales throughout the Kingdom, with much loss of life and property at sea and on land. Loss of nineteen fishing vessels, and fifty-two lives near the Burry river on the Welsh coast.

FEBRUARY (1878)
From the 1879 edition

5. Midhat Pacha is expelled from Turkey. – Railway riots in Quebec before the Parliament House by about 6,000 persons. **7.** Death of Pope Pius IX, at Rome. – A rumour of the entry of the Russians into Constantinople caused great excitement, and a special Cabinet Meeting was held in London. **8.** Opening of the Canadian Parliament by Lord Dufferin. **9.** Funeral of the celebrated caricaturist, George Cruikshank, at Kensal Green Cemetery. – Banquet given by the Royal Geographical Society to Mr. H.M. Stanley, the African explorer. – The terms of the Military Armistice between Russia and Turkey were made known. **13.** Russians take possession of Erzeroum. – The British Fleet anchored near to the Prince's Islands, in the Sea of Marmora. **14.** Entombment of Pope Pius IX took place at Rome in the Basilica. – The notorious Madame Rachel charged with fresh frauds in "beautifying" ladies. **15.** Opening of the Spanish Cortes by the King, with the Queen and his sisters. **16.** Announcement was made that negotiations had been completed between all the Powers for a Congress on the Eastern Question. The British Fleet withdrew to a position about 40 miles south of Constantinople. **20.** Election of the new Pope, Cardinal Pecci, as Leo XIII, by the Cardinals at the Vatican. **21.** The terms of the Treaty of Peace (San Stefano) between Russia and Turkey, in part published. The Russians threatened an ultimatum if the signatures were delayed by Turkey. **22.** Master of the Rolls shot at by a clergyman named Dodwell. **24.** Tumultuous meeting in Hyde Park on the Eastern Question. Mr. Gladstones' house in Harley Street was assailed. – Failure of Messrs. Willis, Percival & Co., London Bankers, for about £700,000.

MARCH (1888)
From the 1889 edition

1. M. Wilson, son-in-law of ex-President Grévy, sentenced to two years' imprisonment and other penalties for trafficking in decorations. – The Panama Canal shareholders resolved to issue bonds for 340,000,000 francs to complete the canal. **2.** The Upper House of Convocation discuss a memorial on "the desecration of the Sabbath by the upper classes". **5.** The Porte telegraphed to Prince Ferdinand that his presence in Bulgaria is illegal. **6.** Waterloo Cup won by Burnaby; Purse by Miss Glendyne; Plate by Winfarthing. **7.** The Prince of Wales held a levee on behalf of the Queen. **9.** Collision between the *City of Corinth* and the *Tasmania* off Dungeness, and wreck of the *Lanoma* in Portland Bay, with loss of 25 hands. **10.** The Prince and Princess of Wales celebrated their silver wedding. **12.** Lying-in-state of the German Emperor. – Fearful snowstorm in America, putting a stop to all business and traffic in New York. **15.** General Boulander's dismissal from the French army announced. – Bank rate reduced from 2½ to 2 per cent. – Marriage of Prince Oscar of Sweden to Miss Ebba Munck at Bournemouth. **16.** Funeral of William I of Germany. – Heavy snowstorms in Scotland and the north of England. **17.** Annual football match between England and Scotland won by England. **22.** A British expeditionary force captured the Thibetan post of Lingtn. **23.** The Grand National won by Playfair. **24.** The Queen arrived at Florence. – University boat-race won by Cambridge. – The Princess of Wales held a Drawing Room on behalf of the Queen. **27.** The *Nile*, the heaviest armoured ship yet built, launched at Pembroke Dockyard. **30.** Resignation of the ministry of M. Tirard, after an adverse vote in the French Chamber: succeeded by M. Floquet. – The Emperor Frederick and the Empress enthusiastically received in Berlin.

APRIL (1898)
From the 1899 edition

1. Special performance at the Royal Theatre in Madrid to raise a fund for increasing the Navy. **2.** The judgment in the Zola trial quashed on appeal. **4.** Great industrial disturbance caused by stoppage in the South Wales coal mines; nearly 100,000 men thrown out of work. **5.** The government of Natal offered the British naval authorities 12,000 tons of steam coal per annum at Durban. – Mr. Balfour stated in the House of Commons the Great Britain had obtained from China a lease of Wei-Hai-Wei, in order to restore the balance of power which had been disturbed by Russia's acquisition of Port Arthur. **8.** The Sirdar with his Anglo-Egyptian force, attacked the Khalifa's Emir Mahmoud, who was encamped on the banks of the Atbara River, within a zareeba, and utterly defeated the opposing forces, capturing their leader. **16.** The United States Senate continued a debate upon the report of their Foreign Relations Committee, and decided to reorganise the independence of the Republic of Cuba. **20.** President McKinley sent an ultimatum to the Madrid Government regarding the situation in Cuba, but before it reached its destination Senor Polo de Bernabe, the Minister at Washington, was instructed to ask for his passport. – Telegraphic communication established between Cape Town and Lantyre. **21.** The Madrid Government notified General Woodford, the United States Minister, that as they had withdrawn their own minister from Washington, diplomatic relations had been broken off. On learning this the United States Government dispatched a squadron from Key West for Havana. – The Rt. Honble. Cecil Rhodes was re-elected a director of the British South Africa Company. **24.** The Regular Army of the United States was increased to 61,000 men, and arrangements made for the enrolment of 125,000 volunteers. **25.** The Senate of the United States (to avoid the difficulties that had arisen owing to the fact that neither their own Government nor that of Spain had declared war) announced that a state of being at war with Spain had existed since April 21st. – Mr. Day became Secretary of State in succession to Mr. Sherman, who resigned in consequence of the work entailed by the outbreak of the war. **27.** The United States squadron, forced to leave Hong Kong owing to the declaration of the 25th, sailed for Manila, the capital of the Philippines. **29.** The House of Representatives at Washington passed a Bill for raising a War Revenue.

MAY (1908)
From the 1909 edition

1. Serious tram accident between Bournemouth and Christchurch; 7 killed and 10 injured. – The Kaiser and the principal German Sovereigns assembled at Vienna, and congratulated the Emperor Francis Joseph on the attainment of the 60th year of his reign. Congratulatory messages were sent from the whole of Europe. **6.** At the annual meeting of the National Art-Collections Fund Mr. Duveen had offered to provide a new wing to the Tate Gallery to house the Turner Collection. **9.** After a most strenuous contest Mr. Winston Churchill (L.) was elected Member for Dundee. **13.** A heavy thunderstorm raged over Lincolnshire; one of the pinnacles of the famous Boston "Stump" displaced by lightning. **14.** The Prince of Wales formally opened the Franco-British Exhibition, in the most deplorable weather. **15.** The Unionist candidate returned for Mid-Shropshire with an increased majority – The Court of Criminal Appeal sat for the first time. **16.** The Bishop of London presided at a large demonstration at the Albert Hall in favour of the Licensing Bill – A demonstration of the Hop and Allied Trades was held in Trafalgar Square, urging that steps should be taken to protect the English hop trade. **19.** A daring robbery took place at the Central Railway Station, Manchester, a package containing goods and securities to the value of £15,000 being removed from a guard's van by a woman who was subsequently arrested in Liverpool. – The Earl of Lytton presided at a representative meeting to support the movement to establish a national theatre as a memorial to Shakespeare. – First appearance for the season of Madame Melba in *La Bohème* at Covent Garden. **20.** In connection with the recent Poor Law Scandals in Mile End, seven of the Guardians were arrested. **26.** The King and the President of the French Republic visited the Franco-British Exhibition. In the evening a State Ball was given at Buckingham Palace. – The decision of the Winchester City Council to remove some railings round a Russian gun captures in the Crimean War and placed in a public position, led to such serious riots that the troops were called out. **28.** The Prince and Princess of Wales opened the new Public Library in Mare Street, Hackney. **30.** The International Balloon Race, starting from the Hurlingham Club, with 31 entries, resulted in four places out of the first five being gained by British competitors.

JUNE (1918)
From the 1919 edition

1. Great fire at Constantinople, covering a distance of over 2½ miles: more than 2,000 houses destroyed, about 20,000 people homeless. **3.** Explosion at Beausenq, France, munitions works: about 100 killed, 50 injured. **5.** The King in residence at the Royal Pavilion, Aldershot. **6.** Highly encouraging survey of the food position given by Mr. Clynes in the House of Commons. **7.** Speech by Mr. Lloyd George, in which he eulogized the unsurpassed sacrifices of the British peoples and their Allies. **9.** Boating accident, with loss of 17 lives, in Ulverton Channel, off Peel Island, Barrow-in-Furness. **10.** 400 people killed by an explosion of a munitions depôt at Jassy. **12.** Statue of John de Witt unveiled in the Hague with State ceremonial. **13.** In the House of Commons Mr. Bonar Law was closely questioned as to the present position of German banks in this country. – Bill for the damming of the Zuyder Zee finally passed by the Dutch States-General. **14.** Bernard A. Kupferburg sentenced at the Old Bailey to 3 years' penal servitude for aiding and abetting Samuel Reardon (sentenced to 18 months' hard labour) wrongfully to apply Government marks to war material with intent to deceive. **15.** Decision of the War Cabinet announced to set up a Committee of Ministers of Home Affairs. – British Colony at Shanghai during "Tank Week" subscribed £429,655. **17.** 34,879 pensions and 3,013 gratuities awarded in Canada during the war. **19.** Debates in both Houses of Parliament on Cabinet control. **20.** Maj.-Gen. the Maharajah of Patiala received in audience by His Majesty, who invested him with the G.B.E. – Mr. Griffith, Sinn Fein, elected M.P. for East Cavan by majority of 1,214 votes over Mr. O'Hanlon, official Nationalist. – Maj.-Gen. Sir E. Northey, K.C.M.G., C.B., appointed Governor and Commander-in-Chief of the East African Protectorate, and H.M. High Commissioner for Zanzibar. **21.** Government announced the abandonment, for the present, of Home Rule and conscription for Ireland. **22.** Redistribution of Departments at the Ministry of Munitions. – Disastrous railway collision near Hammond, Indiana: 59 killed, 115 injured. **24.** First Canadian aerial mail started: special bag carried from Montreal to Toronto. – Capt. Amunsden left Christiania on a N. Polar expedition in the *Maud*. **29.** Peerage conferred on Col. Sir A.H. Lee, K.C.B., M.P. (the donor of the Chequers Estate to the Nation), in recognition of his public services as Director-General of Food Production, 1917–18.

JULY (1928)
From the 1929 edition

2. Royal Assent given to bill enfranchising women on the same terms as men. **5.** Car dashed into hawser by which tractor was hauling timber near Oxford and three occupants were killed. **6.** International Liberal Conference opened in London. – At Gloucester Assizes, Mrs. Beatrice Annie Pace was found not guilty on charge of murdering her husband by administering arsenic, and she was discharged amid remarkable demonstrations of enthusiasm. **7.** Liner *Carmarthenshire* caught fire in the Thames outward bound for China and was beached, passengers being landed. **9.** Electric train collided with light engine outside London Bridge station, one man being killed and several persons injured. **11.** French Cabinet expressed approval with the anti-war pact. **12.** Germany accepted Mr. Kellogg's anti-war pact. **13.** Both majority and minority reports of the tribunal set up to investigate police interrogation of a woman at Scotland Yard urged change in the system. – Labour candidate won the ex-Speaker's seat at Halifax in a triangular fight. – Three young men were sentenced to death at Sussex Assizes for murder of a Brighton man. They appealed unsuccessfully, but were reprieved on eve of day fixed for execution, their sentences being commuted to penal servitude for life. **17.** King inspected new Australian cruisers at Portsmouth, and the reconditioned *Victory*. **18.** Britain's reply accepting the anti-war pact proposed by United States presented. Australia, New Zealand, South Africa, and India all accepted. **19.** Prince of Wales carried out number of engagements at Grimsby, flying there and back. **23.** Queen consulted oculist regarding eye strain – Industrial Transference Board published report declaring that 200,000 miners might not again find employment in coalfields. **25.** King received Sultan of Muscat and Oman. – Indian States Committee, in London, heard case for group of India's ruling Princes for more satisfactory political relationships between their States and Indian Government. **26.** Their Majesties gave garden party at Buckingham Palace. **29.** Light engine and excursion train collided at Ardwick, Manchester, a guard being killed and 22 passengers injured – The Olympic Games were inaugurated at Amsterdam.

AUGUST (1938)
From the 1939 edition

2. The King left the royal yacht and spent a day at his boys' camp at Southwold. **3.** Lord Runiciman arrived in Prague. **4.** Their Majesties and the Princesses disembarked at Aberdeen and motored to Balmoral. – Lord Runiciman met President Benes [of Czechoslovakia] and the Premier and saw representatives of the Sudeten-German Party. **5–7.** Britain's air exercises to test coast defences began. As they ended two bombers crashed, 6 men being killed. **6.** Mr. Malcolm MacDonald arrived in Palestine by air and discussed situation with High Commissioner and Commander of British troops before walking unrecognised through Jerusalem. **7.** Lowerstoft trawler *Aleazar* sank in Irish Sea after collision in thick fog with a cross-Channel steamer, 7 lives being lost. **9.** Prime Minister returned to London to receive treatment for nasal catarrh. – Spanish troops began offensive near Lerida and crossed River Segree. **11.** German monoplane flew 3,942 miles non-stop from Berlin to New York in 25 hours. **14.** The German monoplane arrived back in Berlin after flight of 19 hrs 59 mins. **15.** Spanish Government and General Franco agreed to appointment of British Commission to assist in exchange of prisoners. **17.** Sudetan-Germans, at conference with Czech Ministers, rejected Government's proposals for equality for all citizens, elections on principle of proportionality, and civil servants and schools according to race percentage. **20.** The Duke and Duchess of Gloucester arrived at Nakuru, Kenya, to begin their holiday. **25.** Japanese troops captured Juichang, China. **26.** Grave tension in Jaffa after several serious incidents. In 3 weeks, 174 people were killed or died of wounds and 183 wounded. **27.** After carrying out full-load trials at Hatfield, one of the monoplanes built for Transatlantic service broke its back – Sir John Simon, speaking at Lanark, repeated Mr. Chamberlain's former declaration that it would be a mistake to assume that in event of trouble in

Czechoslovakia Britain would necessarily remain outside. **30.** Berlin Ambassador attended special meeting of British Cabinet which expressed entire agreement with action taken and policy to be pursued [in Czechoslovakia]. Herr Hitler sent for Herr Henlein to discuss position. Dr. Benes explained new proposals for cantonal autonomy to Sudetan-Germans.

SEPTEMBER (1948)
From the 1949 edition

2. Vickers Viscount, four-engined jet-propelled air liner, gave satisfactory demonstration flight. **3.** Dr. Benes, former President of Czechoslovakia died. **4.** Queen Wilhelmina abdicated and became Princesss of the Netherlands, and huge crowds at Amsterdam acclaimed the new Queen Juliana. **5.** Princess Margaret flew to Amsterdam to represent King and Queen at inauguration of Queen Juliana. – New air liner Hermes IV flew for first time and performed perfectly. **6.** Avro Tudor VIII, first all jet-propelled four-engined civil transport aircraft, made its initial test flight. – Berlin Assembly met in British sector. **7.** Indian Premier announced Government had asked Nizam of Hyderabad to disband volunteer force immediately and facilitate return of Indian troops to Secunderabad to restore law and order in the State. **8.** Mr. Attlee announced to be suffering from an early duodenal ulcer which would require dietetic treatment for some weeks. – All political meetings in British sector adjoining Soviet sector in Berlin were banned. **9.** King and Queen attended Braemar Gathering. Princess Margaret returned from Netherlands and flew to Balmoral. – Great crowd attended anti-Communist demonstrations at junction of British and Soviet sectors in Berlin: red flag on top of Brandenburg Gate was torn down and shots were fired into British sector, one person being killed. **10.** British residents in Hyderabad were evacuated by air. **13.** Indian troops invaded Hydarabad on Nizam's refusal to disband volunteer force and severe fighting took place. State of emergency declared throughout India to deal with possible internal disturbances. **17.** Count Bernadotte and United Nations official were shot dead while driving through Jewish area of Jerusalem, assassin being presumed to be member of Stern Gang. **18.** Hyderabad Army formally surrendered and Indian troops entered Secunderabab. **30.** Leader of Stern Gang was arrested in Haifa.

OCTOBER (1958)
From the 1960 edition

1. At Labour Party conference at Scarborough, Mrs. B.A. Castle was elected chairman of party for ensuing year. – British plan for Cyprus officially took effect. Greek Cypriots staged strike throughout island. – Soviet Government sent notes to U.K and U.S.A agreeing to talks on suspension of nuclear tests at Geneva on Oct. 31 and proposing that they should be at foreign ministers' level. **3.** Archbishop

Makarios sent message to Greet Cypriots urging them to react "vigorously" against implementation of British plan. **4.** Comet jet passenger service across Atlantic began. **6.** The Pope was stated to be gravely ill after a stroke. **9.** After suffering a second stroke on previous day Pope Pius XII died in early hours of the morning. **11.** Rocket aimed at moon was successfully launched from Cape Canaveral, but slight error in aiming angle prevented it from reaching its destination and on following day it was believed to have re-entered earth's atmosphere and burnt out over Pacific. **16.** The Queen and the Duke of Edinburgh left Balmoral after their holiday and travelled to Carlisle, which Her Majesty had been prevented from visiting due to her illness in July. – Russian trawler drifted on rocks in Shetlands and sank with loss of more than 20 men. The skipper and two seamen were rescued by Lerwick lifeboat and later handed back to Soviet authorities. **23.** Mr. Krushchev said that Soviet Government was granting credit of £33,000,000 to United Arab Republic towards building of Aswan dam. **30.** Mr. Boris Pasternak, who had been awarded Nobel Prize for literature, declined to receive it after he had been expelled from Writers' Union and criticised in Soviet press. **28.** The Queen opened new session of Parliament, the ceremony being broadcast and televised for the first time. — Cardinal Angelo Giuseppe Roncalli, Patriarch of Venice, was elected Pope, taking title of John XXIII.

NOVEMBER (1968)
From the 1970 edition

3. Many people lost their lives when dam burst at Vallemosso in northern Italy during severe flooding. **7.** In Presidential election, Mr. Nixon narrowly defeated Vice-President Mr. Humphrey; final results showed that Mr. Nixon won 31,770,237 (43.4 per cent) of the popular votes to Mr. Humphrey's 31,270,533 (42.7 per cent). – Thousands of armed policed, backed by troops, quelled anti-Russian march by 3,000 young people in Prague. **8.** Bruce Reynolds, sought for more than five years by police investigating the Great Train Robbery of 1963, was arrested in Torquay; he was remanded in custody. **10.** Her Majesty watched Lent carnival in grounds of residence of British Ambassador. **18.** New York teachers voted to end their strike which had closed most of the city's schools for five weeks. – About 60,000 students throughout Bohemia and Moravia began three-day strike to demonstrate their opposition to the way in which reform policies by Dubcek regime were being slowly eroded under pressure from Russians and conservative forces within Czechoslovak leadership. **19.** Chancellor of the Exchequer flew to Bonn to attend emergency discussions on international monetary crisis. – The French Prime Minister announced spending economies after continued speculation against franc in favour of German Mark. – West Germany decided not to revalue Deutsche Mark, but to take immediate tax measures in import and export sectors aimed at stabilizing internal prices and warding off foreign pressure to revalue. **22.** On his return from Bonn Mr. Jenkins announced new deflationary measures; details of severe curbs in bank lending to private sector were also given. **24.** Despite international monetary crisis, France decided not to devalue franc. **26.** It was reported that U.S. and South Vietnam troops had entered demilitarized zone and fought battle with Vietcong there for the first time since bombing halt on Nov. 1. **28.** John Lennon, of the Beatles pop group, was fined £160 at Marylebone Magistrates' Court for unauthorized possession of drug cannabis. **30.** A rocket, carrying Europe's first space satellite, was successfully launched from the Woomera Range in Australia.

DECEMBER (1978)

From the 1980 edition

6. The Prime Minister told the Commons that Britain would not join the European Monetary System but that the U.K. would be free to join the exchange rate mechanism at a later date if it wished, or to remain outside it, but Mrs. Thatcher said that it was a sad day for Europe that nine member countries had been unable to agree a major new initiative. **10.** The confidential draft of Labour's election manifesto "Keep Britain Labour" was leaked to the Communist *Morning Star* newspaper. **12.** Bakers' Union leaders decided to recommend a full return to work from Dec. 17 after branches voted by a narrow margin to call off the five-week-old bread strike and accept the 14.4 per cent pay offer from the Bakers' Federation. **13.** Thousands of peak-hour commuters experienced long delays in the Midlands when signalmen operating three power boxes controlling the network came out on unofficial strike in support of signals and telecommunications men who were suspended without pay after their refusal to accept a new pay and grading system. **19–26.** Mrs. Gandhi was taken to Tibar jail, New Delhi, after the Lower House of Parliament, the Lok Sabha, voted to expel her and send her to prison for breach of privilege and contempt of the House, the sentence lasting until the present parliamentary session ended; On Dec. 21 it was reported that 12 people had been killed and more than 30,000 arrested in several states across India as party supporters demonstrated against the jailing of Mrs. Gandhi and her expulsion from Parliament; Mrs. Gandhi was released on Dec. 26 after a week in jail. **21.** The Queen received a loyal address from the Isle of Man to mark the millennium of Tynwald. **25.** The Queen's Christmas broadcast to Britain and the Commonwealth on BBC 1 and Independent TV departed from its traditional format and was one of her longest Christmas messages, lasting 20 minutes.

NOTABLE HISTORICAL EVENTS

The Sinking of RMS *Titanic*
As recorded in the 1913 edition
Events of 1911–1912: Accidents and Disasters at Sea

(1912) Apr 14. On her maiden voyage to New York the White Star liner *Titanic* (45,000 tons) collided with an iceberg, and sank a few hours later. Wireless distress signals were sent out, but the vessels that picked up the messages arrived too late to render assistance. Of the 2,206 persons on board the liner, 703 escaped in boats and some hours later were picked up by the *Carpathia*, the number of victims reaching the appalling total of 1,503. Among the latter were Mr. W. T. Stead and Mr. C. M. Hays President of the Grand Trunk Railway. The unparalleled disaster was marked by an absence of panic and a maintenance of discipline. World-wide sympathy was expressed and many relief funds were opened for those who had suffered.

The Outbreak of the First World War
As recorded in the 1915 edition
Diary of the European War

The European Conflagration broke out towards the end of **July [1914]**, and by the beginning of August practically the whole of the Continent was under arms, if not actually engaged in warfare. Up to the last moment hopes were entertained that the dispute between Austria-Hungary and Serbia might be localised, or even settled without recourse to hostilities, but the Dual Monarchy's hand was forced by Germany's declaration of war upon Russia. It speedily became clear, indeed, that the German plans of campaign and the completeness of the vast military organisation had been the deliberate work of years. The first step leading to the outbreak was the presentation, on **July 23**, of Austria-Hungary's ultimatum to Serbia. The latter's reply within the stipulated 48 hours was considered unsatisfactory.

On **July 27** Sir E. Grey announced his proposals for a conference of Germany, France, Italy and Great Britain, and their acceptance by France and Italy; but on the following day Austria-Hungary declared war on Serbia and commenced operations, and on **July 30** there was a partial mobilisation of the Russian Army, followed on the next day by a general mobilisation. War was declared upon Russia by Germany on **Aug. 1**, and on the 2nd French territory was entered at Ciréy by German troops, while Russian forces crossed the German frontier. On **Aug. 3** the British Fleet was mobilised, and Germany sent an ultimatum to Belgium, which led to the British ultimatum to Germany on **Aug. 4**, on which day, at 11pm, war was declared between Great Britain and Germany. On **Aug.10** France declared war upon Austria-Hungary, and Great Britain made a similar declaration two days later.

The End of the First World War: Armistice Declared
As recorded in the 1919 edition
Diary of the War

(1918) **Nov. 9.** Mr. Lloyd George, at the Lord Mayor's banquet, announced the abdication of the Kaiser, and said "Germany's doom was sealed." Flight of the Kaiser to Holland. **10.** French captured Hirson, surrounded Mézières and crossed the Meuse: few German troops remaining on French soil. US troops pushed forward towards Montmédy and the Briery basin. Death of Herr Ballin, Director of the Hamburg-Amerika Line. **11.** Mons entered at dawn by Canadians. Armistice signed by German plenipotentiaries. **11am** firing ceased on all fronts. Allies' terms including the giving up of 6 battle-cruisers, 10 battleships, 8 light cruisers, 50 destroyers and all submarines, specified number of military guns etc immediate evacuation of all invaded countries, release of British prisoners, and the occupation by Allies of the left bank of the Rhine. Messages of congratulation and appreciation sent by the King to the Navy, Army, and Air Force. Scenes of great rejoicing in London and the provinces.

Great War Casualties, 1914–1919
As recorded in the 1940 edition

British Empire		
Total Number Mobilized, 8,904,000		
	Deaths	Wounded
Gt. Britain and Ireland	812,317	1,849,494
Canada	62,817	166,105
Australia	60,456	154,722
New Zealand	18,212	45,946
South Africa	9,032	17,843
Newfoundland	1,609	3,628
Colonies	52,044	78,535
India	73,432	84,715
Total, British Empire	**1,089,919**	**2,400,988**

Allied and Associated Countries			
	Mobilized	Deaths	Wounded
France	8,410,000	1,393,388	1,490,000
Belgium	267,000	38,172	44,686
Italy	5,615,000	460,000	947,000
Portugal	100,000	7,222	13,751
Roumania	750,000	335,706	No record
Serbia	707,000	127,535	133,148
U.S.A.	4,355,000	115,660	205,690
Enemy Countries			
Germany	11,000,000	2,050,466	4,202,028
Austria and Hungary	7,800,000	1,200,000	3,620,000
Bulgaria	1,200,000	101,224	152,400
Turkey	2,850,006	300,000	570,000

OFFICIAL END OF THE WAR

The *Official Termination of the War*, when Treaties of Peace had been ratified by the respective Governments, was **Aug. 31, 1921**. The Ottoman Empire was excluded from the Order in Council, and war with Turkey was declared at an end on Aug. 6, 1924.

The Outbreak of the Second World War

As recorded in the 1940 edition
The War Against Aggression: The First Phase

(1939) Sept. 1. At dawn German troops began invasion of Poland on all fronts – without either ultimatum or declaration. German planes raided many Polish cities and towns, including Warsaw and claimed to have gained upper hand. Few hours after military action began, Polish Ambassador called on Lord Halifax and formally invoked Anglo-Polish Treaty asking for Britain's assistance against aggression. Polish President called the whole nation to arms. British and French Ambassadors in Berlin presented document to German Government warning Germany that unless aggressive action were suspended and all German forces withdrawn from Polish Territory, Britain and France would go to the aid of Poland. Hitler told Signor Mussolini that he would not need military aid from Italy but thanked him for diplomatic and political aid he had given. In declaration to Reichstag, Hitler said that his proposals were rejected and denied that there had been undue pressure.

Herr Förster decreed Danzig part of the Reich. Mr. Chamberlain in Commons outlined Britain's efforts for peace and was supported by all parties. House voted sum not exceeding £500,000,000 for Defence of Realm and prosecution of war. Labour Party in manifesto gave Government's decision full support. State took control of railways. France announced general mobilisation and proclaimed martial law. Italian Council of Ministers announced that Italy would take no initiative in military operations. Britain and France sent favourable replies to President Roosevelt's appeal not to bomb civilians and unfortified cities. Evacuation of children, mothers, blind and disabled from danger zones in Britain began, over 1,000,000 being moved without mishap. **2.** German troops advanced further and made further raids on open towns. **3.** Britain became at war with Germany at **11.15am**. Mr. Chamberlain announced the news in broadcast to the nation. Germany, he said, had given no undertaking to withdraw her troops from Poland by stipulated time and consequently we were at war. France entered the struggle at **5pm**, the time she had fixed. General Viscount Gort appointed Commander-in-Chief of British Field Forces, General Sir Edmund Ironside Chief of Imperial General Staff and General Sir Walter Kirke Commander-in-Chief of the Home Forces. War Cabinet formed and held first meeting. It consisted of Mr. Chamberlain, Sir John Simon, Lord Halifax, Lord Chatfield, Mr. Churchill (new First Lord of the Admiralty), Mr. Hore-Belisha, Sir Kingsley Wood, Sir Samuel Hoare (now Lord Privy Seal) and Lord Hankey (Minister without portfolio). Mr. Eden was appointed Dominions Secretary; Lord Stanhope, Lord President; Sir Thomas Inskip, Lord Chancellor and Sir John Anderson, Home Secretary and Minister of Home Security. Labour and Liberal Parties were invited to accept offices but declined although giving wide co-operation. The King broadcast to the nation, asking the people to stand calm and firm and united.

The End of the Second World War

As recorded in the 1946 edition
Chronicle of the War 1939–45

ALL GERMANY SURRENDERS UNCONDITIONALLY
(1945) May 7. New German Foreign Minister broadcast to German people announcing the unconditional surrender of all German fighting troops. Surrender was signed at **2.41am** in school-room at Rheims serving as General Eisenhower's Headquarters, by General Jodl, German Chief of Staff, in presence of General Bedell Smith, Allied Chief of Staff and other Allied officers. German emissaries were afterwards presented to General Eisenhower and Air Chief Marshal Tedder, whom they assured that they were ready to carry out the terms. German forces in Norway capitulated. Admiral Dönitz ordered U-boats to cease hostilities and return to port. British armoured cars arrived in Copenhagen to join airborne troops flown in.

Field Marshal Montgomery met Marshal Rokossovsky at Wismar. Eighth Army crossed Italian frontier into Austria north of Udine. Garrison at Breslau ceased resistance and surrendered. Fighting still going on in Prague, where populace revolted against Germans. Victory in Europe [VE] celebrated in all Allied capitals.

VE DAY

(1945) May 8. Mr. Churchill broadcast end of hostilities one minute after midnight, although "Cease Fire" had been sounded already all along the front. Agreement signed at Rheims was ratified and confirmed at Berlin, being signed by Air Chief Marshal Tedder, Marshal Zhukov, and General de Lattré de Tassigny for the Allies and by Keitel for the German forces. Huge crowds rejoiced in London, where King and Queen and the Princesses appeared on the balcony of Buckingham Palace several times, once with Mr. Churchill, and were enthusiastically cheered. Prime Minister spoke to great assembly in Whitehall, with his Cabinet standing by his side.

THE ATOMIC BOMB

(1945) Aug. 5. The first atomic bomb dropped by United States aircraft on Hiroshima, important Japanese base on Honshu. President Truman, from cruiser *Augusta* in Mid-Atlantic, announced that British and American scientists had "harnessed the basic power of the universe" and that the bomb had explosive power equal to 20,000 tons of T.N.T. and more than 2,000 times the blast power of largest bomb previously used. Impenetrable cloud of dust and smoke covered target area. **8.** Soviet Foreign Minister announced that the Allies had requested Russia to join in war against Japan and that Russia had agreed. Official photographs of Hiroshima showed that 4 square miles of the city were completely destroyed by one atomic bomb. **9.** Second and more powerful atomic bomb dropped on Nagasaki with devastating results.

JAPAN SURRENDER

(1945) Aug. 14. Broadcasting at midnight, Mr. Attlee announced that Japan had surrendered and that the Emperor had agreed to authorize and ensure signature of necessary terms for carrying out provisions of Potsdam declaration and to order cessation of active operations. President Truman made similar announcement and said General MacArthur had been appointed Supreme Allied Commander to receive the surrender.

The Death of King George VI and the Accession of Queen Elizabeth II

As recorded in the 1953 edition
Home Affairs: The Royal House

SUDDEN DEATH OF THE KING

(1952) Feb. 6. The world was shocked to learn that King George VI, who had retired to rest in his usual health, passed peacefully away in his sleep at Sandringham. It was afterwards learned that cause of death was coronary thrombosis. The Queen and Princess Margaret were at Sandringham, and sad news was broken to the new Queen by Duke of Edinburgh in Kenya. Accession Council signed proclamation of Queen Elizabeth II. Messages of condolence were received from every part of the Commonwealth and in almost every country in the world warm tributes were paid.

QUEEN ELIZABETH II FLIES HOME

(1952) Feb. 6. The new sovereign, Queen Elizabeth II, was resting in her hunting lodge in Kenya when the Duke of Edinburgh broke to her the news of the death of King George. Her Majesty and the Duke drove to airfield at Nanyuki from where they flew to Entebbe, Uganda. There they took off for El Adem, Libya, after being delayed by sudden electrical storm. **7.** Queen Elizabeth and her husband arrived at London Airport after flying from El Adem. Duke of Gloucester welcomed Her Majesty, and when she alighted she was greeted by Mr. Churchill, Mr. Attlee, and leading Privy Councillors. The Queen drove to Clarence House where Queen Mary awaited her. **8.** At her first Privy Council Her Majesty made her Accession Declaration, in which she expressed her resolve to follow her father's shining example of service and devotion. The accession was proclaimed with picturesque ceremonial throughout Britain and the Commonwealth.

The Queen's Coronation

As recorded in the 1954 edition
Home Affairs: The Royal House

QUEEN ELIZABETH IS CROWNED

(1953) June 2. With traditional ceremony and a religious symbolism that stirred millions of people throughout the world, Queen Elizabeth II was crowned in Westminster Abbey, receiving the acclaim of hundreds of thousands of her subjects as, with the Duke of Edinburgh, she made her royal progress through the capital before and after the impressive service. Great throngs lined the decorated streets but even larger multitudes, in their homes and in places of assembly, saw by means of television or heard by wireless, all but the most sacred and personal portions of the ceremony. In the Abbey the Queen, with superb grace and dignity, made the ancient promises to govern well, and confirmed those promises with solemn oath, and after the anointing beneath canopy of cloth of gold and the presentation of the regalia the Archbishop of Canterbury placed the Crown upon her head to the cry from all over the Abbey of "God Save the Queen" and the sound of fanfares. Her Majesty then ascended the throne and the peers, led by Her Majesty's own consort, swore the oath of homage, after which the whole congregation acclaimed their sovereign. The Coronation was completed and shortly afterwards the Queen, the central figure of a colourful procession, left the Abbey to meet again her people, waiting patiently in showers of rain, to show their affection. All the members of the Royal Family were present, including for a time, which covered the actual crowning, the young Duke of Cornwall, in the care of the Queen Mother and Princess Margaret. The Prime Ministers of the Commonwealth, with Sir Winston Churchill at their head, were also there, as were representatives of all the nations. A great roar of cheering met the Queen when, with her husband and wearing her crown, she set out in the golden coach on the longer return journey to the Palace, and the enthusiasm continued throughout the slow progress home. Afterwards the vast concourse near the Mall flocked to the front of the forecourt and presently Her Majesty, her husband and children and all the members of the Royal Family came to the balcony to watch the brilliantly executed fly-past of the Royal Air Force in honour of their sovereign. Other balcony appearances followed and in the evening Her Majesty broadcast to the Commonwealth and Europe and declared that her abiding memory of the day would be not only the solemnity and beauty of the ceremony but the inspiration of the loyalty and affection of her people. At dusk she pressed switch which turned on illuminations and searchlights and was signal for lighting of bonfires and celebrations all over the United Kingdom.

Man's First Landing on the Moon
As recorded in the 1970 edition
Science, Discovery and Invention in 1969

With the words "That's one small step for a man, one giant leap for mankind," American astronaut Neil Armstrong realized an age-old dream of humanity when he took the first step on the surface of the Moon at 3.56am. B.S.T. on Monday, July 21, 1969. America's £10,000,000,000 programme for landing a man on the Moon in this current decade had come to success sooner than many would have believed even a short year before. Perhaps the words uttered by Armstrong were a little uncharacteristic of the more laconic comments he made during the nine days in which the world's gaze was fixed, *via* television, on *Apollo 11* and its historic journey. But they did elicit an immediate response from the millions watching the strange shadowy scene as the American foot in the heavy boot of the spaceman's outfit lowered hesitantly to the lunar surface. Armstrong, with his colleagues, Col. Michael Collins and Col. Edwin (Buzz) Aldrin, took off from Cape Kennedy in their spacecraft at the head of a 7,500,000 lbs. thrust Saturn V rocket on July 16. Two and a half days later they had crossed the point at which the Moon's gravitational pull becomes dominant over that of the Earth and four hours after that they were behind the Moon, going into orbit about it. On Sunday, July 20, Armstrong and Aldrin entered the lunar landing module, code-named *Eagle,* leaving Collins behind in the command ship, *Columbia,* and descended for the first manned landing on the Moon. Using the landing craft's rocket motors they delicately picked their way between craters, avoiding the sport originally chosen because at the last moment its unsuitability became apparent, to drop the last few feet to a level spot in the Sea of Tranquillity. With everything going faultlessly the programme was speeded up for Armstrong to become the first man to set foot on an extra-terrestrial body just over five hours after the landing. He was followed by Aldrin and together they planted the U.S. flag in the dusty surface, collected rock samples and set up scientific experiments. Armstrong spent 2 hours 32 minutes on the lunar surface, Aldrin 1 hour and 43 minutes, before returning to *Eagle* which took off after a stay of 21 hours and 37 minutes. Just under four hours later they had joined up with Collins 69 miles above the Moon's surface ready for the return to Earth. In the official film of the expedition one thing more than any, even more than the footprints in the lunar dust, brought home the immensity of the achievement. That was the view of the cratered and scared surface of the Moon, taken by Collins in the command ship, with the appearance to one side, of a minute pinpoint of light. That light was the Sun reflecting off the ascent stage of *Eagle* as it soared towards the rendezvous in space. That speck grew, the light changed as rocket engines fired and then the module came fully into view, with the sun glinting in innumerable reflections on its insect-like body, a strange man-made object against the stranger lunar background.

Despite forebodings that the operation was directed more towards achieving prestigious ends than scientific ones, as a piece of space one-up-man-ship over the Russians, it appeared afterwards that the scientific rewards of the mission would be considerable. Preliminary examination of the rocks and the first reports of the scientific experiments left behind gave a picture of the Moon and its history entirely different from that of the Earth. The findings were not at all clear but they indicated a present-day Moon uniformly cool throughout, unlike the Earth with its distinct layers of cool crust, warm underlying mantle and molten core. Taking together the findings suggested, said NASA: "The Moon may be like a great shattered brittle ball beneath its crust, fractured into huge rock blocks with fissures and cracks penetrating deep down into the interior; the Mascons, the concentrations of mass which make the Moon exert an uneven gravitational pull on orbiting spacecraft, are probably the Moon's maria themselves, rather than some unseen feature beneath them; lunar dust is fully 50 per cent glass in tiny rods and globe shaped particles." The surprisingly abundant glass, the high store of radioactivity in the lunar samples brought back, the high density of the rocks compared to the rest of the lunar surface and the age of the Moon's surface, at least 3,100 million years, all indicated a lunar history surprisingly different from that of Earth.

BRITISH HOLIDAY AND HEALTH RESORTS

The following is a selection of holiday destination recommendations from editions of *Whitaker's Almanack* dating from 1905 to 1930. The date given in parenthesis specifies the edition the extract was taken from.

Introduction 1905 edition

Everybody, however good his constitution, needs more than ever in these wear-and-tear times to periodically renew his health-springs by a holiday amidst fresh scenes and congenial surroundings.

The sick and the fragile frequently restore their impaired health or lengthen their lives in some cheerful haven enriched by Nature with genial climatic advantages, supplemented by public or private enterprise with modern conveniences and amusements.

The choice of a suitable resort for pleasure or health, recreation or repose, is often difficult; there are so many places to select from in England, Scotland, Ireland and Wales whose claims are as evenly balanced as their attractions are diversified.

Cheap railway fares, steamboats, motor cars, and bicycles have all contributed to largely extend the area within reach of every holidaymaker from which to choose a fresh source of interest.

Individual tastes and temperaments greatly vary, but the love of change is universal; its gratification is Nature's best tonic for mind and body, beneficial to those tired of their toil and to others no less weary of monotony.

Some local authorities are keenly alive to the benefits derived from making widely known the advantages of their respective resorts; others are slowly awakening to the necessity of either following the example of their progressive competitors or falling behind in importance.

To enable an opinion to be formed with as little trouble as possible regarding the resorts which have furnished authentic particulars for this article, a uniform method of presenting the chief characteristics of each place has been adopted.

'How to get there' nowadays, when once 'where to go' has been settled, is a simple matter.

All the railways concerned foster their growing holiday traffic with special fares, travelling conveniences, and shorter journeys. On this occasion space only permitted outlining the systems of the largest lines, which, with their connections, render accessible from the Metropolis the most distant resorts within the British Isles.

The excellent arrangements now made by all the lines to facilitate travelling will do much to stimulate the British public, 'in spite of all temptations to visit other nations,' to first become acquainted with the natural beauty spots throughout their own native country – near-at-hand shrines towards which tourists from every quarter of the globe turn in ever-increasing numbers with ever-increasing zest.

BARRY (1906), Glamorgan. Urban District Council. Pop. 28,000, *Means of access:* Barry Railway (from London, G. W. Ry.). *Location:* 8m. from Cardiff. At the end of a peninsula formed by the curve in the Bristol Channel, surrounded by sea to the west, the south, and the east. *Drainage:* Excellent. *Water Supply:* Constant. *Bathing:* Safe, with fine stretch of sand. *Excursions:* Fine steamers ply daily to Weston-super-Mare, Lynmouth, Minehead, and Ilfracombe. Golf, cricket, and boating.

BATH (1905), Somersetshire. County Borough. Episcopal city. Pop. 49,817. *Means of Access:* 107m. from Paddington, G.W. Ry.; also western main line, Midland Ry. *Location:* 11m. from Bristol, on N. bank of River Avon. *Elevation:* 60 to 550 feet above sea-level. *Neighbourhood:* Woodland, hills, and diversified country. *Climate:* Mild, equable, varies according to elevation and aspect. *Sunshine:* 1,391 hrs., 1903. *Water Supply:* Constant. *Drainage:* Modern. *Soil:* Oolithic limestones, clays and sands. *Baths:* Luxuriously appointed, with every scientific application known to modern balneology. *Mineral waters:* Thermal springs, *Season:* Spring and autumn periods greatest activity.

Bath, situated in a valley and at various levels on slopes of surrounding hills, occupies leading position as fashionable inland watering-place, possessing an unrivalled combination of archaeological, historical, social, and scenic attractions, besides the famous waters to which it owes its origin; their healing virtues tried in 1903 by 100,000 bathers. It was a bathing establishment at the time of the Romans; the wonderfully preserved remains of the city's ancient splendour constitute a unique collection of universal interest. It is now a comfortable residential city, with excellent educational facilities and railway communications. Corporation own hot and cold springs, baths and grand pump-room (a well-organised centre for musical entertainments), and maintain a city band. Theatre Royal, Assembly Rooms (concerts and balls), Art Gallery, Royal Literary and Scientific Institution (library, reading-room, geological museum), abbey church and various old buildings. Royal Victoria Park (50 acres, 1¼m. carriage drive, promenades, lawns, and plantations), Sidney Gardens (band performances, flower shows), recreation ground (county cricket, football, cycling), golf (18 holes; ladies 9 holes – separate clubs), hunting, archery, tennis, boating, angling.

BEDFORD (1923), County Borough. Pop. 39,183. 50 miles from London. Midland and L. & N.W. Railways. A noted educational centre on the banks of the Great Ouse, with charming riverside promenade. Golf Links (18 holes).

BOURNEMOUTH (1905), Hants. County Borough. Pop. 66,000. *Means of access:* L. & S.W. Ry. (107½m. from London) and Midland Ry. *Location:* Extreme S.W. coast of Hants, in sheltered bight between Poole Harbour and Christchurch. *Neighbourhood:* Cliffs, pine-woods, valleys, luxurious growth of trees and shrubs. *Aspect:* South. *Climate:* Mild, equable temperature. *Sunshine:* 1,696 hrs, 1903. *Water Supply:* Constant. *Drainage:* Modern. *Soil:* Sand and gravel. *Front:* High cliffs, covered foliage, intersected rustic paths, broken by deep chines. *Piers:* Bournemouth, 1,238ft., bandstand refreshment kiosk; Boscombe, 600ft. *Beach:* Sandy, no currents, double tides render bathing always practicable. *Bathing:* Mixed. *Baths:* Swimming baths, Turkish and electric at Hydros. *Excursions:* New Forest, 15m.; Corfe Castle, 18m.; Wimborne, 9m.; Christchurch Priory, 4m.; Salisbury, 31m.; Stonehenge, 38m. *Season:* Winter. *Annual Fixtures:* Regatta, cricket week, horse show, tennis, golf, and croquet tournament.

Widely-spread town built within recent years on a heath covered with pines, which surround and permeate the locality, contributing to this fashionable town's position as a health resort, aromatic exhalations from pines benefiting pulmonary complaints. East Cliff (oldest residential quarter) separated from West Cliff (newest portion, more elevated) by River Bourne. Town extended more inland through valley than along coast. Valley affords maximum protection from wind, laid out 2 miles as public pleasure gardens, stream running through. Here Invalids' Walk, sheltered quiet, sunny promenade.

Municipal bands, 2 theatres, winter gardens (vocal and instrumental concerts), Shaftesbury Hall (entertainments, lectures, concerts, gymnasium), art gallery, museum, free library, science, art and technical school, drill hall, 3 arcades, coaching, hunting, golf-links (18 holes; ladies, 9 holes), 3 large parks, provision for all outdoor pastimes, good educational facilities, excellent London railway service, and direct communication Midlands and North. Electric tramways.

BRIGHTON (1924), Sussex. Pop. 142,427. *Means of access:* Southern Railway. 51 miles from London. *Elevation:* 26 to 462 feet. *Aspect:* South. *Sunshine:* (1922), 1,746 hours. *Water Supply:* Constant. *Drainage:* Modern. *Soil:* Chalk. *Front:* 4½ miles. Marine drive with promenade; lawns, ornamental terrace walks. *Piers:* West Pier, 1,100 feet; Palace Pier, 1,710 feet. *Beach:* Shingle. *Excursions:* Paris, 9 hours via Newhaven; Rottingdean, 4½ miles; Devil's Dyke, 5½ miles; Stanmer Park, 3½ miles; Bramber Castle, 10 miles; Hurst 7½ miles; Ditchling Beacon, 7½ miles.

Society's liveliest seaside rendezvous; favourite resort of Londoners. Great educational facilities. Development of the town due to salubrious location, accessibility to London and resemblance thereto, excellent train service, and its enormous capacity for accommodating and amusing all tastes and all classes all the year round. Racecourse meetings; 6 golf links (18 holes); harriers, foxhounds, county cricket ground, numerous parks and recreation grounds, boating, fishing;

Royal Pavilion, once a Royal residence, now used for public amusements and concerts; public library, museum, art galleries.

CLACTON-ON-SEA (1928), Essex. Urban District Council. Pop. 7,049. L. & N.E. Railway. 70 miles from London. *Aspect:* South. *Climate:* Dry, bracing. *Water Supply:* Constant. *Front:* Sea-wall promenade and cliff walk at different levels, the spaces between the terraces clothed in flowers and tamarisk. *Beach:* Sands. Golf links (18 holes). Popular family summer holiday resort and health resort of convalescents.

DOUGLAS (ISLE OF MAN) (1913), Pop. 22,000. *Means of access:* Steamers from Liverpool, Fleetwood, Heysham, also Ireland and Scotland. *Beach:* Firm sands. *Sea Bathing:* Not mixed. *Excursions:* Numerous by steamboats. *Season:* From Whit week to end of September. Yachting, golf links (18 holes), fishing, coaching, tennis, bowls, mountaineering, two theatres, two large ball-rooms, opera house, two variety halls, hippodrome, bands, public baths, etc. *Sunshine:* (1911) 1,873 hrs.

DROITWICH (1928), Worcestershire. Municipal Borough. Pop. 4,588. L.M. & S. Railway and G.W. Railway. 126 miles from London. 19 miles from Birmingham. *Climate:* Mild. *Neighbourhood:* Undulating woodland. A health resort noted for the curative properties of its brine-laden springs.

EDINBURGH (1929), L. & N.E. Railway and L.M. & S. Railway. Edinburgh possesses a picturesque beauty quite unrivalled. Tourists from all parts of the world are attracted to the metropolis of Scotland by its historical associations with Queen Mary, John Knox, and Sir Walter Scott. Besides the Castle, Holyrood Palace, Scott's Monument and John Knox's House, are many historic buildings, museums, libraries, and a celebrated University.

ENGLISH LAKES (1908), The English Lakes District is one of the most attractive to tourists and holiday-seekers; it is rich in literary and historical associations, affords a unique combination of mountains, lakes, rivers and seas; it is rendered easily accessible by modern railway enterprise, the entire area being covered by a well-arranged system of tours specially designed for the ever-increasing number of pleasure-seekers in search of the gems of English beauty spots.

Ambleside, Westmoreland. Urban District Council. Pop. 2,536. *Means of access:* Steamer from Lake Side and Windermere, coach and motor from Waterhead Pier and Windermere, 5m. *Elevation:* From 160 to 300 ft. above sea-level. *Immediate Neighbourhood:* Windermere, Grasmere, Langdale, Coniston, Kirkstone, Troutbeck, etc. *Aspect:* Westerly. To all travellers and visitors it offers direct and appreciable charms, the views are of unsurpassed beauty, and the climate bracing. There are excursions through most picturesque scenery to the lakes and mountains. For amusement there is a golf course (9 holes), boating on the lake, and steamer tugs. *Season:* June–Sept.

Kendal, Westmoreland. Pop. 15,000. L. & N.W. Ry., Mid. Ry. The gateway to the Lakes is a beautiful district on the River Kendal. Excellent fishing and coaching.

Keswick, Cumberland. Pop. 4,451. *Means of access:* By rail from Penrith; coach and motor from Waterhead and Ambleside in connection with lake steamer. One of the best of the northern centres for the Lake district, and is one of the most romantic places in a region rich in romance. About ½m. from Derwentwater and the Lodore Falls within easy reach. Excursions by coach to the picturesque scenery in the surrounding neighbourhood. Good salmon and trout-fishing in lake and river. Golf course (9 holes).

Windermere, Westmoreland. Urban District Council. Pop. 2,379. *Means of access:* Furness Ry., L. & N.W. Ry. *Elevation:* from 116 ft. to 400 ft. above sea-level. A village to the north of Bowness, commanding splendid views. Situated above the famous lake of the same name. Pleasure steamers run the whole length of the lake, and coaches and motors run to Ambleside, Grasmere, and Ullswater. Splendid fishing and boating.

FALMOUTH (1905), Municipal Borough. Pop. 11,789. *Means of access:* G. W. Ry. and by coasting steamship service. *Location:* On south side of Falmouth harbour, 15m. N.N.E. of the Lizard. *Elevation:* Little above sea-level. *Neighbourhood:* Wooded hills. *Aspect:* North-east upon an arm of the sea 10m. in circumference. *Climate:* Temperate, equable. *Sunshine:* 1,696 hrs., 1903. *Season:* Summer and winter. Seaport town and watering-place on the S.W. bank of the River Fal, 8m. below Truro, with a magnificent harbour and excellent facilities for yachting and boating. River and sea excursions.

HARROGATE, (1911), Yorkshire, Municipal Borough. Pop. 32,000. N.E. Ry. *Location:* 18m. N. of Leeds, 20m. W. of York. *Elevation:* 320 ft. to 600 ft. *Neighbourhood:* Open moorlands. *Sunshine:* (1909), 1,399 hrs. *Drainage:* Modern. *Soil:* Alluvial, millstone, grit and shale. *Baths:* Numerous large establishments open all the year round, providing complete modern installations, embracing hydropathic, vapour, heat, light, Peat Plombière swimming baths, and other treatments. *Mineral waters:* About 80 varieties of medicinal springs in a small area, one group sulphur, the other iron. Fashionable, select spa and inland resort, celebrated for its mineral springs and bathing palaces; presents many attractions to health-seekers and visitors. Higher Harrogate, open and bracing; Lower Harrogate, milder and sheltered; favourite town for valetudinarians, invalids, and the retired, also a scholastic centre; claims exemption from high summer and low winter temperatures: the Stray, a verdant public common of 200 acres, intersects the town, and is well laid out to retain its rural charms; the Kursaal, Royal Spa concert-rooms, and gardens are owned by the Corporation, who maintain a military band and an orchestra; covered promenade for water-drinkers; opera house; tennis, lacrosse, golf (18 holes); fox-hunting; coaching.

LLANDRINDOD WELLS, (1925), Central Wales, Urban District Council. L.M. & S. and G.W. Railways. *Elevation:* 750 feet. *Climate:* Bracing. *Mineral Waters:* Sulphur, saline, lithia, chalybeate, etc. A popular health resort. Its great attractions are its mineral springs, but the beauty of its surroundings and the purity of its air also attract many visitors. Golf links (18 holes).

LOWESTOFT (1927), Suffolk. Pop. 44,326. *Means of Access:* L. & N.E. Railway. *Neighbourhood:* Open, sand dunes and broads. *Climate:* Bracing; absence of fog and mist. *Sunshine:* (1925), 1,746 hours. *Water Supply:* Constant. *Drainage:* Modern. *Soil:* Gravel and sand. A large and important fishing town and high-class summer resort. Good centre for exploring the thousands of acres of lagoons and miles of navigable rivers called the Broads. Excellent fishing, boating. New 18-hole golf links laid out by Braid.

MINEHEAD (1906), Somerset. Urban District Council. Pop. 2,511. G. W. Ry. *Location:* On S. shore of Bristol Channel, 24 m. from Taunton. *Neighbourhood:* Sea and moorland. *Aspect:* East. *Climate:* According to situation on shore or hills. *Water supply:* Constant. *Soil:* Sandstone. *Front:* Asphalted esplanade on sea-wall. *Pier:* With landing stage for excursion steamers. *Beach:* Shingle and sand. *Season:* June to September. *Annual Fixture:* Opening meet Devon and Somerset Staghounds (August).

Minehead is a favourite centre, August to December, for members of the Exmoor Hunt; a quiet holiday resort in summer; recommended as a winter residence for invalids.

OBAN (1930), Argyllshire. Pop. 6,344. *Means of Access:* L.M. & S. Railway and steamboat. Oban's natural position, salubrity of climate, and beauty of situation command a high reputation among tourists visiting the Highlands, for whom it is a convenient point of arrival for and departure from the shooting moors. Golf (9 holes). Magnificent drives to numerous places of historic interest.

PERTH (1926), Perthshire. Pop. 33,208. L.M. & S. and L. & N.E. Railways. 22 miles from Dundee, 40 miles from Edinburgh, 450 miles from London. Situated on both sides of the River Tay. It is a great railway centre for tourists and the principal gateway to the Highlands. Golf courses, two (18 holes; ladies, 9 holes).

SHORTLANDS (1929), Kent. Southern Railway. 10 miles from London. Situated midway between Beckenham and Bromley. It is a good residential district, with many places of interest within the neighbourhood.

STAINES (1910), Market town on River Thames, 6m. S.E. of Windsor. Pleasantly situated, and has ample accommodation for the many anglers who make it their headquarters during the season.

TORQUAY (1909), Devon. Market Borough. Pop. 33,625. *Means of access:* G. W Ry., 220m. from London. *Location:* S. E. coast of Devon in the N. recess of Torbay, 25m. S. of Exeter. *Neighbourhood:* Cliffs and hills. *Sunshine:* 1,741 hours, 1907. *Climate:* Mild, soft, equable; luxuriant vegetation. *Water supply:* From Dartmoor; constant, soft. *Drainage:* Modern. *Soil:* Limestone. *Front:* Ornamental promenades and marine drive. *Pier:* 1,500 ft., pavilion, skating rink. *Beach:* Sand and single. *Bathing:* Mixed. *Baths:* Corporation baths (fresh and sea-water, medicated), Turkish. *Excursions:* Rail and river, coaching and marine. *Seasons:* Winter and summer. *Annual Fixtures:* Balls at Easter, Aug., and Christmas; dog show, flower show, regatta, steeple and hurdle races, mobilisation of Fleet.

In a curve of Torbay, on a peninsula between the Rivers Dart and Teign, Torquay is built on seven hills, the highest reaching 400 ft., sheltered N. and E.; lower part is built round harbour (enclosed by quay and piers), the houses rising behind in tiers, affording choice of elevation. A fashionable, high-class watering-place, favourite resort for the delicate, and popular winter residence; claims to be warm in winter and cool in summer. Good yachting facilities in the harbour, and safe anchorage in bay. Convenient centre for excursionists over Dartmoor.

Recreations: Princess Gardens – fêtes, tennis, croquet, bowls, band (plays daily), golf (18 holes and 9 holes), yachting, boating, fishing (sea, river and lake), hunting, polo, chess club, public library, theatre; in the Corporation Bath Saloons – balls, concerts, lectures, skating rink; at the recreation ground – football, hockey, tennis, cycle track; model yacht lake in the King's Gardens.

TUNBRIDGE WELLS (1910), Market Borough. Pop. 35,000. *Means of access:* L.B. & S. C. Ry.; S. E. C. Ry. Inland watering-place. A select residential and health resort. The common, 249 acres, is a splendid sloping sweep of verdant heath, furze and bracken, the highest parts, 440 ft. above sea-level; foot of common are its medicinal springs, pump-room, and Pantiles. Open-air and indoor bathing establishments, golf links (18 holes), good hunting centre, coaching.

FACTS AND FIGURES

A selection of facts and figures from the *Whitaker's Almanack* archive

Agricultural Statistics, Great Britain

	Wheat	Barley	Oats
	Acres	Acres	Acres
1866	3,350,394	2,237,329	2,759,923
1867	3,367,876	2,159,164	2,750,487
1868	3,646,260	2,149,201	2,753,240
1868 over 1867	*278,384 or 8.2 pr ct.	†109,963 or 4.0 pr ct.	*2,753 or 0.3 pr ct.
1868 over 1866	*295,866 or 8.8 pr ct.	†88,128 or 4.0 pr ct.	†6,683 or 0.3 pr ct.
Total Number of Live Stock, June 25.			
1867	4,993,034	28,219,101	2,966,970
1868	5,416,159	30,685,980	2,303,857
1868 over 1867	*423,120 or 8.5 pr ct.	*1,766,879 or 6.1 pr ct.	†663,122 or 22.3 pr ct.
Increase (*) or Decrease (†).			

The amount of land under potatoes in 1868 was 539,554 acres, against 492,217 in 1867 and 498,843 in 1866.

The acreage under hops in 1868 was 64,488, against 64,284 in 1867, and 56,578 in 1866.

It is computed that the extra produce of wheat from the extended acreage under cultivation will be 1,200,000 quarters, which added to the extra yield per acre, will give a surplus wheat yield of 3,000,000 quarters for 1868 over the preceding year.

Probabilities of Life

From the 1869 edition

It will be seen that of 100,000 boys alive at 3, but 94,417 will reach the age of 10, while of girls the number will be 94,551. At 50 the difference is much greater; of females there will then be 65,237 alive, and but 59,123 males. Nine females may reach the age of 100, but none of the other sex.

Average Heights and Weights

From the 1953 edition

The average heights and weights of men in the United Kingdom have been tabulated as follows. The weights include *clothing*, which is generally calculated at one-twenty-fourth of the whole.

	Average Height	Average Weight
Scotsmen	5 ft. 8 ¾ in.	11 st . 11 lb.
Englishmen	5 ft. 7 ¼ in.	11 st. 1 lb.
Irishmen	5 ft. 8 in.	10 st. 13 lb.
Welshmen	5 ft. 6 ½ in.	11 st. 4 lb.

Immigration and Emigration

United Kingdom Passenger Movement 1950 (Including Pleasure Cruises)

	Inwards	Outwards
By Sea:		
Irish Republic	644,000	629,000
Continent of Europe	1,357,000	1,312,000
Out of Europe	269,000	332,000
By Air	710,000	723,000
TOTAL	**2,980,000**	**2,996,000**

Tourists in Great Britain

The total number of foreign visitors arriving in this country rose from 603,000 in 1950 to over 690,000 in 1951, not including tourists from the Republic of Ireland. The large increase in the number of tourists in 1951 is largely accounted for by an increase of 61,000 in the number of foreign visitors from Europe and an increase of over 18,000 in the number of visitors from the Commonwealth.

127,000 United States citizens and 36,000 Canadians visited the United Kingdom in 1951. Tourist earnings from the Dollar Area in the year totalled $69,000,000 (£24,643,000 approximately). The number of visitors from Germany increased by 71 per cent from 24,000 in 1950 to 41,000 in 1951. Expenditure of all overseas visitors in the United Kingdom in 1951 amounted to £73,000,000 compared with £60,900,000 in 1950.

Numbers of Livestock – United Kingdom

The national dairy herd is now only 11 per cent larger than it was in 1939, having decreased in the last year. Sheep numbers are still below pre-war but the number of pigs increased by over a quarter between 1951 and 1952 to 12 per cent above 1939. Poultry numbers, which fell very sharply during the war, now exceed the 1939 total.

Numbers of Livestock (in thousands)	June, 1939	June, 1943	June, 1952*
Cattle: total	8,872	9,259	10,253
Cows and Heifers in milk	2,841	2,910	2,893
Cows in calf but not in milk	480	640	560
Heifers in calf with first calf	564	774	853
Sheep	26,887	20,383	21,653
Pigs	4,394	1,829	4,923
Poultry	74,357	50,729	94,665
* Provisional			

Railways Opened in 1898

Railway	From	To	Date	Miles
G.E., G.N. & Mid.	North Walsham	Mundesley	July 1	5¼
Great Northern	Annesley	Skegby	Apr. 4	5
Great Western	Plymstock	Yealpton	Jan. 15	6½
Great Western	Newbury	Lambourn	Apr. 4	12½
London & S. Western	Barnstaple	Lynton	May 11	20
London & S. Western	Holsworthy	Bude	Aug. 10	10¼
North British	Aberlady	Gullane	May 1	4½
North Sunderland	Chathill	Seahouse	Dec. 14	4
Port Talbot	Port Talbot	Cwmavon	Feb. 14	2
Port Talbot	Cwmavon	Tonmawr	Nov. 1	2
Waterloo and City	Waterloo	Mansion House	July 11	1½

The World's Workers
From the 1939 edition

Country	Total	Employed
Australia (1933)	6,629,839	2,892,557
Belgium (1930)	8,092,004	3,750,285
Brazil (1920)	30,635,605	9,566,822
Canada (1931)	10,362,833	3,927,230
Czechoslovakia (1930)	14,729,536	6,992,313
Egypt (1927)	14,177,864	5,249,864
Eire (1926)	2,971,992	1,307,662
France (1931)	41,228,466	21,611,835
Germany (1933)	65,362,115	32,296,074
Great Britain (1931)	44,795,357	21,074,751
Greece (1928)	6,204,684	2,745,508
Hungary (1930)	8,688,319	3,829,752
India (1931)	352,837,778	141,816,938
Italy (1931)	41,176,671	17,262,521
Japan (1930)	64,450,005	29,619,640
Mexico (1930)	16,552,722	3,352,162
Netherlands (1930)	7,935,565	3,185,816
Palestine (1931)	1,035,821	274,094
Spain (1920)	21,389,812	7,962,416
Sweden (1930)	6,142,191	2,892,324
Switzerland (1930)	4,066,400	1,942,626
Union of S. Africa (1926)	1,676,660	580,166
U.S.A. (1930)	122,775,046	48,829,920
U.S.S.R. (1926)	147,028,000	84,503,400
Yugoslavia (1931)	13,934,038	6,477,819

Average Earnings and Hours of Work

Particulars of the earnings of manual wage-earners and the hours worked in manufacturing industries generally and in some of the non-manufacturing industries and services are collected periodically by the Ministry of Labour. The average weekly hours of work and average weekly earnings of workers in the United Kingdom in 1938 and in 1950–1958 were as follows:

	Hours	Wages (s/d)
1938 October	46.5	53/3
1950 October	40.1	128/0
1951 October	46.1	141/1
1952 October	46.1	151/11
1953 October	46.3	160/1
1954 April	46.5	166/6
1955 April	46.9	182/3
1956 April	46.7	197/9
October	46.6	200/8
1957 April	46.6	204/7
October	46.4	212/5
1958 April	46.2	214/2

READY
REFERENCE

INTERNATIONAL RADIO ALPHABET

Phonetic alphabets were originally developed to avoid confusion when communicating by radio or telephone. The first draft of the International Radio Alphabet was completed by the International Air Transport Association in 1947 and the final version was adopted by the International Telecommunications Union in around 1956.

A	Alfa		N	November
B	Bravo		O	Oscar
C	Charlie		P	Papa
D	Delta		Q	Quebec
E	Echo		R	Romeo
F	Foxtrot		S	Sierra
G	Golf		T	Tango
H	Hotel		U	Uniform
I	India		V	Victor
J	Juliet		W	Whiskey
K	Kilo		X	X-ray
L	Lima		Y	Yankee
M	Mike		Z	Zulu

NOMS DE PLUME

PSEUDONYM	AUTHOR	PSEUDONYM	AUTHOR
Richard Bachman	Stephen King	*Molière*	Jean Baptiste Poquelin
Acton Bell	Anne Brontë		
Currer Bell	Charlotte Brontë	*Toni Morrison*	Chloe Anthony Wofford
Ellis Bell	Emily Brontë		
John le Carré	David Cornwell	*Flann O'Brien*	Brian O'Nolan
Lewis Carroll	Charles Dodgson	*George Orwell*	Eric Arthur Blair
George Egerton	Mary Chavelita Dunne Bright	*Saki*	Hector Hugh Munro
George Eliot	Mary Ann Evans	*Lemony Snicket*	Daniel Handler
Nicci French	Nicci Gerard and Sean French	*Mark Twain*	Samuel Clemens
		Barbara Vine	Ruth Rendell
Dietrich Knickerbocker	Washington Irving	*Mary Westmacott*	Agatha Christie

BOOKER PRIZE WINNERS

1969	P. H. Newby, *Something to Answer For*
1970	Bernice Rubens, *The Elected Member*
1971	V. S. Naipaul, *In a Free State*
1972	John Berger, *G*
1973	J. G. Farrell, *The Siege of Krishnapur*
1974	Nadine Gordimer, *The Conservationist*/Stanley Middleton, *Holiday*
1975	Ruth Prawer Jhabvala, *Heat and Dust*
1976	David Storey, *Saville*
1977	Paul Scott, *Staying On*
1978	Iris Murdoch, *The Sea, The Sea*
1979	Penelope Fitzgerald, *Offshore*
1980	William Golding, *Rites of Passage*
1981	Salman Rushdie, *Midnight's Children**
1982	Thomas Keneally, *Schindler's Ark*
1983	J. M. Coetzee, *Life and Times of Michael K*
1984	Anita Brookner, *Hotel du Lac*
1985	Keri Hulme, *The Bone People*
1986	Kingsley Amis, *The Old Devils*
1987	Penelope Lively, *Moon Tiger*
1988	Peter Carey, *Oscar and Lucinda*
1989	Kazuo Ishiguro, *The Remains of the Day*
1990	A. S. Byatt, *Possession*
1991	Ben Okri, *The Famished Road*
1992	Michael Ondaatje, *The English Patient*/Barry Unsworth, *Sacred Hunger*
1993	Roddy Doyle, *Paddy Clarke Ha, Ha, Ha*
1994	James Kelman, *How Late It Was, How Late*
1995	Pat Barker, *The Ghost Road*
1996	Graham Swift, *Last Orders*
1997	Arundhati Roy, *The God of Small Things*
1998	Ian McEwan, *Amsterdam*
1999	J. M. Coetzee, *Disgrace*
2000	Margaret Atwood, *The Blind Assassin*
2001	Peter Carey, *True History of the Kelly Gang*
2002	Yann Martell, *The Life of Pi*
2003	D. B. C. Pierre, *Vernon God Little*
2004	Alan Hollinghurst, *The Line of Beauty*

* Also the winner of the Booker of Bookers prize in 1993 and the Best of Booker prize in 2008

2005	John Banville, *The Sea*
2006	Kiran Desai, *The Inheritance of Loss*
2007	Anne Enright, *The Gathering*
2008	Aravind Adiga, *The White Tiger*
2009	Hilary Mantel, *Wolf Hall*
2010	Howard Jacobson, *The Finkler Question*
2011	Julian Barnes, *The Sense of an Ending*

POETS LAUREATE

The post of Poet Laureate was officially established when John Dryden was appointed by royal warrant as Poet Laureate and Historiographer Royal in 1668, although Ben Jonson was considered to have been the first recognised laureate after having a pension of 100 marks a year conferred upon him. The post is attached to the royal household and was originally conferred on the holder for life; in 1999 the length of appointment was changed to a ten-year term.

Ben Jonson (b.1572–d.1637), appointed 1616
Sir William D'Avenant (b.1606–d.1668), appointed 1638
John Dryden (b.1631–d.1700)*, appointed 1668
Thomas Shadwell (b.1642–d.1692), appointed 1689
Nahum Tate (b.1652–d.1715), appointed 1692
Nicholas Rowe (b.1674–d.1718), appointed 1715
Laurence Eusden (b.1688–d.1730), appointed 1718
Colley Cibber (b.1671–d.1757), appointed 1730
William Whitehead (b.1715–d.1785), appointed 1757
Thomas Warton (b.1728–d.1790), appointed 1785
Henry Pye (b.1745–d.1813), appointed 1790
Robert Southey (b.1774–d.1843), appointed 1813
William Wordsworth (b.1770–d.1850), appointed 1843
Alfred, Lord Tennyson (b.1809–d.1892), appointed 1850
Alfred Austin (b.1835–d.1913), appointed 1896
Robert Bridges (b.1844–d.1930), appointed 1913
John Masefield (b.1878–d.1967), appointed 1930
Cecil Day Lewis (b.1904–d.1972), appointed 1968
Sir John Betjeman (b.1906–d.1984), appointed 1972
Ted Hughes (b.1930–d.1998), appointed 1984
Andrew Motion (b.1952–), appointed 1999
Carol Ann Duffy (b.1955–), appointed 2009

* John Dryden, a Catholic, was stripped of his laureateship in 1689 for refusing to swear the oath of allegiance to the new Protestant monarchy.

PRIME MINISTERS

The accession of George I, who was unfamiliar with the English language, led to a disinclination on the part of the Sovereign to preside at meetings of his Ministers and caused the appearance of a Prime Minister, a position first acquired by Robert Walpole in 1721 and retained by him without interruption for 20 years and 326 days. The office of Prime Minister was officially recognised in 1905.

The Prime Minister, by tradition also First Lord of the Treasury and Minister for the Civil Service, is appointed by the Sovereign and is usually the leader of the party which enjoys, or can secure, a majority in the House of Commons. Other ministers are appointed by the Sovereign on the recommendation of the Prime Minister, who also allocates functions among ministers and has the power to obtain their resignation or dismissal individually.

Over the centuries there has been some variation in the determination of the dates of appointment of Prime Ministers. Where possible, the date given is that on which a new Prime Minister kissed the Sovereign's hands and accepted the commission to form a ministry. However, until the middle of the 19th century the dating of a commission or transfer of seals could be the date of taking office. Where the composition of the government changed, eg became a coalition, but the Prime Minister remained the same, the date of the change of government is given.

Year Appointed	Name	Party
1721	Sir Robert Walpole	Whig
1742	The Earl of Wilmington	Whig
1743	Henry Pelham	Whig
1754	The Duke of Newcastle	Whig
1756	The Duke of Devonshire	Whig
1757	The Duke of Newcastle	Whig
1762	The Earl of Bute	Tory
1763	George Grenville	Whig
1765	The Marquess of Rockingham	Whig
1766	The Earl of Chatham	Whig
1768	The Duke of Grafton	Whig
1770	Lord North	Tory
1782 *Mar.*	The Marquess of Rockingham	Whig
1782 *Jul.*	The Earl of Shelburne	Whig
1783 *Apr.*	The Duke of Portland	Coalition
1783 *Dec.*	William Pitt	Tory
1801	Henry Addington	Tory
1804	William Pitt	Tory
1806	The Lord Grenville	Whig
1807	The Duke of Portland	Tory

Year Appointed	Name	Party
1809	Spencer Perceval	*Tory*
1812	The Earl of Liverpool	*Tory*
1827 *Apr.*	George Canning	*Tory*
1827 *Aug.*	Viscount Goderich	*Tory*
1828	The Duke of Wellington	*Tory*
1830	The Earl Grey	*Whig*
1834 *Jul.*	The Viscount Melbourne	*Whig*
1834 *Dec.*	Sir Robert Peel	*Tory*
1835	The Viscount Melbourne	*Whig*
1841	Sir Robert Peel	*Tory*
1846	Lord John Russell (later The Earl Russell)	*Whig*
1852 *Feb.*	The Earl of Derby	*Tory*
1852 *Dec.*	The Earl of Aberdeen	*Peelite*
1855	The Viscount Palmerston	*Liberal*
1858	The Earl of Derby	*Conservative*
1859	The Viscount Palmerston	*Liberal*
1865	The Earl Russell	*Liberal*
1866	The Earl of Derby	*Conservative*
1868 *Feb.*	Benjamin Disraeli	*Conservative*
1868 *Dec.*	William Gladstone	*Liberal*
1874	Benjamin Disraeli	*Conservative*
1880	William Gladstone	*Liberal*
1885	The Marquess of Salisbury	*Conservative*
1886 *Feb.*	William Gladstone	*Liberal*
1886 *Jul.*	The Marquess of Salisbury	*Conservative*
1892	William Gladstone	*Liberal*
1894	The Earl of Rosebery	*Liberal*
1895	The Marquess of Salisbury	*Conservative*
1902	Arthur Balfour	*Conservative*
1905	Sir Henry Campbell-Bannerman	*Liberal*
1908	Herbert Asquith	*Liberal*
1915	Herbert Asquith	*Coalition*
1916	David Lloyd-George	*Coalition*
1922	Andrew Bonar Law	*Conservative*
1923	Stanley Baldwin	*Conservative*
1924 *Jan.*	Ramsay MacDonald	*Labour*
1924 *Nov.*	Stanley Baldwin	*Conservative*
1929	Ramsay MacDonald	*Labour*
1931	Ramsay MacDonald	*Coalition*
1935	Stanley Baldwin	*Coalition*

Year Appointed	Name	Party
1937	Neville Chamberlain	*Coalition*
1940	Winston Churchill	*Coalition*
1945 *May*	Winston Churchill	*Conservative*
1945 *Jul.*	Clement Attlee	*Labour*
1951	Sir Winston Churchill	*Conservative*
1955	Sir Anthony Eden	*Conservative*
1957	Harold Macmillan	*Conservative*
1963	Sir Alec Douglas-Home	*Conservative*
1964	Harold Wilson	*Labour*
1970	Edward Heath	*Conservative*
1974 *Feb.*	Harold Wilson	*Labour (minority government)*
1974 *Oct.*	Harold Wilson	*Labour*
1976	James Callaghan	*Labour*
1979	Margaret Thatcher	*Conservative*
1990	John Major	*Conservative*
1997	Tony Blair	*Labour*
2007	Gordon Brown	*Labour*
2010	David Cameron	*Coalition*

RANKS IN THE ARMED FORCES

(The numbers indicate equivalent ranks in each service)

Royal Navy

1. Admiral of the Fleet
2. Admiral (Adm.)
3. Vice-Admiral (Vice-Adm.)
4. Rear-Admiral (Rear-Adm.)
5. Commodore (Cdre)
6. Captain (Capt.)
7. Commander (Cdr)
8. Lieutenant-Commander (Lt.-Cdr)
9. Lieutenant (Lt.)
10. Sub-Lieutenant (Sub-Lt.)
11. Midshipman

Army

1. Field Marshal
2. General (Gen.)
3. Lieutenant-General (Lt.-Gen.)
4. Major-General (Maj.-Gen.)
5. Brigadier (Brig.)
6. Colonel (Col.)
7. Lieutenant-Colonel (Lt.-Col.)
8. Major (Maj.)
9. Captain (Capt.)
10. Lieutenant (Lt.)
11. Second Lieutenant (2nd Lt.)

Royal Air Force

1. Marshal of the RAF
2. Air Chief Marshal
3. Air Marshal
4. Air Vice-Marshal
5. Air Commodore (Air Cdre)
6. Group Captain (Gp Capt.)
7. Wing Commander (Wg Cdr)
8. Squadron Leader (Sqn Ldr)
9. Flight Lieutenant (Flt Lt.)
10. Flying Officer (FO)
11. Pilot Officer (PO)

'BEST PICTURE' OSCAR WINNERS

1928	Wings	1971	The French Connection
1929	The Broadway Melody	1972	The Godfather
1930	All Quiet on the Western Front	1973	The Sting
1931	Cimarron	1974	The Godfather Part II
1932	Grand Hotel	1975	One Flew Over the Cuckoo's Nest
1933	Cavalcade	1976	Rocky
1934	It Happened One Night	1977	Annie Hall
1935	Mutiny on the Bounty	1978	The Deer Hunter
1936	The Great Ziegfeld	1979	Kramer vs Kramer
1937	The Life of Emile Zola	1980	Ordinary People
1938	You Can't Take It With You	1981	Chariots of Fire
1939	Gone With the Wind	1982	Gandhi
1940	Rebecca	1983	Terms of Endearment
1941	How Green Was My Valley	1984	Amadeus
1942	Mrs Miniver	1985	Out of Africa
1943	Casablanca	1986	Platoon
1944	Going My Way	1987	The Last Emperor
1945	The Lost Weekend	1988	Rain Man
1946	The Best Years of Our Lives	1989	Driving Miss Daisy
1947	Gentleman's Agreement	1990	Dances With Wolves
1948	Hamlet	1991	The Silence of the Lambs
1949	All the King's Men	1992	Unforgiven
1950	All About Eve	1993	Schindler's List
1951	An American in Paris	1994	Forrest Gump
1952	The Greatest Show on Earth	1995	Braveheart
1953	From Here to Eternity	1996	The English Patient
1954	On the Waterfront	1997	Titanic
1955	Marty	1998	Shakespeare in Love
1956	Around the World in 80 Days	1999	American Beauty
1957	The Bridge on the River Kwai	2000	Gladiator
1958	Gigi	2001	A Beautiful Mind
1959	Ben-Hur	2002	Chicago
1960	The Apartment	2003	The Lord of the Rings: The Return of the King
1961	West Side Story	2004	Million Dollar Baby
1962	Lawrence of Arabia	2005	Crash
1963	Tom Jones	2006	The Departed
1964	My Fair Lady	2007	No Country for Old Men
1965	The Sound of Music	2008	Slumdog Millionaire
1966	A Man for All Seasons	2009	The Hurt Locker
1967	In the Heat of the Night	2010	The King's Speech
1968	Oliver!	2011	The Artist
1969	Midnight Cowboy		
1970	Patton		

'BEST ACTOR' OSCAR WINNERS

1928 Emil Jannings, *The Last Command*
1929 Warner Baxter, *In Old Arizona*
1930 George Arliss, *Disraeli*
1931 Lionel Barrymore, *A Free Soul*
1932 Wallace Beery, *The Champ*; Fredric March, *Dr. Jekyll and Mr. Hyde*
1933 Charles Laughton, *The Private Life of Henry VIII*
1934 Clark Gable, *It Happened One Night*†
1935 Victor McLaglen, *The Informer*
1936 Paul Muni, *The Story of Louis Pasteur*
1937 Spencer Tracy, *Captains Courageous*
1938 Spencer Tracy, *Boys Town*
1939 Robert Donat, *Goodbye, Mr. Chips*
1940 James Stewart, *The Philadelphia Story*
1941 Gary Cooper, *Sergeant York*
1942 James Cagney, *Yankee Doodle Dandy*
1943 Paul Lukas, *Watch on the Rhine*
1944 Bing Crosby, *Going My Way*†
1945 Ray Milland, *The Lost Weekend*†
1946 Fredric March, *The Best Years of Our Lives*†
1947 Ronald Colman, *A Double Life*
1948 Laurence Olivier, *Hamlet*†
1949 Broderick Crawford, *All the King's Men*†
1950 José Ferrer, *Cyrano de Bergerac*
1951 Humphrey Bogart, *The African Queen*
1952 Gary Cooper, *High Noon*
1953 William Holden, *Stalag 17*
1954 Marlon Brando, *On The Waterfront*†
1955 Ernest Borgnine, *Marty*†
1956 Yul Brynner, *The King and I*
1957 Alec Guinness, *The Bridge on the River Kwai*†
1958 David Niven, *Separate Tables*
1959 Charlton Heston, *Ben-Hur* †
1960 Burt Lancaster, *Elmer Gantry*
1961 Maximilian Schell, *Judgment at Nuremberg*
1962 Gregory Peck, *To Kill a Mockingbird*
1963 Sidney Poitier, *Lilies of the Field*
1964 Rex Harrison, *My Fair Lady*†
1965 Lee Marvin, *Cat Ballou*
1966 Paul Scofield, *A Man for All Seasons*†
1967 Rod Steiger, *In the Heat of the Night*†
1968 Cliff Robertson, *Charly*
1969 John Wayne, *True Grit*

1970 George C. Scott, *Patton**†
1971 Gene Hackman, *The French Connection*†
1972 Marlon Brando, *The Godfather**†
1973 Jack Lemmon, *Save the Tiger*
1974 Art Carney, *Harry and Tonto*
1975 Jack Nicholson, *One Flew Over the Cuckoo's Nest*†
1976 Peter Finch, *Network*
1977 Richard Dreyfuss, *The Goodbye Girl*
1978 Jon Voight, *Coming Home*
1979 Dustin Hoffman, *Kramer vs Kramer*†
1980 Robert De Niro, *Raging Bull*
1981 Henry Fonda, *On Golden Pond*
1982 Ben Kingsley, *Gandhi*†
1983 Robert Duvall, *Tender Mercies*
1984 F. Murray Abraham, *Amadeus*†
1985 William Hurt, *Kiss of the Spider Woman*
1986 Paul Newman, *The Color of Money*
1987 Michael Douglas, *Wall Street*
1988 Dustin Hoffman, *Rain Man*†
1989 Daniel Day-Lewis, *My Left Foot*
1990 Jeremy Irons, *Reversal of Fortune*
1991 Anthony Hopkins, *The Silence of the Lambs*†
1992 Al Pacino, *Scent of a Woman*
1993 Tom Hanks, *Philadelphia*
1994 Tom Hanks, *Forrest Gump*†
1995 Nicholas Cage, *Leaving Las Vegas*
1996 Geoffrey Rush, *Shine*
1997 Jack Nicholson, *As Good As It Gets*
1998 Roberto Benigni, *Life Is Beautiful*
1999 Kevin Spacey, *American Beauty*†
2000 Russell Crowe, *Gladiator*†
2001 Denzel Washington, *Training Day*
2002 Adrien Brody, *The Pianist*
2003 Sean Penn, *Mystic River*
2004 Jamie Foxx, *Ray*
2005 Philip Seymour Hoffman, *Capote*
2006 Forest Whitaker, *The Last King of Scotland*
2007 Daniel Day-Lewis, *There Will Be Blood*
2008 Sean Penn, *Milk*
2009 Jeff Bridges, *Crazy Heart*
2010 Colin Firth, *The King's Speech* †
2011 Jean Dujardin, *The Artist*†

* indicates the actor refused the award
† indicates actor won their award appearing in that year's best picture

'BEST ACTRESS' OSCAR WINNERS

1928	Janet Gaynor, *7th Heaven*
1929	Mary Pickford, *Coquette*
1930	Norma Shearer, *The Divorcee*
1931	Marie Dressler, *Min and Bill*
1932	Helen Hayes, *The Sin of Madelon Claudet*
1933	Katharine Hepburn, *Morning Glory*
1934	Claudette Colbert, *It Happened One Night†*
1935	Bette Davis, *Dangerous*
1936	Luise Rainer, *The Great Ziegfeld†*
1937	Luise Rainer, *The Good Earth*
1938	Bette Davis, *Jezebel*
1939	Vivien Leigh, *Gone with the Wind†*
1940	Ginger Rogers, *Kitty Foyle*
1941	Joan Fontaine, *Suspicion*
1942	Greer Garson, *Mrs Miniver†*
1943	Jennifer Jones, *The Song of Bernadette*
1944	Ingrid Bergman, *Gaslight*
1945	Joan Crawford, *Mildred Pierce*
1946	Olivia de Havilland, *To Each His Own*
1947	Loretta Young, *The Farmer's Daughter*
1948	Jane Wyman, *Johnny Belinda*
1949	Olivia de Havilland, *The Heiress*
1950	Judy Holliday, *Born Yesterday*
1951	Vivien Leigh, *A Streetcar Named Desire*
1952	Shirley Booth, *Come Back, Little Sheba*
1953	Audrey Hepburn, *Roman Holiday*
1954	Grace Kelly, *The Country Girl*
1955	Anna Magnani, *The Rose Tattoo*
1956	Ingrid Bergman, *Anastasia*
1957	Joanne Woodward, *The Three Faces of Eve*
1958	Susan Hayward, *I Want To Live!*
1959	Simone Signoret, *Room at the Top*
1960	Elizabeth Taylor, *Butterfield 8*
1961	Sophia Loren, *Two Women*
1962	Anne Bancroft, *The Miracle Worker*
1963	Patricia Neal, *Hud*
1964	Julie Andrews, *Mary Poppins*
1965	Julie Christie, *Darling*
1966	Elizabeth Taylor, *Who's Afraid of Virginia Woolf?*
1967	Katharine Hepburn, *Guess Who's Coming to Dinner*
1968	Katharine Hepburn, *The Lion in Winter*; Barbra Streisand, *Funny Girl*
1969	Maggie Smith, *The Prime of Miss Jean Brodie*
1970	Glenda Jackson, *Women in Love*
1971	Jane Fonda, *Klute*
1972	Liza Minnelli, *Cabaret*
1973	Glenda Jackson, *A Touch of Class*
1974	Ellen Burstyn, *Alice Doesn't Live Here Anymore*
1975	Louise Fletcher, *One Flew over the Cuckoo's Nest†*
1976	Faye Dunaway, *Network*
1977	Diane Keaton, *Annie Hall†*
1978	Jane Fonda, *Coming Home*
1979	Sally Field, *Norma Rae*
1980	Sissy Spacek, *Coal Miner's Daughter*
1981	Katharine Hepburn, *On Golden Pond*
1982	Meryl Streep, *Sophie's Choice*
1983	Shirley MacLaine, *Terms of Endearment†*
1984	Sally Field, *Places in the Heart*
1985	Geraldine Page, *The Trip to Bountiful*
1986	Marlee Matlin, *Children of a Lesser God*
1987	Cher, *Moonstruck*
1988	Jodie Foster, *The Accused*
1989	Jessica Tandy, *Driving Miss Daisy*
1990	Kathy Bates, *Misery*
1991	Jodie Foster, *The Silence of the Lambs†*
1992	Emma Thompson, *Howards End*
1993	Holly Hunter, *The Piano*
1994	Jessica Lange, *Blue Sky*
1995	Susan Sarandon, *Dead Man Walking*
1996	Frances McDormand, *Fargo*
1997	Helen Hunt, *As Good As It Gets*
1998	Gwyneth Paltrow, *Shakespeare in Love†*
1999	Hilary Swank, *Boys Don't Cry*
2000	Julia Roberts, *Erin Brockovich*
2001	Halle Berry, *Monster's Ball*
2002	Nicole Kidman, *The Hours*
2003	Charlize Theron, *Monster*
2004	Hilary Swank, *Million Dollar Baby†*
2005	Reese Witherspoon, *Walk the Line*
2006	Helen Mirren, *The Queen*
2007	Marion Cotillard, *La Vie en Rose*
2008	Kate Winslet, *The Reader*
2009	Sandra Bullock, *The Blind Side*
2010	Natalie Portman, *Black Swan*
2011	Meryl Streep, *The Iron Lady*

† indicates actor won their award appearing in that year's best picture

TYPES OF CHEESE

Cheese	Country	Characteristics
Brie	France	Soft, cow's milk, downy rind
Camembert	France	Soft, cow's milk, downy rind
Cheddar	England	Hard, cow's milk, white to yellow
Dolcelatte	Italy	Semi-soft, cow's milk, mould-ripened, blue/green veined
Edam	The Netherlands	Semi-hard, skimmed cow's milk, mild, red wax rind
Emmenthal	Switzerland	Hard, cow's milk, creamy
Gorgonzola	Italy	Semi-hard, cow's milk, mould-ripened, blue/green veined
Gouda	The Netherlands	Semi-hard, cow's milk, mild, yellow wax rind
Gruyère	Switzerland	Hard, cow's milk, small holes
Feta	Greece	Soft, ewe's or goat's milk, salty
Lancashire	England	Hard, cow's milk, white, crumbly
Manchego	Spain	Semi-hard, ewe's milk, mild or sharp
Mozzarella	Italy	Soft, cow's or water buffalo's milk, white
Munster	France	Semi-soft, cow's milk, bacteria-ripened
Parmesan	Italy	Very hard, cow's milk, bacteria-ripened, long cure
Roquefort	France	Semi-hard, ewe's milk, blue veined
Stilton	England	Semi-hard, cow's milk, mould-ripened, blue veined

BEEF CUTS

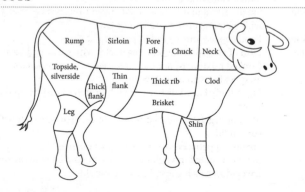

CULINARY TERMS

Term	Definition
Al dente	Of pasta that is firm when bitten (*trans.* to the tooth)
Au gratin	Covered with breadcrumbs and/or cheese and cooked until golden brown
Balti	Spicy dish, stewed until most of the liquid has evaporated; served in a wok-like pot
Béchamel	White sauce infused with carrot, onion, celery, black peppercorns and bay leaf
Blanch	To boil food in water briefly
Bourguignonne	Cooked in a red wine sauce with mushrooms and onions
Braise	To cook slowly with a small amount of liquid
Bruschetta	Sliced ciabatta topped with garlic, olive oil, tomatoes and basil
Alla cacciatora	Cooked with tomatoes, mushrooms, onions and herbs
Canapé	Appetiser, small piece of bread or toast with savoury topping
Chasseur	Sauce made with mushrooms, white wine, shallots and herbs
Dhal	Thick, spicy stew prepared with split pulses
En croûte	Wrapped in pastry and baked
Entrecôte	Boneless steak of beef cut from the sirloin
Entrée	Dish served before the main course
Flambé	To cover food with alcohol and ignite before serving
Florentine	Dish where spinach is used as a key ingredient
Frikkadel	Fried ball of minced meat
Frittata/Tortilla	Thick omelette often containing potatoes, vegetables, cheese and ham
Gnocchi	Small potato and flour dumplings
Haute cuisine	Fine cuisine, elaborately prepared
Hollandaise	White sauce made with egg, oil/butter and lemon juice
Hors d'oeuvre	Appetiser served before a meal
à la Lyonnaise	Sautéed meat or vegetables with chopped onions cooked in butter, vinegar and chopped parsley
Millefeuille	Small rectangular pastries made from thin layers of puff pastry with whipped cream and jam or fruit
En papillote	Food cooked and served in parchment paper
Ratatouille	Dish of stewed or sautéed vegetables with garlic and basil
Roux	Cooked mixture of flour and fat used to thicken sauces
Sauté	To quickly fry in a shallow pan
Soufflé	Light, fluffy baked dish made with beaten egg whites and egg yolks
Tagine	Meat or vegetable stew cooked in an earthenware dish with a conical lid
Tapas	Spanish appetisers, can make up a whole meal
Tikka	Meat marinated in yoghurt and spices, cooked in a clay oven
Timbale	Layered rice dish cooked in a tall mould

THE EARTH

Dimensions

Surface area = **510,064,472km²** (196,936,994 miles²), of which water makes up **70.92** per cent and land **29.08** per cent
Equatorial diameter = **12,742.01km** (7,917.51 miles)
Polar diameter = **12,713.50km** (7,899.80 miles)
Equatorial circumference = **40,030.20km** (24,873.60 miles)
Polar circumference = **40,007.86km** (24,859.73 miles)

Equator = 0°
North Pole = 90° N.
South Pole = 90° S.
Tropic of Cancer = 23°27' N.
Tropic of Capricorn = 23°27' S.
Arctic Circle = 66°33' N.
Antarctic Circle = 66°33' S.

The Tropics and the Arctic and Antarctic circles are affected by the slow decrease in obliquity of the ecliptic, of about 0.47 arcseconds per year. The effect of this is that the Arctic and Antarctic circles are currently moving towards their respective poles by about 14 metres a year, while the Tropics move towards the Equator by the same amount.

The Earth, broadly speaking, consists of three layers:

Crust: Thin outer layer, with an average depth of 50 km/30 miles beneath the continents and around 5–10 km (3–6 miles) beneath the ocean floors

Mantle: Lies between the crust and the core and is about 2,865 km/1,780 miles thick

Core: Extends from the mantle to the Earth's centre and is about 6,964 km/4,327 miles in diameter

The Atmosphere

The atmosphere is the air or mixture of gases enveloping the Earth. Various layers are identified by scientists, based on rate of temperature change, composition, etc. Most weather conditions form in the troposphere, and this is also the layer where most pollutants released into the atmosphere by human activity accumulate. The stratosphere is the layer in which most atmospheric ozone is found.

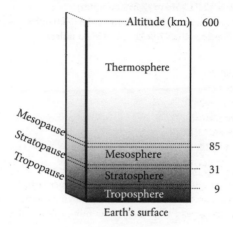

The component gases of the atmosphere are:

Gas	% by Vol.	Gas	% by Vol.
Nitrogen	78.08	Methane	0.00017
Oxygen	20.95	Krypton	0.00011
Argon	0.934	Hydrogen	0.00005
Carbon dioxide	0.038	Nitrous oxide	0.00005
Neon	0.00182	Ozone	0.00004
Helium	0.00052	Xenon	0.000009

EARTHQUAKES

Movements on or in the Earth generate seismic waves. These can be measured in a variety of ways, and there are a number of different scales for comparing the relative size of earthquakes based on seismic waves, usually called seismic magnitudes. The nature of seismic waves means that any one earthquake can have many different seismic magnitudes. The main magnitude scales are:

Name	Period of Measurement (seconds)
Richter magnitude	0.1–1
Body wave magnitude	1–5
Surface wave magnitude	20
Moment magnitude	>200

The point of initiation of an earthquake is known as the hypocentre (usually given in terms of latitude, longitude and depth below the surface). The epicentre is the surface projection of the hypocentre.

Richter Scale

Named after Charles Richter, who invented seismic magnitude scales in 1935.

Magnitude	Intensity
1	Detectable only by instruments
2	Barely detectable, even near epicentre
3	Similar to vibrations from a heavy goods vehicle
4–5	Detectable within 32km (20 miles) of the epicentre; possible slight damage within a small area
6	Moderately destructive; chimneys fall, houses move on foundations
7	Major earthquake; bridges twist, walls fracture, buildings collapse
8	Great earthquake; surface waves seen, objects thrown in the air
9	Widespread destruction

The World's Most Destructive Earthquakes
(by number of fatalities, Richter scale)

Date	Location	Fatalities	Magnitude
23 January 1556	China, Shaanxi	830,000	~8
27 July 1976	China, Tangshan	255,000*	7.5
9 August 1138	Syria, Aleppo	230,000	Unknown
26 December 2004	Sumatra	227,898	9.1
12 January 2010	Haiti	222,570	7.0

* Official number; real figure possibly as high as 655,000

WEATHER

Wind Force Measures
The Beaufort Scale of wind force is used internationally in communicating weather conditions. Devised originally by Admiral Sir Francis Beaufort in 1805 as a scale of 0–12, it was extended to Force 17 by the US Weather Bureau in 1955. Each scale number represents a certain strength or velocity of wind at 10m (33ft) above ground in the open.

Scale No.	Wind Force	KPH	MPH	Knots
0	Calm	0–1	0–1	0–1
1	Light air	1–5	1–3	1–3
2	Light breeze	6–11	4–7	4–6
3	Gentle breeze	12–19	8–12	7–10
4	Moderate breeze	20–28	13–18	11–16
5	Fresh breeze	29–38	19–24	17–21
6	Strong breeze	39–49	25–31	22–27
7	Near gale	50–61	32–38	28–33
8	Gale	62–74	39–46	34–40
9	Strong gale	75–88	47–54	41–47

Scale No.	Wind Force	KPH	MPH	Knots
10	Whole gale	89–103	55–63	48–55
11	Storm	104–117	64–72	56–63
12	Hurricane	118–133	73–82	64–71
13	–	134–148	83–92	72–80
14	–	149–166	93–103	81–89
15	–	167–183	104–114	90–99
16	–	184–201	115–125	100–108
17	–	202–219	126–136	109–118

Weather Records (UK)

Highest daily temperature: 38.5°C Faversham, Kent (2003)
Lowest daily temperature: –27.2°C Braemar, Aberdeenshire (1895, 1982); Altnaharra, Highland (1995)
Highest monthly sunshine: 383.9hrs Eastbourne, Sussex (1911)
Highest gust speed (low-level): 123 knots Fraserburgh, Aberdeenshire (1989)
Highest 24-hour rainfall: 316.4mm Seathwaite, Cumbria (2009)

WORLD GEOGRAPHICAL STATISTICS

Oceans

Area	Km²	Miles²
Pacific	165,250,000	63,800,000
Atlantic	82,440,000	31,830,000
Indian	73,440,000	28,360,000
Southern*	20,327,000	7,848,300
Arctic	14,090,000	5,440,000

* In 2000 the International Hydrographic Organisation approved the description of the 20,327,000km² (7,848,300 miles²) of circum-Antarctic waters up to 60°S. as the Southern Ocean. The division by the Equator of the Pacific into the North and South Pacific and the Atlantic into the North and South Atlantic makes a total of seven oceans.

Seas

Area	Km²	Miles²
South China	3,685,000	1,423,000
Caribbean	2,753,000	1,063,000
Mediterranean	2,509,900	969,100
Bering	2,304,000	890,000
Okhotsk	1,580,000	611,000
Gulf of Mexico	1,550,000	600,000
Japan	978,000	377,600
Hudson Bay	819,000	316,000
Andaman	798,000	308,000
East China	750,000	290,000
North Sea	570,000	220,000
Red Sea	453,000	174,900
Black Sea	422,000	163,000
Baltic Sea	386,000	149,000
Yellow Sea	380,000	146,700
Persian Gulf	241,000	93,000

Highest Mountains

Mountain, Location	Height	
	Metres	Feet
Mt Everest [Qomolangma]	8,850	29,035
K2 [Qogir]*	8,611	28,251
Kangchenjunga	8,586	28,169
Lhotse	8,501	27,890
Makalu	8,463	27,766
Cho Oyu	8,201	26,906

* Formerly Godwin-Austen

The culminating summits in the other major mountain ranges are:

Mountain, Location	Height	
	Metres	Feet
Victory Peak [Pik Pobedy], Tien Shan	7,439	24,406
Mt Aconcagua, Andes	6,959	22,831
Mt McKinley (S. Peak), Alaska	6,194	20,320
Kilimanjaro, Tanzania	5,895	19,340
Hkakabo Razi, Myanmar	5,881	19,296
Mt Elbrus (W. Peak), Caucasus	5,642	18,510
Citlaltépetl, Mexico	5,610	18,406
Jaya Peak, New Guinea	5,030	16,500
Vinson Massif, Antarctica	4,892	16,050
Mt Blanc, Alps	4,807	15,771

BRITISH ISLES (by country)	Height	
	Metres	Feet
Ben Nevis, Scotland	1,344	4,406
Snowdon, Wales	1,085	3,559
Carrantuohill, Rep. of Ireland	1,041	3,414
Scafell Pike, England	977	3,210

Largest Lakes

The areas of some of these lakes are subject to seasonal variation.

Lake, Location	Area Km²	Miles²
Caspian Sea, Iran/Azerbaijan/Russia/ Turkmenistan/Kazakhstan	386,400	149,200
Michigan–Huron, USA/Canada*	117,610	45,300
Superior, Canada/USA	82,100	31,700
Victoria, Uganda/Tanzania/Kenya	69,484	26,828
Tanganyika, Dem. Rep. of Congo/ Tanzania/Zambia/Burundi	32,900	12,700
Baikal, Russia	31,500	12,200
Great Bear, Canada	31,328	12,096
Malawi [Nyasa], Tanzania/Malawi/ Mozambique	29,600	11,430

* Lakes Michigan and Huron are regarded as lobes of the same lake. The Michigan lobe has an area of 57,750km² (22,300 miles²) and the Huron lobe an area of 59,570km² (23,000 miles²)

UNITED KINGDOM (by country)

Lough Neagh, Northern Ireland	396	153
Loch Lomond, Scotland	71.12	27.46
Lake Windermere, England	14.74	5.69
Lake Vyrnwy (artificial), Wales	4.53	1.75
Llyn Tegid [Bala], Wales	4.38	1.69

Deepest Lakes

Lake, Location	Greatest Depth	
	Metres	Feet
Baikal, Russia	1,637	5,371
Tanganyika, Burundi/Tanzania/Dem. Rep. of Congo/Zambia	1,436	4,710
Caspian Sea, Azerbaijan/Iran/ Kazakhstan/Russia/Turkmenistan	1,025	3,363
O'Higgins [San Martin], Chile/Argentina	836	2,743
Malawi [Nyasa], Malawi/Mozambique/ Tanzania	704	2,310
Ysyk, Kyrgyzstan	668	2,192
Great Slave, Canada	614	2,015
Quesnel, Canada	610	2,001
Crater, Oregon, USA	592	1,943
Matano, Indonesia	590	1,936
Buenos Aires [General Carrera], Argentina/Chile	586	1,923
Hornindalsvatnet, Norway	514	1,686

All these lakes would be sufficiently deep to submerge the Empire State Building – in the case of Lake Baikal, more than four times over.

Largest Deserts

Area	Km²	Miles²
Sahara	8,600,000	3,300,000
Arabian	2,330,000	900,000
Gobi	1,300,000	500,000
Kalahari	930,000	360,000
Great Victoria	424,400	163,900
Taklimakan Shamo	320,000	123,550

Longest Rivers

River, Location	Length	
	Km	Miles
Nile, Africa	6,650	4,132
Amazon, S. America	6,448	4,007
Yangtze [Chang Jiang], China	6,300	3,915
Mississippi-Missouri-Red Rock, N. America	5,970	3,710
Yenisey-Selenga, Mongolia/Russia	5,539	3,442
Huang He [Yellow River], China	5,463	3,395
BRITISH ISLES (by country)		
Shannon, Rep. of Ireland	372	231
Severn, Britain	354	220
Thames, England	330	205
Tay, Scotland	193	120
Clyde, Scotland	170	106

COLLECTIVE NOUNS FOR ANIMALS

Animal	Collective noun
Ants	army, bike, colony, swarm
Apes	shrewdness
Bears	sloth
Camels	caravan, flock
Caterpillars	army
Cats	clowder, cluster
Chickens	brood, clutch, peep
Crows	hover, murder, parcel
Dogs	cowardice, kennel, pack
Doves	dole, flight
Flamingos	flurry, regiment, stand
Flies	business, cloud, swarm
Foxes	earth, lead, skulk, troop
Frogs	army, colony
Goldfinches	charm, chattering
Goldfish	troubling
Grasshoppers	cloud
Hares	down, drove, husk, trip
Hawks	kettle, mews
Hedgehogs	array
Jellyfish	brood, smuck
Larks	exaltation
Leopards	leap
Lions	flock, pride, troop
Magpies	tiding, tittering
Moles	labour, movement
Monkeys	troop
Mules	barren, pack, span
Otters	bevy, family
Owls	parliament, stare
Peacocks	muster
Penguins	colony, rookery
Pigs	herd, drove

Rabbits	bury, colony, nest, warren	Spiders	cluster, clutter
Raccoons	nursery	Squirrels	drey
Rats	colony	Starlings	chattering, murmuration
Ravens	unkindness		
Rhinoceros	crash	Swans	bank, wedge, whiteness
Rooks	clamour, parliament	Tigers	ambush
Seals	harem, herd, pod, rookery	Toads	knab, knot
		Turkeys	posse, raffle, rafter
Snakes	nest, pit	Turtles	bale, dule, turn
Snipe	walk, whisper, wish, wisp	Wasps	bike, herd, nest, pledge
		Whales	herd, pod, school
Sparrows	host, quarrel		

NAMES OF MALE, FEMALE AND YOUNG ANIMALS

Animal	Male	Female	Young
Ant	drone	queen, worker	larvae
Bear	boar	sow	cub
Cat	tom	queen	kitten
Deer	buck, stag	doe	fawn
Donkey	jack, jackass	jennet, jenny colt,	foal
Elephant	bull	cow	calf
Fox	reynard	vixen	kit, cub, pup
Giraffe	bull	doe	calf
Goat	buck, billy	doe, nanny	kid, billy
Goose	gander	goose	gosling
Gorilla	male	female	infant
Hedgehog	boar	sow	pup, piglet
Hippopotamus	bull	cow	calf
Mouse	buck	doe	kitten, pinkie, pup
Rabbit	buck	doe	kit
Sheep	buck, ram	ewe, dam	lamb, lambkin, cosset
Swan	cob	pen	cygnet
Whale	bull	cow	calf

ARRANGEMENT OF THE ORCHESTRA

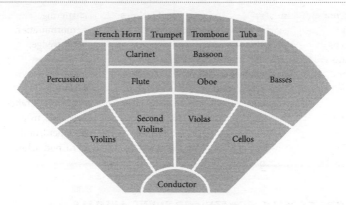

MUSICAL COMPOSITIONS AND SECTIONS

Term	Meaning
Aria	A self-contained piece for solo voice, often with an accompaniment and occurring within a larger work
Canon	A device in which one melody is repeated, often with creative variation, at regular overlapping intervals
Concerto	A work, usually in three parts, for orchestra and one or more solo instruments
Étude	French 'study': a piece, often difficult, originally designed to help perfect a particular technique or style
Mass	A sacred composition for choir (either accompanied or *a cappella*) in which the Eucharistic liturgy is set to music
Nocturne	A piece inspired by, or evocative of, the night
Opera	A composition in which vocal and orchestral scores are combined to create a piece of dramatic narrative theatre
Oratorio	A large work for choir, orchestra and soloist, similar to an opera but with a focus on sacred topics
Requiem	A mass for the dead
Rhapsody	A lively, one-movement work, often patriotic
Sonata	An instrumental piece for one or two instruments, often comprising four movements: fast, slow, moderate, fast
Symphony	An orchestral piece, generally in several movements
Toccata	An instrumental piece, often designed to demonstrate the dexterity and technical proficiency of a performer

PRESIDENTS OF THE USA

Year Inaugurated	Name	Party
1789	George Washington (1732–99)	*Federalist*
1797	John Adams (1735–1826)	*Federalist*
1801	Thomas Jefferson (1743–1826)	*Democratic-Republican*
1809	James Madison (1751–1836)	*Democratic-Republican*
1817	James Monroe (1758–1831)	*Democratic-Republican*
1825	John Quincy Adams (1767–1848)	*Democratic-Republican*
1829	Andrew Jackson (1767–1845)	*Democrat*
1837	Martin Van Buren (1782–1862)	*Democrat*
1841	William Harrison (1773–1841) (died in office)	*Whig*
1841	John Tyler (1790–1862) (elected as Vice-President)	*Whig*
1845	James K. Polk (1795–1849)	*Democrat*
1849	Zachary Taylor (1784–1850) (died in office)	*Whig*
1850	Millard Fillmore (1800–74) (elected as Vice-President)	*Whig*
1853	Franklin Pierce (1804–69)	*Democrat*
1857	James Buchanan (1791–1868)	*Democrat*
1861	Abraham Lincoln (1809–65) (assassinated in office)	*Republican*
1865	Andrew Johnson (1808–75) (elected as Vice-President)	*National Union*
1869	Ulysses S. Grant (1822–85)	*Republican*
1877	Rutherford B. Hayes (1822–93)	*Republican*
1881	James A. Garfield (1831–81) (assassinated in office)	*Republican*
1881	Chester A. Arthur (1830–86) (elected as Vice-President)	*Republican*
1885	Grover Cleveland (1837–1908)	*Democrat*
1889	Benjamin Harrison (1833–1901)	*Republican*
1893	Grover Cleveland (1837–1908)	*Democrat*
1897	William McKinley (1843–1901) (assassinated in office)	*Republican*
1901	Theodore Roosevelt (1858–1919) (elected as Vice-President)	*Republican*
1909	William Howard Taft (1857–1930)	*Republican*
1913	Woodrow Wilson (1856–1924)	*Democrat*

Year Inaugurated	Name	Party
1921	Warren G. Harding (1865–1923) (died in office)	Republican
1923	Calvin Coolidge (1872–1933) (elected as Vice-President)	Republican
1929	Herbert Hoover (1874–1964)	Republican
1933	* Franklin D. Roosevelt (1882–1945) (died in office)	Democrat
1945	Harry S. Truman (1884–1972) (elected as Vice-President)	Democrat
1953	Dwight D. Eisenhower (1890–1969)	Republican
1961	John F. Kennedy (1917–63) (assassinated in office)	Democrat
1963	Lyndon B. Johnson (1908–73) (elected as Vice-President)	Democrat
1969	Richard Nixon (1913–94)	Republican
1974†	Gerald Ford (1913–2006)	Republican
1977	James Carter (1924–)	Democrat
1981	Ronald Reagan (1911–2004)	Republican
1989	George H.W. Bush (1924–)	Republican
1993	William Clinton (1946–)	Democrat
2001	George W. Bush (1946–)	Republican
2009	Barack Obama (1961–)	Democrat

* Re-elected 5 November 1940, the first case of a third term; re-elected for a fourth term 7 November 1944

† Appointed under the provisions of the 25th Amendment

SECRETARIES-GENERAL OF THE UNITED NATIONS

1946–52	Trygve Lie (Norway)
1953–61	Dag Hammarskjöld (Sweden)
1961–71	U Thant (Burma)
1972–81	Kurt Waldheim (Austria)
1982–91	Javier Pérez de Cuellar (Peru)
1992–96	Boutros Boutros-Ghali (Egypt)
1997–2006	Kofi Annan (Ghana)
2007–	Ban Ki-moon (Republic of Korea)

POPES

1523	Clement VII	1700	Clement XI
1534	Paul III	1721	Innocent XIII
1550	Julius III	1724	Benedict XIII
1555	Marcellus II	1730	Clement XII
1555	Paul IV	1740	Benedict XIV
1559	Pius IV	1758	Clement XIII
1566	St Pius V	1769	Clement XIV
1572	Gregory XIII	1775	Pius VI
1585	Sixtus V	1800	Pius VII
1590	Urban VII	1823	Leo XII
1590	Gregory XIV	1829	Pius VIII
1591	Innocent IX	1831	Gregory XVI
1592	Clement VIII	1846	Blessed Pius IX
1605	Leo XI	1878	Leo XIII
1605	Paul V	1903	St Pius X
1621	Gregory XV	1914	Benedict XV
1623	Urban VIII	1922	Pius XI
1644	Innocent X	1939	Pius XII
1655	Alexander VII	1958	Blessed John XXIII
1667	Clement IX	1963	Paul VI
1670	Clement X	1978	John Paul I
1676	Blessed Innocent XI	1978	John Paul II
1689	Alexander VIII	2005	Benedict XVI
1691	Innocent XII		

ROMAN EMPERORS

Augustus	27 BC–AD 14	Domitian	81–96
Tiberius	14–37	Nerva	96–98
Gaius Caesar	37–41	Trajan	98–117
(Caligula)		Hadrian	117–38
Claudius I	41–54	Antoninus Pius	138–61
Nero	54–68	Marcus Aurelius	161–80
Galba	68–69	Lucius Verus	161–69
Otho	69	Commodus	177–92
Vitellius	69	Pertinax	193
Sabinus	69	Didius Julianus	193
Vespasian	69–79	Septimius Severus	193–211
Titus	79–81	Caracalla	211–17

Geta	211–12	Constans	337–50
Macrinus	217–18	Constantius II	337–61
Elagabalus	218–22	Julian	361–63
Alexander Severus	222–35	Jovian	363–64
Maximinus Thrax	235–38	Valentinian I	364–75
Gordian I	238	Valens	364–78
Gordian II	238	Gratian	375–83
Pupienus	238	Valentinian II	375–92
Balbinus	238	Maximus	383–88
Gordian III	238–44	Eugenius	392–94
Philip	244–49	Theodosius I	394–95
Decius	249–51	Arcadius	395–408
Hostilianus	251	Theodosius II	408–50
Gallus	251–53	Marcian	450–57
Aemilianus	253	Leo I	457–74
Valerian	253–59	Leo II	474
Gallienus	253–68	Zeno	474–91
Claudius II	268–70		
Aurelian	270–75	**Western Emperors**	
Tacitus	275–76	Honorius	395–423
Florianus	276	Maximus	408–11
Probus	276–82	Constantius III	421
Carus	282–83	Johannes	423–5
Carinus	283–84	Valentinian III	425–55
Numerianus	283–84	Petronius Maximus	455
Diocletian	284–305	Avitus	455–56
Maximian	285–305	Majorian	457–61
Constantius I	305–6	Libius Severus	461–65
Galerius	305–11	Anthemius	467–72
Severus	306–7	Olybrius	472
Maxentius	307–12	Glycerius	473–74
Constantine I	306–37	Julius Nepos	474–75
Constantine II	337–40	Romulus Augustus	475–76

SEVEN WONDERS OF THE WORLD

The following sights were identified by classical observers as the pre-eminent architectural and sculptural achievements of the ancient world. Only the pyramids of Egypt are still in existence.

The Colossus of Rhodes

A bronze statue of Greek sun god, Helios, later identified with Apollo, set up about 280 BC. According to legend it stood 33m (110ft) tall at the harbor entrance of the seaport of Rhodes.

The Hanging Gardens of Babylon

These adjoined Nebuchadnezzar's palace, 96 km (60 miles) south of Baghdad. The terraced gardens, ranging from 25–90m (75ft to 300ft) above ground level, were watered from storage tanks on the highest terrace.

The Pharos of Alexandria

A marble watch tower and lighthouse on the island of Pharos in the harbour of Alexandria, built c.270 BC.

The Pyramids of Egypt

The pyramids are found from Gizeh, near Cairo, to a southern limit 96km (60 miles) distant. The oldest is that of Djoser, at Saqqara, built c.2650 BC. The Great Pyramid of Cheops (built c.2580 BC) covers 5.3 hectares (230.4 x 230.4m or 756 x 756ft) at the base and was originally 146.6m (481ft) in height.

The Statue of Zeus

Located at Olympia in the plain of Elis, 12m (40ft) tall and constructed of marble inlaid with ivory and gold by the sculptor Phidias, about 430 BC.

The Temple of Artemis at Ephesus

Ionic temple erected about 350 BC in honour of the goddess and burned by the Goths in AD 262.

The Tomb of Mausolus

Built at Halicarnassus, in Asia Minor, by the widowed Queen Artemisia about 350 BC. The memorial originated the term mausoleum.

GREEK AND ROMAN GODS

Greek Name	Roman Name	Symbolising
The Olympians	*Consentes Dii*	
Aphrodite	Venus	Beauty, love and procreation
Apollo	Apollo	Music, poetry and the Sun
Ares	Mars	War
Artemis	Diana	Hunting and animals
Athene	Minerva	Education and wisdom
Demeter	Ceres	The Earth and agriculture
Dionysus	Bacchus	Revelry, theatre and wine
Hades	Pluto	Death and the Underworld
Hebe	Juventas	Youth
Helios	Sol	The Sun
Hephaestus	Vulcan	Fire and crafts
Hera	Juno	Fidelity and marriage
Hermes	Mercury	Messenger of the gods
Hestia	Vesta	Family and the home
Persephone	Proserpine	Death or fertility
Poseidon	Neptune	The sea
Zeus	Jupiter	Ruler of the gods

The Olympians were the principal gods in Greek mythology (their Roman counterparts were known as the *Consentes Dii*) and lived at the top of Mount Olympus, the tallest peak in Greece. The previous occupants of Mount Olympus were the Titans, a powerful group of deities led by Cronus who ruled the Earth. The Olympians, led by Zeus, overthrew the Titans in the Titan War and imprisoned them in Tartarus, an abyss found beneath the Underworld.

There were never more than 12 Olympians at any one time, but the gods listed above have all been recognised as Olympians at some point

THE SOLAR SYSTEM

	Mean Distance from Sun (km 10⁶)	Period of Rotation on Axis (days)	Diameter (km)
Sun	–	25–35*	–

Planets†

	Mean Distance from Sun (km 10⁶)	Period of Rotation on Axis (days)	Diameter (km)
Mercury	58	58.646	4,878
Venus	108	243.019r	12,100
Earth	150	0.997	12,756
Mars	228	1.026	6,794
Jupiter	778	0.410e	142,800
Saturn	1,427	0.426e	120,000
Uranus	2,870	0.718r	52,400
Neptune	4,497	0.671	48,400

* depending on latitude, *r* retrograde, *e* equatorial
† In August 2006 Pluto was reclassified by the International Astronomical Union as a dwarf planet

Satellites of the Planets

	Mean Distance From Planet (km)	Period of Revolution Round Planet (days)
EARTH		
Moon	384,400	27.322
MARS		
Phobos	9,378	0.319
Deimos	23,459	1.262
JUPITER		
Metis	127,960	0.295
Adrastea	128,980	0.298
Amalthea	181,300	0.498
Thebe	221,900	0.675
Io	421,600	1.769
Europa	670,900	3.551
Ganymede	1,070,000	7.155
Callisto	1,883,000	16.689
Leda	11,094,000	239

	Mean Distance From Planet (km)	Period of Revolution Round Planet (days)
Himalia	11,480,000	251
Lysithea	11,720,000	259
Elara	11,737,000	260
Ananke	21,200,000	631r
Carme	22,600,000	692r
Pasiphae	23,500,000	735r
Sinope	23,700,000	758r
SATURN		
Pan	133,583	0.575
Atlas	137,670	0.602
Prometheus	139,353	0.613
Pandora	141,700	0.629
Epimetheus	151,42	0.694
Janus	151,42	0.695
Mimas	185,20	0.942
Enceladus	238,020	1.370
Tethys	294,66	1.888
Telesto	294,66	1.888
Calypso	294,66	1.888
Dione	377,40	2.737
Helene	377,40	2.737
Rhea	527,04	4.518
Titan	1,221,830	15.945
Hyperion	1,481,100	21.277
Iapetus	3,561,300	79.330
Phoebe	12,952,000	550.48r
URANUS		
Cordelia	49,770	0.335
Ophelia	53,790	0.376
Bianca	59,170	0.435
Cressida	61,780	0.464
Desdemona	62,680	0.474
Juliet	64,350	0.493
Portia	66,090	0.513
Rosalind	69,940	0.558
Belinda	75,260	0.624
Puck	86,010	0.762

	Mean Distance From Planet (km)	Period of Revolution Round Planet (days)
Miranda	129,390	1.413
Ariel	191,020	2.520
Umbriel	266,300	4.144
Titania	435,910	8.706
Oberon	583,520	13.463
Caliban	7,169,000	579
NEPTUNE		
Naiad	48,230	0.294
Thalassa	50,070	0.311
Despina	52,530	0.335
Galatea	61,950	0.429
Larissa	73,550	0.555
Proteus	117,650	1.122
Triton	354,760	5.877
Nereid	5,513,400	360.136

r retrograde

Dwarf Planets
Ceres, Eris, Haumea, Makemake, Pluto

RECORD-BREAKING ANIMALS AND PLANTS

Mammals

Fastest mammal: cheetah (eastern and southern Africa) – up to 110 km/h (68mph)

Tallest mammal: giraffe (western and southern Africa) – up to 5.5m (18ft) in height

Largest mammal: blue whale (Pacific, Indian and Southern oceans) – up to 35m (115ft) in length

Largest land mammal: African bush elephant (central Africa) – up to 3.2m (10.5ft) in height, 7m (22.9ft) in length and 10,000kg (1,574.7 stone) in weight

Loudest mammal: blue whale – up to 188db

Birds

Fastest bird: peregrine falcon (worldwide) – up to 350km/h (217mph)

Fastest land bird: ostrich (north Africa) – up to 65km/h (40mph)

Biggest wingspan: wandering albatross (Southern ocean) – up to 3.7m (12.1ft)

Longest migration: Arctic tern (Arctic to Antarctic) – average 80,500km (50,000 miles)

Fish, Amphibians and Reptiles

Biggest fish: whale shark (Pacific, Atlantic and Indian oceans) – up to 13m (43ft) in length

Biggest amphibian: Chinese giant salamander (China) – up to 1.8m (5.9ft) in length

Biggest reptile: estuarine or saltwater crocodile (south-east Asia, northern Australia) – up to 6m (19.7ft) in length

Biggest spider: Goliath bird-eating spider (South America) – leg span of 30cm (11.8in)

Longest snake: reticulated python (south-east Asia) – up to 10m (32.8ft) in length

Plants

Tallest living tree: Hyperion (Redwood National Park, Northern California) – 115.5m (378.9ft) tall

Biggest tree: Lindsey Creek tree (Pacific Coast, USA) – trunk volume of 2,550 cubic m (90,000 cubic ft), mass of 3,630,000kg (580,800 stone)

Biggest seed: double coconut or coco de mer (Seychelles) – up to 20kg (3.15 stone)

Biggest leaves: raffia palm (Madagascar, South America, tropical Africa) – up to 21m (68.9ft) long and 3m (9.8ft) wide

	Kingdom ANIMALIA	Phylum CHORDATA	Class MAMMALIA	Order PRIMATES	Family HOMINIDAE	Genus HOMO	Species SAPIENS
Hydra							
Earthworm							
Crab							
Insect							
Fish							
Frog							
Lizard							
Bird							
Rat							
Wolf							
Elephant							
Giraffe							
Tree Shrew							
Lemur							
Monkey							
Ape							
Early Human							
Modern Human							

PARTS OF A FLOWER

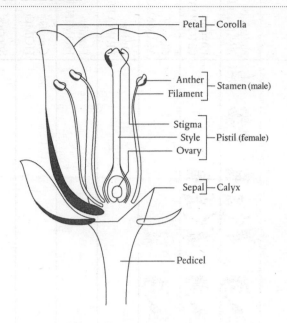

THE HUMAN BODY

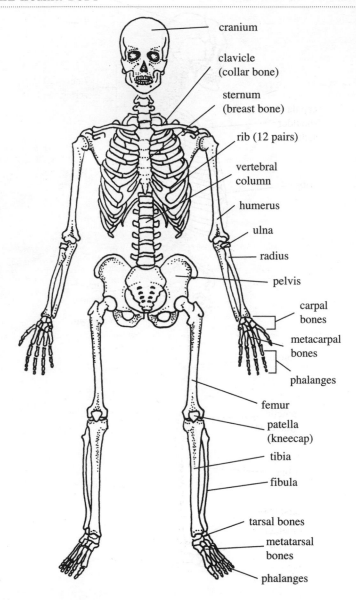

cranium

clavicle
(collar bone)

sternum
(breast bone)

rib (12 pairs)

vertebral
column

humerus

ulna

radius

pelvis

carpal
bones

metacarpal
bones

phalanges

femur

patella
(kneecap)

tibia

fibula

tarsal bones

metatarsal
bones

phalanges

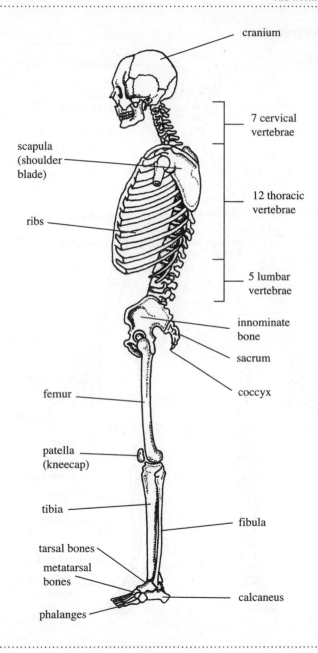

cranium

7 cervical
vertebrae

scapula
(shoulder
blade)

12 thoracic
vertebrae

ribs

5 lumbar
vertebrae

innominate
bone

sacrum

coccyx

femur

patella
(kneecap)

tibia

fibula

tarsal bones

metatarsal
bones

calcaneus

phalanges

ATHLETICS

World Records
MEN
Track

100m Usain Bolt (Jamaica) 2009	9.58sec
200m Usain Bolt (Jamaica) 2009	19.19sec
400m Michael Johnson (USA) 1999	43.18sec
800m David Rudisha (Kenya) 2000	1min 41.01sec
1,500m Hicham El Guerrouj (Morocco) 1998	3min 26.00 sec
Marathon Patrick Makau (Kenya) 2011	2hr 03min 38 sec
110m hurdles Dayron Robles (Cuba) 2008	12.87sec
400m hurdles Kevin Young (USA) 1992	46.78sec

Field

High jump Javier Sotomayor (Cuba) 1993	2.45m
Pole vault Sergey Bubka (Ukraine) 1994	6.14m
Long jump Mike Powell (USA) 1991	8.95m
Triple jump Jonathan Edwards (GB) 1995	18.29m
Shotput Randy Barnes (USA) 1990	23.12m
Discus Jurgen Schult (GDR) 1986	74.08m
Hammer Yuriy Sedykh (USSR) 1986	86.74m
Javelin Jan Zelezny (Czech Rep.) 1996	98.48m
Decathlon Roman Sebrle (Czech Rep.) 2001	9,026pts

WOMEN
Track

100m Florence Griffith-Joyner (USA) 1988	10.49sec
200m Florence Griffith-Joyner (USA) 1988	21.34sec
400m Marita Koch (GDR) 1985	47.60sec
800m Jarmila Kratochvilova (Czechoslovakia) 1983	1min 53.28sec
1,500m Qu Yunxia (China) 1993	3min 50.46sec
Marathon Paula Radcliffe (GB) 2003	2hr 15min 25sec
100m hurdles Yordanka Donkova (Bulgaria) 1988	12.21sec
400m hurdles Yuliya Pechonkina (Russia) 2003	52.34sec

Field

High jump Stefka Kostadinova (Bulgaria) 1987	2.09m
Pole vault Yelena Isinbayeva (Russia) 2009	5.06m
Long jump Galina Chistyakova (USSR) 1988	7.52m
Triple jump Inessa Kravets (Ukraine) 1995	15.50m
Shotput Natalya Lisovskaya (USSR) 1987	22.63m
Discus Gabriele Reinsch (GDR) 1988	76.80m
Hammer Betty Heidler (GER) 2011	79.42m
Javelin Barbora Spotakova (Czech Rep.) 2008	72.28m
Heptathlon Jackie-Joyner Kersee (USA) 1988	7,291pts

CRICKET

World Cup Winners
First held 1975

Year	Winner	Year	Winner
1975	West Indies	1996	Sri Lanka
1979	West Indies	1999	Australia
1983	India	2003	Australia
1987	Australia	2007	Australia
1992	Pakistan	2011	India

Test Cricket
Leading Batsmen as at April 2012
Sachin Tendulkar (India) 15,470 runs at an average of 55.44
Ricky Ponting (Australia) 13,346 at 52.75
Rahul Dravid (India) 13,288 at 52.31
Jacques Kallis (South Africa) 12,379 at 56.78
Brian Lara (West Indies) 11,953 at 52.88

Leading Bowlers as at April 2012
Muttiah Muralitharan (Sri Lanka) 800 wickets at an average of 22.72
Shane Warne (Australia) 708 at 25.41
Anil Kumble (India) 619 at 29.65
Glenn McGrath (Australia) 563 at 21.64
Courtney Walsh (West Indies) 519 at 24.44

County Champions
First held 1864

Year	Winner
2000	Surrey
2001	Yorkshire
2002	Surrey
2003	Sussex
2004	Warwickshire
2005	Nottinghamshire
2006	Sussex
2007	Sussex
2008	Durham
2009	Durham
2010	Nottinghamshire
2011	Lancashire

ASSOCATION FOOTBALL

World Cup Winners
First held 1930

Year	Venue	Winner	Year	Venue	Winner
1930	Uruguay	Uruguay	1978	Argentina	Argentina
1934	Italy	Italy	1982	Spain	Italy
1938	France	Italy	1986	Mexico	Argentina
1950	Brazil	Uruguay	1990	Italy	West Germany
1954	Switzerland	West Germany	1994	USA	Brazil
1958	Sweden	Brazil	1998	France	France
1962	Chile	Brazil	2002	S. Korea/Japan	Brazil
1966	England	England	2006	Germany	Italy
1970	Mexico	Brazil	2010	South Africa	Spain
1974	West Germany	West Germany			

World Cup: Golden Boot Winners
The Golden Boot (also known as the Golden Shoe) is awarded to the top goal-scorer of the tournament.

YEAR	PLAYER	NUMBER OF GOALS
1982	Paolo Rossi (Italy)	6
1986	Gary Lineker (England)	6
1990	Salvatore Schillaci (Italy)	6
1994	Hristo Stoichkov (Bulgaria)	6
	Oleg Salenko (Russia)	6
1998	Davor Suker (Croatia)	6
2002	Ronaldo (Brazil)	8
2006	Miroslav Klose (Germany)	5
2010	Thomas Müller (Germany)	5

Premier League Champions

Year	Winner	Year	Winner
1993	Manchester United	2003	Manchester United
1994	Manchester United	2004	Arsenal
1995	Blackburn Rovers	2005	Chelsea
1996	Manchester United	2006	Chelsea
1997	Manchester United	2007	Manchester United
1998	Arsenal	2008	Manchester United
1999	Manchester United	2009	Manchester United
2000	Manchester United	2010	Chelsea
2001	Manchester United	2011	Manchester United
2002	Arsenal	2012	Manchester City

FA Cup Winners

First held 1872

Year	Winner	Year	Winner
1981	Tottenham Hotspur	1997	Chelsea
1982	Tottenham Hotspur	1998	Arsenal
1983	Manchester United	1999	Manchester United
1984	Everton	2000	Chelsea
1985	Manchester United	2001	Liverpool
1986	Liverpool	2002	Arsenal
1987	Coventry	2003	Arsenal
1988	Wimbledon	2004	Manchester United
1989	Liverpool	2005	Arsenal
1990	Manchester United	2006	Liverpool
1991	Tottenham Hotspur	2007	Chelsea
1992	Liverpool	2008	Portsmouth
1993	Arsenal	2009	Chelsea
1994	Manchester United	2010	Chelsea
1995	Everton	2011	Manchester City
1996	Manchester United	2012	Chelsea

UEFA Champions League Winners
First held 1993

Year	Winner	Year	Winner
1993	Olympique de Marseille	2003	AC Milan
1994	AC Milan	2004	FC Porto
1995	AFC Ajax	2005	Liverpool
1996	Juventus	2006	FC Barcelona
1997	Borussia Dortmund	2007	AC Milan
1998	Real Madrid	2008	Manchester United
1999	Manchester United	2009	FC Barcelona
2000	Real Madrid	2010	Inter Milan
2001	Bayern Munich	2011	FC Barcelona
2002	Real Madrid	2012	Chelsea

GOLF

Majors*

Jack Nicklaus (USA)	18	Ben Hogan (USA)	9
Tiger Woods (USA)	14	Gary Player (South Africa)	9
Walter Hagen (USA)	11		

* Majors = Masters, US Open, British Open, PGA

US Masters Champions

First held 1934

Year	Winner	Year	Winner
1981	Tom Watson (USA)	1998	Mark O'Meara (USA)
1982	Craig Stadler (USA)	1999	José María Olazábal (Spain)
1983	Severiano Ballesteros (Spain)	2000	Vijay Singh (Fiji)
1984	Ben Crenshaw (USA)	2001	Tiger Woods (USA)
1985	Bernhard Langer (W. Germany)	2002	Tiger Woods (USA)
1986	Jack Nicklaus (USA)	2003	Mike Weir (Canada)
1987	Larry Mize (USA)	2004	Phil Mickelson (USA)
1988	Sandy Lyle (GB)	2005	Tiger Woods (USA)
1989	Nick Faldo (GB)	2006	Phil Mickelson (USA)
1990	Nick Faldo (GB)	2007	Zach Johnson (USA)
1991	Ian Woosnam (GB)	2008	Trevor Immelman (South Africa)
1992	Fred Couples (USA)	2009	Angel Cabrera (Argentina)
1993	Bernhard Langer (Germany)	2010	Phil Mickelson (USA)
1994	José María Olazábal (Spain)	2011	Charl Schwartzel (South Africa)
1995	Ben Crenshaw (USA)	2012	Bubba Watson (USA)
1996	Nick Faldo (GB)		
1997	Tiger Woods (USA)		

US Open Champions

First held 1895

Year	Winner	Year	Winner
1981	David Graham (Australia)	1989	Curtis Strange (USA)
1982	Tom Watson (USA)	1990	Hale Irwin (USA)
1983	Larry Nelson (USA)	1991	Payne Stewart (USA)
1984	Fuzzy Zoeller (USA)	1992	Tom Kite (USA)
1985	Andy North (USA)	1993	Lee Janzen (USA)
1986	Raymond Floyd (USA)	1994	Ernie Els (South Africa)
1987	Scott Simpson (USA)	1995	Corey Pavin (USA)
1988	Curtis Strange (USA)	1996	Steve Jones (USA)

Year	Winner
1997	Ernie Els (South Africa)
1998	Lee Janzen (USA)
1999	Payne Stewart (USA)
2000	Tiger Woods (USA)
2001	Retief Goosen (South Africa)
2002	Tiger Woods (USA)
2003	Jim Furyk (USA)
2004	Retief Goosen (South Africa)
2005	Michael Campbell (New Zealand)

Year	Winner
2006	Geoff Ogilvy (Australia)
2007	Angel Cabrera (Argentina)
2008	Tiger Woods (USA)
2009	Lucas Glover (USA)
2010	Graeme McDowell (GB)
2011	Rory McIlroy (GB)
2012	Webb Simpson (USA)

Open Champions

First held 1860
Played over 72 holes since 1892

Year	Winner
1982	Tom Watson (USA)
1983	Tom Watson (USA)
1984	Severiano Ballesteros (Spain)
1985	Sandy Lyle (GB)
1986	Greg Norman (Australia)
1987	Nick Faldo (GB)
1988	Severiano Ballesteros (Spain)
1989	Mark Calcavecchia (USA)
1990	Nick Faldo (GB)
1991	Ian Baker-Finch (Australia)
1992	Nick Faldo (GB)
1993	Greg Norman (Australia)
1994	Nick Price (Zimbabwe)
1995	John Daly (USA)
1996	Tom Lehman (USA)
1997	Justin Leonard (USA)

Year	Winner
1998	Mark O'Meara (USA)
1999	Paul Lawrie (GB)
2000	Tiger Woods (USA)
2001	David Duval (USA)
2002	Ernie Els (South Africa)
2003	Ben Curtis (USA)
2004	Todd Hamilton (USA)
2005	Tiger Woods (USA)
2006	Tiger Woods (USA)
2007	Padraig Harrington (Ireland)
2008	Padraig Harrington (Ireland)
2009	Stewart Cink (USA)
2010	Louis Oosthuizen (South Africa)
2011	Darren Clarke (GB)

PGA Championship Winners

First held 1916

Year	Winner
1982	Raymond Floyd (USA)
1983	Hal Sutton (USA)
1984	Lee Trevino (USA)
1985	Hubert Green (USA)
1986	Bob Tway (USA)

Year	Winner
1987	Larry Nelson (USA)
1988	Jeff Sluman (USA)
1989	Payne Stewart (USA)
1990	Wayne Grady (Australia)
1991	John Daly (USA)

Year	Winner	Year	Winner
1992	Nick Price (South Africa)	2002	Rich Beem (USA)
1993	Paul Azinger (USA)	2003	Shaun Micheel (USA)
1994	Nick Price(South Africa)	2004	Vijay Singh (Fiji)
1995	Steve Elkington (Australia)	2005	Phil Mickelson (USA)
1996	Mark Brooks (USA)	2006	Tiger Woods (USA)
1997	Davis Love III (USA)	2007	Tiger Woods (USA)
1998	Vijay Singh (Fiji)	2008	Padraig Harrington (Ireland)
1999	Tiger Woods (USA)	2009	Y. E. Yang (Rep. of Korea)
2000	Tiger Woods (USA)	2010	Martin Kaymer (Germany)
2001	David Toms (USA)	2011	Keegan Bradley (USA)

Ryder Cup Winners

First held 1927

Played over 2 days 1927–61; over 3 days 1963 to date

Year	Winner	Year	Winner
1983	USA	1997	Europe
1985	Europe	1999	USA
1987	Europe	2002	Europe
1989	Match drawn	2004	Europe
1991	USA	2006	Europe
1993	USA	2008	USA
1995	Europe	2010	Europe

HORSE RACING

Grand National Winners

First run in 1839

Year	Winning Horse	Year	Winning Horse
1981	Aldaniti	1992	Party Politics
1982	Grittar	1993	*Race declared void*
1983	Corbiere	1994	Minnehoma
1984	Hallo Dandy	1995	Royal Athlete
1985	Last Suspect	1996	Rough Quest
1986	West Tip	1997	Lord Gyllene
1987	Maori Venture	1998	Earth Summit
1988	Rhyme 'N' Reason	1999	Bobbyjo
1989	Little Polveir	2000	Papillon
1990	Mr Frisk	2001	Red Marauder
1991	Seagram	2002	Bindaree

Year	Winning Horse	Year	Winning Horse
2003	Monty's Pass	2008	Comply or Die
2004	Amberleigh House	2009	Mon Mome
2005	Hedgehunter	2010	Don't Push It
2006	Numbersixvalverde	2011	Ballabriggs
2007	Silver Birch	2012	Neptune Collonges

MOTOR RACING

Formula One World Champions

First held 1950

Year	Winner	Year	Winner
1982	Keke Rosberg (Finland)	1999	Mika Hakkinen (Finland)
1983	Nelson Piquet (Brazil)	2000	Michael Schumacher (Germany)
1984	Niki Lauda (Austria)	2001	Michael Schumacher (Germany)
1985	Alain Prost (France)	2002	Michael Schumacher (Germany)
1986	Alain Prost (France)	2003	Michael Schumacher (Germany)
1987	Nelson Piquet (Brazil)	2004	Michael Schumacher (Germany)
1988	Ayrton Senna (Brazil)	2005	Fernando Alonso (Spain)
1989	Alain Prost (France)	2006	Fernando Alonso (Spain)
1990	Ayrton Senna (Brazil)	2007	Kimi Raikkonen (Finland)
1991	Ayrton Senna (Brazil)	2008	Lewis Hamilton (GB)
1992	Nigel Mansell (GB)	2009	Jenson Button (GB)
1993	Alain Prost (France)	2010	Sebastian Vettel (Germany)
1994	Michael Schumacher (Germany)	2011	Sebastian Vettel (Germany)
1995	Michael Schumacher (Germany)		
1996	Damon Hill (GB)		
1997	Jacques Villeneuve (Canada)		
1998	Mika Hakkinen (Finland)		

ROWING

The University Boat Race
First held 1829

1829–2012: Cambridge 81 wins, Oxford 76; one dead heat (1877)

Year	Winner	Year	Winner
1981	Oxford	1997	Cambridge
1982	Oxford	1998	Cambridge
1983	Oxford	1999	Cambridge
1984	Oxford	2000	Oxford
1985	Oxford	2001	Cambridge
1986	Cambridge	2002	Oxford
1987	Oxford	2003	Oxford
1988	Oxford	2004	Cambridge
1989	Oxford	2005	Oxford
1990	Oxford	2006	Oxford
1991	Oxford	2007	Cambridge
1992	Oxford	2008	Oxford
1993	Cambridge	2009	Oxford
1994	Cambridge	2010	Cambridge
1995	Cambridge	2011	Oxford
1996	Cambridge	2012	Cambridge

RUGBY LEAGUE

World Cup Winners
First held 1954

Year	Winner	Year	Winner
1954	Great Britain	1977	Australia
1957	Australia	1988	Australia
1960	Great Britain	1992	Australia
1968	Australia	1995	Australia
1970	Australia	2000	Australia
1972	Great Britain	2008	New Zealand
1975	Australia		

RUGBY UNION

World Cup Winners
First held 1987

Year	Winner	Year	Winner
1987	New Zealand	2003	England
1991	Australia	2007	South Africa
1995	South Africa	2011	New Zealand
1999	Australia		

Six Nations Champions
First held 2000

Year	Winner	Year	Winner
2000	England	2007	France
2001	England	2008	Wales
2002	France	2009	Ireland
2003	England	2010	France
2004	France	2011	England
2005	Wales	2012	Wales
2006	France		

SNOOKER

World Champions
First held 1927

Year	Winner	Year	Winner
1990	Stephen Hendry (Scotland)	2002	Peter Ebdon (England)
1991	John Parrott (England)	2003	Mark Williams (Wales)
1992	Stephen Hendry (Scotland)	2004	Ronnie O'Sullivan (England)
1993	Stephen Hendry (Scotland)	2005	Shaun Murphy (England)
1994	Stephen Hendry (Scotland)	2006	Graeme Dott (Scotland)
1995	Stephen Hendry (Scotland)	2007	John Higgins (Scotland)
1996	Stephen Hendry (Scotland)	2008	Ronnie O'Sullivan (England)
1997	Ken Doherty (Ireland)	2009	John Higgins (Scotland)
1998	John Higgins (Scotland)	2010	Neil Robertson (Australia)
1999	Stephen Hendry (Scotland)	2011	John Higgins (Scotland)
2000	Mark Williams (Wales)	2012	Ronnie O'Sullivan (England)
2001	Ronnie O'Sullivan (England)		

TENNIS

Australian Open Men's Singles Champions
First held 1905

Year	Winner	Year	Winner
1983	Mats Wilander (Sweden)	1998	Petr Korda (Czech Republic)
1984	Mats Wilander (Sweden)	1999	Yevgeny Kafelnikov (Russia)
1985	Stefan Edberg (Sweden)	2000	Andre Agassi (USA)
1986	Not played	2001	Andre Agassi (USA)
1987	Stefan Edberg (Sweden)	2002	Thomas Johansson (Sweden)
1988	Mats Wilander (Sweden)	2003	Andre Agassi (USA)
1989	Ivan Lendl (Czechoslovakia)	2004	Roger Federer (Switzerland)
1990	Ivan Lendl (Czechoslovakia)	2005	Marat Safin (Russia)
1991	Boris Becker (Germany)	2006	Roger Federer (Switzerland)
1992	Jim Courier (USA)	2007	Roger Federer (Switzerland)
1993	Jim Courier (USA)	2008	Novak Djokovic (Serbia)
1994	Pete Sampras (USA)	2009	Rafael Nadal (Spain)
1995	Andre Agassi (USA)	2010	Roger Federer (Switzerland)
1996	Boris Becker (Germany)	2011	Novak Djokovic (Serbia)
1997	Pete Sampras (USA)	2012	Novak Djokovic (Serbia)

Australian Open Women's Singles Champions
First held 1922

Year	Winner	Year	Winner
1983	Martina Navratilova (USA)	1998	Martina Hingis (Switzerland)
1984	Chris Evert (USA)	1999	Martina Hingis (Switzerland)
1985	Martina Navratilova (USA)	2000	Lindsay Davenport (USA)
1986	Not played	2001	Jennifer Capriati (USA)
1987	Hana Mandlikova (Czechoslovakia)	2002	Jennifer Capriati (USA)
		2003	Serena Williams (USA)
1988	Steffi Graf (Germany)	2004	Justine Henin (Belgium)
1989	Steffi Graf (Germany)	2005	Serena Williams (USA)
1990	Steffi Graf (Germany)	2006	Amelie Mauresmo (France)
1991	Monica Seles (Yugoslavia)	2007	Serena Williams (USA)
1992	Monica Seles (Yugoslavia)	2008	Maria Sharapova (Russia)
1993	Monica Seles (Yugoslavia)	2009	Serena Williams (USA)
1994	Steffi Graf (Germany)	2010	Serena Williams (USA)
1995	Mary Pierce (France)	2011	Kim Clijsters (Belgium)
1996	Monica Seles (USA)	2012	Victoria Azarenka (Belarus)
1997	Martina Hingis (Switzerland)		

French Open (Roland Garros) Men's Singles Champions
First held 1891

Year	Winner	Year	Winner
1983	Yannick Noah (France)	1998	Carlos Moya (Spain)
1984	Ivan Lendl (Czechoslovakia)	1999	Andre Agassi (USA)
1985	Mats Wilander (Sweden)	2000	Gustavo Kuerten (Brazil)
1986	Ivan Lendl (Czechoslovakia)	2001	Gustavo Kuerten (Brazil)
1987	Ivan Lendl (Czechoslovakia)	2002	Albert Costa (Spain)
1988	Mats Wilander (Sweden)	2003	Juan Carlos Ferrero (Spain)
1989	Michael Chang (USA)	2004	Gaston Gaudio (Argentina)
1990	Andres Gomez (Ecuador)	2005	Rafael Nadal (Spain)
1991	Jim Courier (USA)	2006	Rafael Nadal (Spain)
1992	Jim Courier (USA)	2007	Rafael Nadal (Spain)
1993	Sergi Bruguera (Spain)	2008	Rafael Nadal (Spain)
1994	Sergi Bruguera (Spain)	2009	Roger Federer (Switzerland)
1995	Thomas Muster (Austria)	2010	Rafael Nadal (Spain)
1996	Yevgeny Kafelnikov (Russia)	2011	Rafael Nadal (Spain)
1997	Gustavo Kuerten (Brazil)	2012	Rafael Nadal (Spain)

French Open (Roland Garros) Women's Singles Champions
First held 1897

Year	Winner	Year	Winner
1983	Chris Evert (USA)	1998	Arantxa Sanchez Vicario (Spain)
1984	Martina Navratilova (USA)	1999	Steffi Graf (Germany)
1985	Chris Evert (USA)	2000	Mary Pierce (France)
1986	Chris Evert (USA)	2001	Jennifer Capriati (USA)
1987	Steffi Graf (Germany)	2002	Serena Williams (USA)
1988	Steffi Graf (Germany)	2003	Justine Henin (Belgium)
1989	Arantxa Sanchez Vicario (Spain)	2004	Anastasia Myskina (Russia)
1990	Monica Seles (Yugoslavia)	2005	Justine Henin (Belgium)
1991	Monica Seles (Yugoslavia)	2006	Justine Henin (Belgium)
1992	Monica Seles (Yugoslavia)	2007	Justine Henin (Belgium)
1993	Steffi Graf (Germany)	2008	Ana Ivanovic (Serbia)
1994	Arantxa Sanchez Vicario (Spain)	2009	Svetlana Kuznetsova (Russia)
1995	Steffi Graf (Germany)	2010	Francesca Schiavone (Italy)
1996	Steffi Graf (Germany)	2011	Li Na (China)
1997	Iva Majoli (Croatia)	2012	Maria Sharapova (Russia)

Wimbledon Men's Singles Champions
First held 1877

Year	Winner	Year	Winner
1981	John McEnroe (USA)	1997	Pete Sampras (USA)
1982	Jimmy Connors (USA)	1998	Pete Sampras (USA)
1983	John McEnroe (USA)	1999	Pete Sampras (USA)
1984	John McEnroe (USA)	2000	Pete Sampras (USA)
1985	Boris Becker (W. Germany)	2001	Goran Ivanisevic (Croatia)
1986	Boris Becker (W. Germany)	2002	Lleyton Hewitt (Australia)
1987	Pat Cash (Australia)	2003	Roger Federer (Switzerland)
1988	Stefan Edberg (Sweden)	2004	Roger Federer (Switzerland)
1989	Boris Becker (W. Germany)	2005	Roger Federer (Switzerland)
1990	Stefan Edberg (Sweden)	2006	Roger Federer (Switzerland)
1991	Michael Stich (Germany)	2007	Roger Federer (Switzerland)
1992	Andre Agassi (USA)	2008	Rafael Nadal (Spain)
1993	Pete Sampras (USA)	2009	Roger Federer (Switzerland)
1994	Pete Sampras (USA)	2010	Rafael Nadal (Spain)
1995	Pete Sampras (USA)	2011	Novak Djokovic (Serbia)
1996	Richard Krajicek (Netherlands)	2012	Roger Federer (Switzerland)

Wimbledon Women's Singles Champions
First held 1884

Year	Winner	Year	Winner
1981	Chris Evert (USA)	1997	Martina Hingis (Switzerland)
1982	Martina Navratilova (USA)	1998	Jana Novotna (Czech Republic)
1983	Martina Navratilova (USA)	1999	Lindsay Davenport (USA)
1984	Martina Navratilova (USA)	2000	Venus Williams (USA)
1985	Martina Navratilova (USA)	2001	Venus Williams (USA)
1986	Martina Navratilova (USA)	2002	Serena Williams (USA)
1987	Martina Navratilova (USA)	2003	Serena Williams (USA)
1988	Steffi Graf (W. Germany)	2004	Maria Sharapova (Russia)
1989	Steffi Graf (W. Germany)	2005	Venus Williams (USA)
1990	Martina Navratilova (USA)	2006	Amelie Mauresmo (France)
1991	Steffi Graf (Germany)	2007	Venus Williams (USA)
1992	Steffi Graf (Germany)	2008	Venus Williams (USA)
1993	Steffi Graf (Germany)	2009	Serena Williams (USA)
1994	Conchita Martinez (Spain)	2010	Serena Williams (USA)
1995	Steffi Graf (Germany)	2011	Petra Kvitova (Czech Republic)
1996	Steffi Graf (Germany)	2012	Serena Williams (USA)

US Open Men's Singles Champions
First held 1881

Year	Winner	Year	Winner
1983	Jimmy Connors (USA)	1999	Andre Agassi (USA)
1984	John McEnroe (USA)	2000	Marat Safin (Russia)
1985	Ivan Lendl (Czechoslovakia)	2001	Lleyton Hewitt (Australia)
1986	Ivan Lendl (Czechoslovakia)	2002	Pete Sampras (USA)
1987	Ivan Lendl (Czechoslovakia)	2003	Andy Roddick (USA)
1988	Mats Wilander (Sweden)	2004	Roger Federer (Switzerland)
1989	Boris Becker (Germany)	2005	Roger Federer (Switzerland)
1990	Pete Sampras (USA)	2006	Roger Federer (Switzerland)
1991	Stefan Edberg (Sweden)	2007	Roger Federer (Switzerland)
1992	Stefan Edberg (Sweden)	2008	Roger Federer (Switzerland)
1993	Pete Sampras (USA)	2009	Juan Martin Del Potro (Argentina)
1994	Andre Agassi (USA)	2010	Rafael Nadal (Spain)
1995	Pete Sampras (USA)	2011	Novak Djokovic (Serbia)
1996	Pete Sampras (USA)		
1997	Patrick Rafter (Australia)		
1998	Patrick Rafter (Australia)		

US Open Women's Singles Champions
First held 1887

Year	Winner	Year	Winner
1983	Martina Navratilova (USA)	1997	Martina Hingis (Switzerland)
1984	Martina Navratilova (USA)	1998	Lindsay Davenport (USA)
1985	Hana Mandlikova (Czechoslovakia)	1999	Serena Williams (USA)
1986	Martina Navratilova (USA)	2000	Venus Williams (USA)
1987	Martina Navratilova (USA)	2001	Venus Williams (USA)
1988	Steffi Graf (Germany)	2002	Serena Williams (USA)
1989	Steffi Graf (Germany)	2003	Justine Henin (Belgium)
1990	Gabriela Sabatini (Argentina)	2004	Svetlana Kuznetsova (Russia)
1991	Monica Seles (Yugoslavia)	2005	Kim Clijsters (Belgium)
1992	Monica Seles (Yugoslavia)	2006	Maria Sharapova (Russia)
1993	Steffi Graf (Germany)	2007	Justine Henin (Belgium)
1994	Arantxa Sanchez Vicario (Spain)	2008	Serena Williams (USA)
1995	Steffi Graf (Germany)	2009	Kim Clijsters (Belgium)
1996	Steffi Graf (Germany)	2010	Kim Clijsters (Belgium)
		2011	Samantha Stosur (Australia)